C0-AKL-024

You Can't Not Do It

The Journal Of an Older Activist

Ruth Stamm Dear

Edited by Rima Lunin Schultz

Plain View Press
P. O. 33311
Austin, TX 78764

plainviewpress.com
sbright1@austin.rr.com
1-800-878-3605

Copyright Ruth Stamm Dear, 2001. All rights reserved.
ISBN: 1-891386-24-7
Library of Congress Number: 2001095503

Errata:
p. 97 - chapter heading: Grief (not Grie)
p. 135 - Henny (not Henry)
p. 184 - screed (not creed)

Acknowledgments

Thanks to Gertrude Rubin, Wayne Vanek, Robert Wiebe and Renée Buecker for their initial encouragement, to Sr. Gladys Schmitz whose remark supplied the title, to publisher Susan Bright for her support and interest, and, especially, to Rima Lunin Schultz for her belief in the possibility of this book, her hard work, and persistence, truly a friend and a sister. Thanks to Lauren Carrozzi for donating proof reading time to Plain View Press.

Title Page photo is by Steve Dalber.

Contents

Selected Articles and Speeches by Ruth Dear

Introduction

The publication of Ruth Dear's *You Can't Not Do It: The Journal of An Older Activist*, is a significant event. Ruth has spent a lifetime engaged in political movements whose goals are economic and social justice. She has picketed, protested, demonstrated and practiced civil disobedience in order to challenge racism, anti-Semitism, homophobia and gender and age oppression. She has been jailed for her protest of militarism and nuclear proliferation and has protested the United States involvement in war and in "peace-keeping" and covert activities in other countries. For those of us who watch the news, listen to broadcasts, read newspapers and magazines and say "What can be done? What can I do?" and question how individuals can influence the global-scale challenges that confront us every day, Ruth Dear's journal offers encouragement to engage in activism. Tempered with years of experience, including moments of disillusionment and painful acknowledgement of personal limitations, this is an honest account of Ruth Dear's inner struggle about how to live a socially responsible life as an older activist. Diminished in physical strength as a natural aspect of aging, and experiencing loss in her private life, Ruth Dear writes about how she is motivated to go on — *"You Can't Not Do It"*.

I have had the pleasure of assisting Ruth Dear in getting her journal ready for publication. I met Ruth Dear in 1995 at a meeting of the Oak Park, Illinois, chapter of the Women's International League for Peace and Freedom where I was a guest speaker talking about Jane Addams and her peace initiatives. I also spoke about the way in which I was using biography as social history in a women's history project I was directing. Jane Addams's biography was one of the many that engrossed me, but the real agenda of the project was to write about women whose lives had not yet been recovered by historians. When Ruth came up to me after my talk and introduced herself I was pleased to meet a woman I knew about through her reputation as a peace movement activist. I had been in audiences when Ruth had addressed gatherings in Oak Park — Hiroshima Day observances, anti-war rallies — and remembered her pithy, focused, and radical comments.

It was the right time for Ruth and me to meet. An activist all her life and a writer of contemporary political and social essays as well as a journalist for the publications of the organizations to which she belonged, Ruth had spent little time writing about her own life or reflecting on the connections between the personal and the public events therein. While she has become more receptive to the recent explosion of autobiography and memoir that is rooted in the 1960s idea that the personal is political, Ruth does not like to write about herself. Yet she had come, by 1995, to feel her own need to pull together her ideas and experiences, not, she informed me, in the traditional autobiographical format, but in some other manner. Would I come over and look at her papers and offer some ideas about how she might go about beginning such a project? I replied, "Yes," and we set up our first meeting.

My efforts to see whether I could be of assistance were not without self-interest. I have to admit that my first thought was "great! this woman most likely has wonderful papers about her life as an activist" and, as a historian of women's history interested in writing the biographies of grassroots women like Ruth Dear, I wanted to read the material. So our lives intersected at a time when both of us — for very disparate reasons — had intellectual and personal reasons for thinking about the representation of women's lives through biography, autobiography and memoir.

Ruth and I soon discovered that our connections to each other were going to be deeper and more profound than just the happenstance of mutual interests. In attempting to find the right format through which Ruth could write her memoirs, we embarked on a long conversation that turned into a friendship which continues to grow and deepen. Thinking more traditionally than Ruth about writing a memoir, I suggested that Ruth collect her thoughts about her life in the process of a series of oral interviews that I would conduct with her. My idea was that the transcripts could be used as material for her memoir.

When I think back now on this process I have to laugh. Both of us were wrong for this setup. Ruth hated to respond to the typical questions interviewers are supposed to ask; I could not maintain the neutral voice of the interviewer and wanted to engage with Ruth in a dialogue not an interview. The oral interview process did give two "strangers" permission to spend long hours together talking. What we learned was that we had a lot in common, starting with our backgrounds. We had a shared sense of our immigrant Jewish heritage and we both had families whose lives were changed forever in Europe and in the United States by ideas of social revolution. She was of my parents' generation and had, in common with them, a youth and young adulthood spent in the secular Jewish and radical workers' culture formed by immigrants and first-generation Americans. We used a common political vocabulary, implicitly understanding its nuances. We were readers. Books and words had served as our connection to worlds outside our limited local space and, at times, had been our escape from the restrictions we had both felt as nonconformist women.

We spent time reading through Ruth's papers. One day she asked me "Would my journal be of interest?" Ruth then disclosed that she had been keeping a journal since her husband, George Dear, had died in 1985. I began reading the journal entries, finding them a window into Ruth's past. They were more than the writings of a grieving widow. I suggested to Ruth that they were a form of political memoir that deserved publication. After thinking out the pros and cons of publishing excerpts from her journal, Ruth determined it was the right direction to pursue. We then began our work in earnest to prepare a manuscript based on the journals and using the daily entry as the format. Ruth's journal takes us through one decade of her life, from 1985 to 1995. In its analysis of contemporary affairs and through its critique of contemporary culture the journal provides the reader with a context for understanding Ruth's point of view. There are also excerpts from Ruth's published articles that appeared in the *Nonviolent Activist* of the War Resisters League, *WIN* magazine and *Hyde Park Kenwood Voices* in the 1970s and document her earlier activities.

Dear's political memoir *"You Can't Not Do It": The Journal of An Older Activist* begins with the recently-widowed Ruth coming to terms with her husband's death. George Dear, her husband, best friend and comrade, had been her link (and she his) to a lifelong engagement in political activism. They were partners whose shared experiences kept alive their intense commitment to social justice and peace goals. George's illness in the 1980s came at a time when political events in the United States and internationally reflected the success of conservative attacks on liberals and the abandonment of many collectivist goals.

For Ruth, a private person who values her independence and autonomy, the practical and emotional dimensions of this loss forced her to seek unlikely support systems in a unique religious community, Third Unitarian Church, in the Austin neighborhood. Her journal recounts the inner dialogue Ruth engaged in before she was ready to join Third Church and speaks to issues of identity, belief and community. Ruth's journal broadens to cover a variety of political and social movement themes including ageism and feminism, peace and nonviolent resistance to war. Her journal is a testament to her ongoing efforts to engage in social justice and peace initiatives.

There are many reasons why *"You Can't Not Do It"* deserves careful reading by not only Ruth's generation of activists, but also by the generation that came of age politically in the 1960s, and those who have come to maturity since then, many of whom were influenced by the 1970s countercultural values. Ruth is able to cut across the generational boundaries because her own development as an activist was not confined to her young adult years. Instead, she was able to make connections with anti-war activists during the Viet Nam conflict (she led in opposition to the war meeting with Viet Namese women in Moscow in 1963) and in the 1980s found herself organizing with high school students and others against the Gulf War in the 90s. Historians are finding connections across generations in the peace, civil rights, and women's liberation movements in the United States and Ruth Dear's life illustrates this phenomenon. Ruth's engagement in Women's Strike for Peace in the 1960s and her involvement off and on with the Women's International League for Peace and Freedom are part of the longtime efforts of American women to resist militarism and war. The 1960s generation of war resisters found women like Dear already engaged in anti-war politics; some of the 60s leaders had been wheeled in baby carriages when their mothers protested Strontium 90 in milk and the proliferation of nuclear weapons after World War II. Dear supported New Left initiatives and welcomed contact with young radicals. She corresponded with draft resisters serving prison sentences, joined a group of supporters of Students for a Democratic Society (SDS) and joined the Pledge of Resistance.

Ruth Dear was invigorated by the 1960s women's liberation movement. Gender issues had affected her participation in radical politics. For example, she recalls how only late in life she began to think of herself as a writer. From the 1930s she had contributed articles and reviews to the radical magazines and informal publications of the organizations in which she was an active member. Yet she had seen these pieces as "organization" work, an aspect of her activism rather than an original contribution qualifying her as a writer. Her husband's interest in the craft of writing had been more direct and personal. Ruth's journal attests to her literary talent and keen sense of language honed after a lifetime of experience as a commentator and journalist. She was ready to hear the feminist message which resonated in her own experience. Her leadership in the Gray Panthers in Chicago was a natural expansion of the values and goals of feminism. Unwilling to be labeled or constrained by social codes constructed by the male patriarchy through its political control of the State and its hegemony over mass culture, Ruth Dear's collectivist activism is in part based on her respect for individual expression and freedom. She marched with other women to Take Back the Night.

Ruth's journal speaks to one of her ongoing concerns — balancing her advocacy of collectivism and her desire to protect individual rights and free expression in society. There is a strong parallel in her search for balance in her personal relationships. Ruth's journal speaks out about the dilemma of a private person's search for a community that allows her a connection based on mutuality rather than dependency, that respects her views and does not demand conformity. After much soul-searching she achieves this balance through her membership in Third Unitarian, but it is never an entirely satisfactory resolution. Ruth defines herself as a radical pacifist and criticizes institutionalized religion and charitable endeavors preferring the construction of a social system that provides for the basic needs of all people. In her early years she had little contact with churches or synagogues. As time passed, however, her path intersected with religiously-inspired radicals. Her observations of the role of religious inspiration in social movements has resulted in her broadened perspective on the roots of radicalism in society. Her explanation and understanding of historical change, still deeply grounded in Marxist interpretation of social, economic and class systems, has never been doctrinaire. Her journal honestly deals with the contradictions within ideologies, whether metaphysical or materialist in conception.

I have been privileged to work with Ruth Dear on her political memoir in the form of this journal. We share a deep bond of sisterhood and have taken turns mentoring, advising, encouraging, and editing each other's writings. We are both still figuring out how to live a good life staying loyal to our beliefs and values, yet adjusting to changing times and learning new things everyday. Together we await the next wave of activism for social justice and global peace, noticing with great satisfaction recent evidence of gathering momentum among workers and social activists of many stripes, including students, who challenge the widening gap between the rich and poor worldwide, and concern themselves with the earth's environment. We fear the beginnings of a new nuclear arms race with its risks for global survival. *"You Can't Not Do It"* is not a blueprint for radicals; it is, however, a strong statement about the resiliency and strength of the radical spirit.

Rima Lunin Schultz

Rima Lunin Schultz, left, and Ruth Stamm Dear, right, at a social action forum for Women's History Month, March 2001, at Third Unitarian Church, Chicago. In the background is the Paul Robeson Memorial mural.

Background

I. Beginnings

Many radicals come to their beliefs through painful struggle with their early background. I was fortunate. Both parents were Anarchists who met in the movement at the turn of the century in New York City and provided a stimulating environment with a strong commitment to social justice. My mother, Anna Kobilsky, affectionately called Anyuta, graduated from St. George's college of midwifery in Odessa, Russia, and was a member of the Social Revolutionary Party there. Besides English, she spoke Russian, Yiddish and Polish. My father, Simyon Aronstam, anglicized by immigration authorities to Simon Stamm, came from Kurland, now Latvia, and was fluent in German and Russian as well as Yiddish and English. In the U.S., he worked as an accountant and Mama went into nursing until my brother Tommy was born in 1904 when she was thirty-three. About three years before, they had decided to live together, refusing to recognize the authority of the state to legalize their union. Ten years after Tommy, I was born.

My parents were a study in contrasts. Papa was a feisty, gregarious person with a short fuse. Mama was very retiring, reserved, not very happy, a great reader. The atmosphere at once was lively, affectionate, quarrelsome, relatives and friends coming and going. Sunday nights, Papa's friends would gather around the dining room table, talking, singing, drinking tea out of glasses, while Mama rushed around providing refreshments. From time to time, people would stay over: a Russian cousin, Lazar, who, to my parents' disgust, enlisted in World War I to "help Russia"; a "Mr. Loeb" who, I learned much later, needed a safe house during the Palmer Red Raids of the early twenties; Lazar's girlfriend Mira who once explained to me that a *mishmash* was the result of going out in the rain with a face all made up.

Secular Yiddish culture was a large part of this environment since my parents were part of a Yiddish revival movement. My father collaborated on a radical Jewish paper. My mother spoke Yiddish to me when I was a baby. We had little regard for ritual or religion except for some dietary preferences and prejudices and yearly attendance at Aunt Mary and Uncle Joe's seder. Religious holidays were noted but not observed except b my seizing the opportunity to stay home from school.

Even before I realized I was being taught a cultural heritage, there was a pot-pourri of impressions: loaded words like *pogrom, quota, gentile, assimilationists* in a pejorative tone; names of writers, artists and radicals — Zhitlovsky, Louis Levine (Lewis Corey), Jacob Gordon of the Yiddish Art Theater, Trotsky, Mendelsohn, Emma Goldman whom Mama had known; Jewish sayings ("As Gott will, schiesst a besom" — God willing, a broom will shoot). Mama would refer to stories by Sholem Aleichem and Peretz. A particularly haunting one by Peretz concerned a distraught young wife who in the midst of great poverty finally remonstrated with her Talmudic student husband; for interrupting him at his studies, he told her she would lose her place in heaven at his feet, whereupon she hanged herself. A powerful feminist lesson!

Among our prize possessions were two matching glass-fronted oak cases crammed with all manner of books: a complete set of Turgenev, Lissagaray's *History of the [Paris] Commune*, Kraft-Ebing's *Psychopathia Sexualis*, Ibsen's plays, the Old Testament in a *Masterpieces of Hebrew Literature* series, John Stuart Mill's *The Subjection of Women*, and, much later, works by Freud as well as *What Every Girl Should Know* by Margaret Sanger, placed there for my edification in lieu of verbal explanation.

Papa died suddenly on a fall night in 1921. I remember "Your father is dying." There was a lot of commotion, Dr. Rabbe, a family friend, was in attendance. Beyond that and the day of the funeral, I have no recollection, until we were in our apartment in Harlem, although right after this traumatic, tragic event, I stayed with Papa's sisters, Minna and Vera, and Vera's daughter Violet, at 1029 Boston Road in the Bronx. Years later, when I went to this building, the halls and roof were familiar but I could not remember the specifics of living there.

There followed hard times, both financially and emotionally. With $300 in the bank and no money coming in, drastic adjustments were made. Tommy, who was in his last year of high school, graduated and went to work as a stock clerk at Lane Bryant whose owner was a friend of the family. We moved to a seven-room apartment on 124th Street in what was then white Harlem. There, on the top floor of the building, aptly named "Sans Souci," as it was indeed free of care, we lived in the back three rooms while Mama rented out the other four — an uncertain, anxiety-filled undertaking as roomers came and went. With the help of two older cousins who established trust funds for us, we got by. For a while we were on welfare but this lasted only till this additional source of income was discovered. One day I came home from school to find Ma much distressed after a nasty visit from a social worker, and, as a result, we both retained a strong prejudice against that profession.

The atmosphere at home was very different after Papa died. Few people came to the house aside from relatives and an occasional friend of Tommy's. I was very lonely as there were no children in the building and the new school was about eight blocks away. No schoolmates were in the neighborhood. Because of this and my radical background and beliefs I felt apart. In school I was often too shy to volunteer answers and burned with frustration when other students did and received credit. I am still uncomfortable in school buildings — long, soulless corridors — and, in fact, in most institutions.

Books became a refuge. A few years ago, going through some old photographs with my niece, Karen, I found a snapshot of myself at the Lane

Bryant annual boat ride, sitting on the upper deck, bent over a book with Ma and her sisters, Fanny and Mary, talking animatedly in the background. In this way, I survived uncomfortable situations. The branch library was just down the street and after the Bobbsey Twins and Louisa May Alcott, under my mother's guidance I began to read classic fiction as well as turn of the century social novels. One of my pleasantest memories is sitting on the window seat-cum-radiator of the front room, overlooking Mt. Morris Park, with a book in my lap. Complementing this interest in books was an interest in word derivation and usage. One day, Tommy brought home a secondhand copy of *Webster's Unabridged Dictionary* and thereafter, when asked about a meaning, he would say "Look it up!"

Of course there were bright spots: sledding down the hill in the park, the Pickwick Club at the library, plays, trips to Coney Island and Rye Beach and, most pleasurable of all, two summers at Pioneer Youth Camp at Rifton, New York. As this was socialist and trade union sponsored, there were like-minded companions. The summer of 1927, the framed Anarchists, Sacco and Vanzetti, had exhausted the last of their appeals and they were executed August 22nd, something we 13-year-olds discussed passionately. Later, reading their letters, Vanzetti's comment, "All my life I would have talked on street corners to scorning men," struck home — a pertinent comment on movement activity.

A year or so later, we senior girls at camp read and discussed Radclyffe Hall's *Well of Loneliness* which had just come out, feeling very in. We also learned a lesson in cliquism. Camper participation was encouraged in a number of ways including the running of the afternoon store by one of the senior girls. There we hung around at closing time and received some goodies. To our surprise, the director raised this at a camp meeting and, after heated discussion, the majority agreed that this preferential treatment was wrong, but Gabby, the storekeeper, just did not get the point. This incident inspired my only attempt at fiction aside from an operetta we wrote based on the Wobbly song book. Camp was educational in another way: a friend instructed me in the details of sexual intercourse which Margaret Sanger had somehow omitted from her booklet.

When I was twelve, Tommy married for the first time and moved out and I had my own little room. In Mama's opinion, Lily wasn't up to Tommy's level of intelligence, but then nobody was. Although, naturally, we were all intelligent, he was looked on as the most. Only much later, in a consciousness raising group, did I discover that other women with brothers were similarly regarded. I finally rebelled at this intellectual arrogance, and my mother never raised it again when remarking on friends. Of course this was partly based on a prizing of awareness, of social consciousness, of being in touch with issues and developments, but it was intellectual arrogance none the less.

My school career was not great. Barely scraping through Morris High School, I was partly bored and partly uninterested in the curriculum. But in my senior year I joined the Social Problems Club which offered friendships and a political outlet which became a major interest.

Expecting a less rigid, more adult atmosphere in Hunter College I was sadly disappointed. Tommy, unable himself to attend, suggested taking basic science as this was least likely to be a vehicle for capitalist propaganda, but this was not for me and I ended up by majoring in languages. Although it was assumed I'd go into teaching, a slight lisp disqualified me as the authorities were then very persnickety about speech. The only other option was office work for which I eventually took some business courses. As this was in the depths of the Depression, college graduates were earning ten or twelve dollars a week as saleswomen at Macy's department store, there seemed little future in finishing at Hunter and I dropped out in my senior year.

I continued to live at home, Ma putting little pressure on me as I had been diagnosed as epileptic some five years before — a diagnosis which many years later was proven false — so I lived with the uncertainty and stigma and the fear of not being able to hold a job. All my energies now went into the movement which offered hope and vision and acceptance as well as a different kind of learning.

II. A New World; The Trotskyist Movement

Shortly after I entered college, I joined the newly formed Spartacus Youth League of the Communist League of America (Left Opposition) and about the same time my brother joined the adult group. This was in 1931 in the context of the Depression, a period of extreme destitution, homelessness, failing farms, wage cutting, unemployment without any framework for relief. George Dear, my comrade and husband, told me years later that when he went out to the Campbell Soup factory in New Jersey, in reply to a want ad, he found hundreds of men had already gathered outside. Finally a representative appeared and asked who would work for one cent an hour and got no takers. Upping the offer, penny by penny, he stopped at a nickel when someone raised a hand, and this established the wage rate.

This was also a time of tremendous ferment which led to organization and resistance. When someone was evicted for nonpayment of rent, the furniture on the street, neighbors and others would gather and put it back. Movement rent parties were held so that guests could make cash contributions. Both Communist and Socialist parties organized the unemployed and led "hunger marches." The great mass of workers who had no representation, as the American Federation of Labor was composed mostly of skilled craftspeople, started to unionize, strike and even occupy factories on an industry-wide basis. Farmers demonstrated for assistance. We high school and college students, too, organized in the National Student League and the Student League for Industrial Democracy and held one-day strikes for peace. Resistance abroad — the Spanish Civil War, sit-down strikes in France — fed into this powerful social upheaval.

Participation in the movement was the opening of a new world to me, a place to be expressive, to voice radical convictions, and to function and be heard, to work with others, a focus for my life. My family had been sympathetic to the Bolsheviks at the time of the 1917 October Revolution and, later, to Trotsky, so this was a clicking into place of ideas and feelings. In fact, this movement became my life. Usually I'd go down to the office on East Tenth Street and stay into the evening for meetings. Afterwards, we'd go to a cafeteria on Fourteenth Street, "The Crusader," to socialize, hash over events, relieve tensions. Ideologically, what appealed to me was Trotsky's adherence to the principle of socialist internationalism against the narrowing vision of building socialism in one country, Russia, and the subsequent neglect of its development in other countries.

In the office, I met George who came in from Princeton on a visit. A few years later we became partners, sharing our lives, our activity and our commitment until his death in 1985.

In the youth group I studied Marxism intensively. Believing, with Lenin, that a radical party was to be the vanguard, we were educating ourselves for this. It was an absorbing world of action as well as ideas. Regularly, we would gather to mail out *The Militant*, singing Wobbly songs as we worked. It was also a world of fierce polemics against the system, the Stalinists, the reformists, and even against one another over differences of opinion.

We were the recipients of much abuse, verbal and physical, by Stalinists who considered us counter-revolutionaries. Once, waiting in a group to leaflet returning veterans of the Spanish Civil War, we were surrounded by Communist Party members who tried to grab the flyers. In the resultant scuffle I found myself sitting on the ground, a young woman with long hair bending over me. Grabbing hold of that hair, I yanked, the first and only time to engage in physical violence.

In this movement I learned and sharpened skills in speaking and writing. Since we were always spreading the word, I drafted flyers and articles, spoke on street corners from a portable wooden platform, discussed and analyzed. A recent Channel 11 program on Mexican muralist Diego Rivera recalled picketing Rockefeller Center, chanting, "Save Rivera's murals!" To the surprise of the authorities, he had included Lenin and Trotsky as well as several local comrades unknown to them, and they ordered the paintings destroyed. Only once was I arrested for activity, pasting up leaflets in Newark together with another SYLer, held overnight and released when someone came to bail us out.

In 1934, our movement split over a proposal by Trotsky to join the Socialist Parties. The "Old Man" had let us down. Proposing to go it alone, a group of us formed the Revolutionary Workers League ("Oehlerites") and issued *The Fighting Worker*. A year or so later, when our national office, in order to reach workers in basic industry, was moved to Chicago, I came out here for a while and stayed with a sympathetic family, living on a pittance Mama sent. I was lucky compared to others who slept in the office, an apartment in a half-empty building on Division Street. One young man would chew paper to quiet hunger pangs.

In those Depression days, our usual means of travel from New York to Chicago was by thumb. One could get a cabin for a dollar and eat hamburgers and coffee for a nickel each. With a male comrade, I would usually stand in front to attract attention as drivers were readier to take a chance with a woman along. Once a trucker asked George and me to keep him awake by singing.

George and I finally made a permanent move to Chicago in 1937, when we decided to live together. Once there, he was hired by the Works Progress Administration (WPA) to help build a curb on the north side. In 1939, U.S. Steel's South Works plant, tooling up for war, hired him as a laborer and he of course joined the Steelworkers union local named for Hilding Andersen, one of the workers shot in the back during the Republic Steel strike, two years earlier. Exempt from the draft as an essential worker, George remained there all through World War II and beyond, eventually becoming a machinist, while I found some office jobs.

At first we lived in a ratty room somewhere near headquarters. Here, one morning, police broke in while we were still in bed. A slightly dotty neighbor had heard us talking about typewriters and since this was slang for machine guns, he'd called the cops. Their first question was my age, and when satisfied that I was twenty-three, they were about to leave when they saw literature on the table. We were hauled down to the station for questioning and finally let go.

Shortly after this, my mother came from New York to live with us and as she had a small income, we moved to a four-room apartment. When George got the job at the steel mill, we moved to Thirty-fifth Street, a block east of Cottage Grove, the dividing line between black and white Chicago.

My brother Tommy also came to Chicago, did some organizing in Detroit, and, then, discouraged, proposed the Revolutionary Workers League national office be moved back to New York. This caused a painful rift, both personal and political, as he became very angry and verbally abusive in meetings because, for the first time, I opposed his position. He did return to his [second] wife, May, and lived in New York thereafter.

During World War II, when our small group collapsed after several splits, I felt lost, bereft, adrift. This was the end of a very turbulent, exciting period, as people, clobbered by the Depression, protested, organized and revolted, not only here but also in other parts of the world. While we made some social gains, the dark shadow of fascism in Germany hung over us as we watched movements there being crushed.

III. Peace Becomes an Over-riding Issue

I think I first heard about pacifism in the 20s when Mama and Tommy were discussing Gandhi's massive campaign against British rule in India. In college, in the early 30s, I participated in one-day strikes for peace based on the Oxford Peace Pledge. In the radical movement, we read Wilhelm Liebknecht's work on militarism and opposed wars such as U.S. intervention in Nicaragua. In fact the ideological underpinning of our movement was that this is an era of wars and revolutions. Although leery of class peace, we recognized that in wartime the demand for peace becomes a radical one.

As Trotskyists we had very early agitated about the rise of German fascism — "premature antifascists," we were dubbed — and warned that the anti-Semitism was a ploy to divide the working class. Indeed, among the first victims were the trade unions and the left. When World War II broke out, sentiment here became pro-British and the persecution and murder of the Jewish people was used as justification for U.S. entry into the war. I could not believe that the U.S. and Britain were concerned with anything but preventing Germany from becoming a strong rival power.

This was a very painful, difficult time. On one hand, I was accused of not wanting to fight fascism and on the other, I could not find a vehicle to express my passionate opposition to it and to the slaughter of innocent people on all sides. For a short time, a few of us issued a bulletin stating our position but soon we were visited by the FBI and eventually we folded. Then George and I discovered the Washington Park Open Forum where a largely black group of people met every Sunday in a free speech area set aside by court order. Here there was outspoken opposition to the war because of Britain's colonial role in Africa. Thus we found a platform for our views, literally, and continued to use it throughout the war.

Up until this time I regarded pacifism as ineffectual at best or inimical to revolutionary struggle, at worst. But now pacifists were standing up to the military, refusing to serve, getting stiff prison sentences. They were a small, courageous, determined voice speaking out against the war and I began to feel common ground with them. Then came the bomb, the end of the war, revelations about the Allies' conduct of the war, the cold war, the Korean war on which I did research and wrote a paper to present to a group of like-minded friends.

In the mid-50s we became friends with a Quaker couple who introduced us to Circle Pines Center, a cooperative camp in Michigan which again opened up a world of involvement, warmth, integration, openness to peace and social justice issues. Though passionately concerned with the building civil rights struggle, I found no avenue for direct intervention though we did support CORE (Congress on Racial Equality). The peace movement, on the other hand, offered opportunity. While the anti-nuclear protest was not all that I wished for in a peace platform, it offered a way to oppose at least one aspect of a militarized society.

When Women Strike for Peace (WSP) was formed in 1960, I was attracted by its activist stance and its emphasis on loose, grass roots organization. I joined Chicago Women for Peace, writing, editing, demonstrating. This was my first connection with the women's peace movement. The older organization, Women's International League for Peace and Freedom (WILPF), had always struck me as conservative, legislatively oriented, not big on action. Then, since many WILers were in Women for Peace(WFP) — in fact its founders had come from WILPF — I became better acquainted with their program which was a broader one on social justice issues than WSP/WFP's. Attending the second national conference of WSP in Urbana, Illinois, following on the heels of the Birmingham civil rights demonstrations, we had difficulty getting through a resolution on civil rights and failed utterly to pass one protesting the war in Viet Nam. In 1963, after helping to organize a Chicago delegation to go to Washington to protest the House Un-American Activities Committee's (HUAC) summoning of our national and some New York leaders to testify, and overcoming some local opposition in the process, I decided to join the South Side branch of WILPF where I was active for about four years. In fact, it was from a WILPF conference in Indianapolis that George, Marjorie Collins and I decided to drive down to Mississippi to see and report on the Mississippi Freedom Movement in 1964.

In 1968, Don Rose, editor of *Hyde Park-Kenwood Voices*, offered me a regular column, "The Peace Voice," and shortly thereafter, Maris Cakars of *WIN Magazine* suggested I do a monthly column, "Dovetales" — a wrap-up of publications, announcements, oddments of concern to the movement. And for a while I was happy to do my bit as correspondent and commentator, free of meetings and other organizational responsibilities.

As resistance to the Viet Nam war heated up, once again I became actively involved, attending demonstrations and trials, supporting Chicago Area Draft Resisters (CADRE). In the early 70s I joined War Resisters League (WRL), expressing reservations about their pledge not to support even civil wars, feeling I could not tell oppressed people how to conduct their struggle. With this, I acknowledged myself a radical pacifist — a radical first and a pacifist second, to quote a sister contributor to *WIN*. The appeal of WRL was its emphasis on direct action, its secular character, its dedication to unilateral disarmament and its opposition to "the violence of the status quo." Upon moving to Oak Park in 1974, we joined the newly formed Oak Park chapter. We also helped organize Metro West Peace Center, the annual Hiroshima Day observance in Scoville Park, and other events.

When the Pledge of Resistance was formed in the early 80s to oppose U.S. intervention in Central America, I became involved in the local chapter and then in the Chicago area steering committee, glad to support another group dedicated to resistance and direct action. I experienced my first arrests in 50 years as part of the Pledge. During the Gulf War, I supported the local coalition against it ("No blood for oil!"), demonstrated downtown, etc.

Looking back, I see that my peace concern was expressed in every organization I joined, even if it was not directly peace related: Women Mobilized for Change, Citizens for a Democratic Society (an SDS support group), Gray Panthers. I hope the writings and speeches included in this volume reflect more clearly these interconnections.

Ruth Dear   November 26, 1995

Photo Captions, pg 20:
Anna Kobilsky Stamm, Ruth's mother.
Anna Kobilsky Stamm and Simon Stamm, Ruth Stamm Dear's parents.
Ruth Dear, on the left, and friends from the Spartacus Youth League, 1930s, New York city.
Ruth Dear's brother, Thomas Stamm.
Stamm family celebration of Ruth's niece Karen's marriage to Peter Aschenbrenner, 1980.

Chapter One
Grief

March 8, 1985

International Women's Day and first bloom of season — a tiny vinca, bluely opening. Also, daffodil shoots in the South strip, crocus shoots in the ash arc and red tulip shoots in the patio border. Picked up armfuls and armfuls of twigs, George sawed up the fallen limb between ours and the neighbors' garden so now we have firewood which we will soon leave behind.

Leaving the yard with life springing up all over, so much joy (and the frustration of caring for so much), I feel pain, yet have no reasonable alternative. Especially at this time of year, the house sparkles with sunshine coming through the high windows.

August 4, 1985

George died suddenly June 13, 1985, in West Suburban Hospital of myocardial infraction, edema of the lungs, enlarged heart etc., having had an operation for a strangulated bowel April 9 and was home convalescing after 19 days in the hospital and went back to hospital on June 12 on the doctor's advice.

So-o-o no more life companion, no more loving mate, no one to share life with in the same way. Then, going through his writings, disposing of extra copies, giving some theater art books to Playwrights, going through his files and getting rid of most of them, each undertaking a painful ordeal; disposing of a life in this summary fashion without really adequate time for reflection. I felt I was throwing away a life of a *living*, writing, thinking feeling person who kept all mementos, it seems, holding on for dear life! I was under the gun of little space for these things, and not wanting to *write* his biography which, in a way, was laid out before me. Did I have the right? Who else? Is this what I would want for myself? I hold on to every bit of writing I did, as an expression of *my* living, breathing self and my history.

I had and still have remarkable support from friends and co-workers and this carried me thru the first week. His memorial, a beautiful service with tributes from all over his life, dating back to the 30s. It was a sincere, loving, supportive tribute but it was their George, not my Joe.

It strikes me as important that I write this on the a.m. of Metro-West Hiroshima commemoration — our 5th? — which George did so much to organize and continue and this year will take place without him and without his radical and basic input which I cannot replace. Also it relates I suppose to my personal feelings of a holocaust — at one blow, losing him, my(our!) place of abode, our way of life, and having to pick up from this and go on, wounded inside, emptied of another, needing help but reluctant to keep asking.

August 8, 1985

This morning about 9:30 AM, I took George's ashes to near-by Thatcher Woods and spread them in a glade on the south side, above the rapidly disappearing, under-scum pond. Rain and time will dissipate them; I had mingled them at home with good potting soil. I gave him back to the earth in a lovely woodsy spot and hope his spirit will rest there — if such there be. As with all these partings, it was a wrenching experience but at the same time a holy one because of the quiet woods, dappled sunlight, fresh green, and brought me back to enjoyment of these things as though a patina had been removed.

December 22, 1985

Disturbed by being asked how I get spiritual renewal, I tried to express it in terms of movement, humanity, etc. Later I realized I had omitted nature as a source, too. It seems to me that people who have a ready-made handle for their beliefs and refer often (and maybe glibly?) to spirit do not really understand those of us who feel just as deeply about our beliefs. When I decide to *get arrested,* e.g., it is out of deep commitment and support and desire to be an even more responsible part of this. I was buoyed by feelings for nonviolent activist Barbara Deming, war tax resister Martha Tranquilli, self-immolated Alice Herz, as if by some (old) sisterhood and also reassurance because of age. So I feel my spirituality (feeling of dedication and one with others — solidarity — desire for social justice and vision of how things could be) goes very deep. And when I think of it, there are many of us who function this way, and it seems to me that reference to prayer, spirit etc., *are* too public. I do not have one source, one shrine, one building, one God and one jargon or ready terminology for it, and I really think it unconscionably presumptuous of people not to look beyond that to a common human spirit. Should I ask then how you get spiritual renewal from these things which seem ritualized and pat to me?

May 20, 1986

Reading May Sarton's journal, *At Seventy*, I'm impressed by how well she conveys the joy and attraction of gardening and the tension and labor involved — the pressure of having to keep up with it and put in ordered plants, bulbs, etc. Also her ups and downs and the love of and desire for visitors, public readings, an admiring audience as well as her love/concern for so many different friends and the inevitable desire for solitude that results, a need to replenish herself, get herself back on track, writing, answering letters (which she seems very compulsive about). Obviously I write this down because I see similarities of temperament (though she seems much more outgoing). How I long to have a center like that — a continuing work or *daemon* of writing — to be able to structure time around it, though even when in the 60s and 70s I was doing my "Dovetales" column for *WIN* or my Hyde Park-Kenwood *Voices* "Peace Notes" columns, it didn't work that way. I make many observations to myself and would like to share them.

I'm preparing for a talk to West Suburban National Organization of Women (NOW) on "Ageing and Feminism" and I was inspired by Stud Terkel's interview with Jean Gump of Plowshares, by feelings about being one with older women and doing civil disobedience, by Barbara MacDonald's story, "Look Me in the Eye," to kind of revolve the talk about women functioning in movements today, by those I see all around me. Sarton has further nourished this by her observations and by the circle of friends — women in their 80s and 90s — literary and other craftswomen, doers all.

May 30, 1986

Making a life with Joe [George] in Chicago, especially after Ma left for New York in 1953, having lived 14 years with us, I became more centered on the home and was finally able to develop an independence *re* housekeeping and feel it was our place — not Ma's — so I could fill a "wifely" role in that respect. I miss that personal center, that feeling of a household and a relationship based there. So in addition to missing George terribly, I miss the grounding. I am freer — and emptier. I don't want to just fill it with the movement. If I do, I want to do what is creative, rewarding and meaningful to me.

* * *

Carrying the "No Contra Aid" banner in Oak Park Memorial Day parade with the Pledge of Resistance people and the constant applause we received from people lining the streets, all along the parade route, buoyed my spirits. One young man called, "They're letting everybody in" or some such and Sr. Gladys said someone pulled his nose at us — those were the only visible disapprovals. It was heartening. We were at the rear of the parade in the left-wing, independent St. Giles Family Mass Community contingent. They had "Oak Parkers for Peace" and antiwar signs in general. John Poole refused to march because of the military character of the parade, especially the Berwyn-Cicero contingent in fatigues or camouflage at the head of the line. Several of us demurred, Gladys particularly expressing our feelings that the peace signs were too general. Luckily Jean had one about Contras and then others of our group arrived with the big banner (they'd overslept) and we strung it out and at least six at a time held it. Maybe if I'd seen the front of the parade I'd have felt a stronger disinclination to participate but I felt we had made a very specific contribution and obviously expressed the reactions of many to the military display.

December 31, 1986

I started going to 10 a.m. discussions at Third Church, a unique congregation of Oak Park and Chicago's west side Austin neighborhood people with a heavy emphasis on social action. I stayed for Don Wheat's sermons and readings and several times I was much moved by the quality and message. And I was even somewhat attracted to idea of joining an ongoing group many of whom I know, a place to anchor though a bit repelled by Old Left ideologues (who are not many). i.e. a place to belong. But the whole idea of a *church* membership seems to me also repellent, a big barrier to cross. Apostasy? But I don't profess Judaism or Judaic religion. Why then take part in another? I'm sure atheists belong — in fact, I *know* they do. Isn't that what some friends did years ago in Hyde Park? and George and my feelings of scorn for that need to belong to *anything*? Any such step reminds me of our big ideological barrier to joining the Hyde Park Co-op, our final acceptance and now the idea that it might have compromised us seems laughable to me. But this is somewhat different, tho many people think I do belong anyway. Am I afraid of "sullying" my image?

May 14, 1987

Today I am resting after being at Armed Forces (AF) Week vigil for 1 1/2 hours yesterday. Tomorrow is civil disobedience at the AF parade which last week I decided to join. I thought I had decided that I would probably not do more CD but felt moved to participate after hearing plans two weeks ago at Religious Task Force Pledge Council meeting since Sr. Gladys had decided to do it and I had said I'd be her support person. So today I've been a bit strung up, my stomach acting up a bit at the prospect, I suppose. Funny, I seem more nervous about details of what to wear or bring than the action itself tho that is looming at the back of my mind. I guess to do it, I have to do it with someone I know and feel a larger group is involved and has backing. A large motivating factor is the Armed Forces aspect. Yesterday, at Daley Plaza, overwhelmed by tanks, guns, army navy trucks and personnel cluttering up the whole plaza.

Thinking about my initial reaction to Ruth L's mastectomy — waking up in the night, lying beside Joe, and crying — -I wondered was this a belated reaction to George's colostomy? At the time, I put a brave face on it in order to lend support (and, I suppose, to support myself so to speak) and didn't have the luxury of crying.

August 28, 1987

Writing now in a good mood, after having done CD 8/22 at Arlington Heights, Illinois base and arrested and held for seven hours. Amazed that I made no reference here to my first CD (arrest) on the eve of George's death though it is inescapably bound up in my mind. I guess the aftermath and the first entry being two months after his death, buried it.

Well, this was a big thing this time. I was one of the "high commitment group" which headed the march to the base, committed to CD if stopped by cops. Nothing happened till we arrived at the gate. Then people pushed and shoved at it, a tug of war with police behind the gate. I held back, not liking the physical crush and yes, afraid of being hurt. As there seemed to be a standoff — after the gate was broken open, the rope across it pulled apart, and the cops were standing 2-3 deep I decided to go elsewhere. At another gate people were massing for some confrontation. I started to go there, looked through the fence and saw Brooke, Gladys, and John had been arrested. I returned to gate, feeling terrible I hadn't been there and feeling I'd never be able to live with myself if I didn't at least try to get arrested.

A chain was strung between the gateposts, low to the ground, and I summoned up all my courage and stepped over it at the first opportunity — a tremendous psychological, emotional step too. I felt I had done it! — more so than the time at the Federal Building, perhaps because this was an individual act not as part of a simultaneous action with others. After that, feelings of boredom and tedium, some good moments in the cell with singing. However, tiring and confusing and wearing. Feelings mixed but next day, elation. I had completed a rite of passage. I felt one of the elite.

Why didn't I feel this before? Actually I did. I came home June 12, 1985, set up by having done it only to have George come home from the doctor and tell me he was told to go into hospital. So, of course, even tho I was glad I had done it, those feelings became submerged in the terrible aftermath. This time, there was not this terrible event to check them.

Seven Hours in Arlington Heights Jail

August 22, 1987
by Ruth Dear

Stepping over the chain barring the main gate to the base, I was immediately handcuffed, hands behind my back, and led to the waiting wagon where a dozen others greeted me. At Arlington Heights jail, women were separated from men and the cuffs were removed. Most were stripped of their valuables, IDs and shoes. All the thirty-six women ended up in one large cell and the waiting began, six hours of it.

At intervals we were summoned, one by one, to be queried and then fingerprinted. We began to sing and, as spirits rose, women formed a circle and danced. When singing stopped, there were lively conversations in small groups which at times created an almost unbearable noise level. Though a bench ran around two sides of the cell, several of us sat or stretched out on the floor. There was only one open stainless steel toilet and when someone had to go, others lined up, facing out, to make a living screen. A cop threatened a few times that we'd be sent to Cook County jail if we didn't post bond but we had agreed on bail solidarity and ignored him. He also promised us food which never materialized. Finally, at about nine o'clock at night we were called to the courtroom in groups. I was impressed and moved to see the place packed with supporters. Again we waited about an hour to be questioned and have bond set by the judge. Our offense was "criminal trespass" and most were released on our own recognizance and given dates to appear in September.

All in all, it was an uplifting, draining, tiring — and in the end, liberating experience. A high point was an elderly DeKalb woman's answer to the judge's query if she had been arrested before. "I'm ashamed to say I haven't," she said.

February 10, 1988

Don't I ever appreciate things before it's too late? What a *mensch* I had in George and how little I appreciated that! It seems to me it would be good to have a memorial *before* someone died, in the sense of an appreciation/tribute. I would have been able to see him thru others' eyes and realize the multi-dimensionality, the whole person, so that I could value and evaluate him properly. In any case, he, so to speak, provided me with a memorial which is still very sustaining: an appreciation of his life and contributions as well as my own, in a sense, since we shared much of it together. On the other hand, it takes his death, his not being here, for me to evaluate without all the emotional reactions, frictions, conflicts of daily intercourse, to see someone that way. I can see why people believe in an afterlife, it gives one a second chance!

July 12, 1988

From *The Unbearable Lightness of Being* near end where Tereza decides relationship wasn't so bad or better than she thought, I was moved to look at ours and came to a similar conclusion. After all if it was so poor, why do I miss George so terribly?

Felt guilty also about forgetting George's birthday, the 15th of May, partly because absorbed in the trial for the Arlington Heights action and leaving May 16 for Yugoslavia. I want to forget the pain yet I don't want to forget!

July, 1988

Excellent commentary on WBEZ: on the one hand the U.S. approves *glasnost* which includes public debate at high levels and on the other hand the Democratic Party is congratulated for stifling public discussion at their convention. Listening to and watching commentators, they reflect this attitude and praise a "well-managed" convention, where Jesse Jackson was in a sense bought off by his people's inclusion in the National Committee of the party and the inclusion by Dukakis' people of J's campaign people. J does continue to articulate his program which is progressive but not one bit radical, accepting military spending though reducing it. The media fall in with all this hoopla and regurgitate it *ad nauseam* causing more *nausea*. Somehow people who work hard at resistance and solidarity seem to forget all this in the rosy glow of winning an election. Even though I'd like Dukakis to win rather than Bush, it seems to me that to vote for him and his reactionary VP is to forget the future.

Perhaps none of the official left parties will ever grow strong; my vote for them is important and weighs more because of the small number of votes they do get. One thing has been borne out by the Jackson campaign and that is that Blacks do indeed support a progressive agenda (as do many whites) and that no matter how much of a sellout Jackson would make as president or vice president, the climate (as with Chicago Mayor Harold Washington) would be more hospitable to social concerns. I have learned not to make a big issue with friends and co-workers of the elections — if a vote doesn't matter that much, in my opinion, then it is unwise to give it more prominence than it deserves. So I view myself as standing somewhat outside this quadrennial hoopla and going forward with real social justice work. People don't *listen* at this time because they have persuaded themselves that the "lesser evil" is a good thing and they are doing it, thus actually voting *against* Bush. Maybe since Jackson had such success articulating a program, people will be demanding more. A White House changing of the guard is just that and now Dukakis will be guarding the *status quo* at the beck or behest of the Establishment.

August 21, 1988

I really enjoyed the discussion at Joe Powers' Friday night to welcome back John Poole. I enjoy that clash of ideas and exchange with friends. I also felt strengthened by having plowed through the *Swords into Plowshares* book and having distanced myself somewhat from the religious bias. I don't know how good my review for NVA is, I had a terrible time writing it, only a little at a time, and fearful of handling or mishandling it. I think I was distancing myself from all those good (mostly) Catholics at the same time that I tried to go past their religious phraseology which after a while I find hard to take. Well, it *is* alien like I suppose Marxist terminology was to others. But I felt I was on firmer ground, accepting their actions and motivations but declining to go along with their scheme. I also feel a little ashamed of my flirting with the idea of joining Third Church. I was looking for a home, a center, something to belong to. However, they tend to be predictable and the churchly rituals, though very muted, still repel me somewhat. I guess I have to accept something wholeheartedly in order to join or at least feel comfortable.

Just a word more on *Plowshares* review: it was very painful, in a way, to grapple with because of new sensibilities or sensitivities about religion. Not the flat-out negative I had thought it was — "opium of the people"? And yet I *knew* I would put it together. Although I mined the book for quotes and ideas, it seemed to me I was perhaps not doing it justice and on the other hand, it seemed to me I had done it thoroughly for such a short review. Yet I did misstate "divine obedience" as "civil obedience" and before that I had misread "divine obedience" as "divine disobedience" so I have trouble with the religion and the obedience aspect. In fact, emotionally, I can't stand the humility, humbling oneself, genuflecting before some higher power. Probably I'll never understand it. I guess I've heard Christian meekness and passivity condemned so much that it seems utterly foreign to intelligent, autonomous humanity.

September 23, 1988

Reading the journal of Florida Scott-Maxwell (*The Measure of My Days*) I was made sharply aware of the fact that I write concretely about me in contrast to her putting her thoughts in more general or abstract terms such as her obsession with equality as some compelling force that would produce homogeneity and erase idiosyncrasies. Odd that someone who, as a Jungian analyst, dealt with individual personalities all her professional life, should have these fears. It is a profoundly moving book because it reflects her turmoil and feelings about life (at 85!) both past and present, as well as, in a sense, being forced back upon a journal due to physical handicaps such as some sight loss, dexterity loss, etc., as well as pain and discomfort. It is a question of how to accommodate to these things and how one learns to take them somewhat in stride although they are disquieting.

In any case, I wonder why I have not used these journal pages to fashion a philosophy, or grope with one, as she seemed to be doing. Too concerned with me? Yet the other also reflects concern or concerns but is put in a more helpful general way, a larger way.

Maybe I should try to grapple more with issues like religion, spirit, psychology, etc. in these pages. I certainly do so intellectually or emotionally in my head. I really do *not* want to write essays — or maybe I do? Is that why from time to time a column appeals to me? I must go now as my *tutee*, Margaret, is coming at 10!

October 13, 1988

The desire to write keeps haunting me. Maybe, as with Florida Scott-Maxwell, it would ease things a bit? I swing — and sometimes teeter — between images of myself: one capable, respected, the other, old and not quite able to cope or keep step.

Reading Naipaul's *The Enigma of Arrival* at first was very soothing and engaging: his feeling for nature, the English countryside, his taking courage and heart and solace from nature. His observation is sometimes annoying and arbitrary and sexist and repetitious, but that's part of his mood weaving. He seems to be a permanent DP, judging from this and *The Bend in the River*.

* * *

Niece Karen wrote me yesterday that she feels ambivalent about Socialist Workers Party (SWP) having a memorial or meeting about Trotsky. Her father, Tommy, would have gone so she feels maybe she should. How well I know that feeling! You keep doing something because of another person's views or emphasis, because you feel you should. And it takes a while to free oneself of that burden to do what one really *prefers* without feeling one is letting down the person hovering over one. Like my deciding so-called theory was not for me, that I preferred involvement and action to accomplish a goal. "No practice without theory" became for me a sort of strait jacket until I realized my feelings were valid and that without practice, theory was sterile and withered.

October 21, 1988

Well I did try civil disobedience October 14 at the Armed Forces celebration protest action but cops on horseback prevented that plus no mass arrests. About 19 did get arrested. All the so-called hurdles successfully covered if not jumped.

Started Brad Lyttle's book on *The Chicago Anti-Viet Nam War Movement* and was plunged into that era and involvement again. Disappointed that we were not mentioned at least in founding Citizens for a Democratic Society (CDS), a support group for Students for a Democratic Society (SDS), but objectively I guess Flacks etc. was more to the fore. And Brad's connections were with David Finke, CADRE etc. We were supporters of CADRE and I suppose not up front in organizing CDS — but this was true of Milt Cohen who is mentioned.

Listening to all the to-do about the word *liberal* ("Big L"), I am reminded of the McCarthy period when the same atmosphere was created around *communist*. And in similar fashion, Dukakis, the Democrat, is retreating and sometimes disavowing the label. In a way, it is worse because during McCarthy, cold-war liberals, while disavowing communism, still claimed to be liberals. Now they don't even do that, it seems.

Hearing about US being a debtor nation and that fact sinking in made me realize that fascism could be a logical next step — a really right wing Bush vs. centrist Dukakis, the latter a so-called lesser evil. The mounting political reaction, CIA types, nationalist hate groups, fundamentalists, racists, Nazis, survivalists plus big business corporate interests could mesh into an openly militarist storm trooper-like group. There would be no lack of recruits in a depression. However what keeps it at a more covert level is the lack of a well-organized militant class conscious working class challenging power.

It seems to me no one on the national scene is articulating this. Jesse Jackson did to some extent though it was in a framework of his bid for power. However he showed there is a strong constituency out there. And the Democratic establishment showed that no way would this constituency be recognized or acknowledged.

The media critics talk of the candidates not dealing with the issues but they don't raise them or indicate what they really are so they are reduced to reflecting what the two campaigns say.

And I keep hoping — though experience should have taught me not to — that people will realize what they are supporting in voting for Dukakis and draw back from it. Well, they haven't had the experience, most of them, of seeing Germany go from bourgeois, socialist-dominated democracy to fascism and how that "lesser evil" was no help. I surely value those insights and education from the Trotskyist movement. But it is painful to see them held up by so few — to my knowledge, of course.

I am hoping, by the way, to be able to use or refer to some of my material on women's resistance during the Viet Nam War in my Lyttle review. Another painful episode — a contribution not acknowledged by War Resisters League Feminist Task Force despite enthusiastic response from some at first such as the letter from Mab Segrest. I am surprised at no mention of my *Voices* column or *WIN* though Lyttle does deal with the important groups and is quite faithful about the facts, it seems to me.

Ladies Day at the Induction Center

by Ruth Dear
From "Peace Notes" column in *Hyde Park Kenwood Voices* October 1967.

Chicago, October 18, six a.m., dark, crescent of partly eclipsed moon showing, cold. Bringing posters in car to 615 West Van Buren. Some women already there; piles of Women for Peace posters. We deposit a huge colorful drawing, rolled up, on ground.

Police are stationed in front of induction center and along sidewalk. Line forms a long oval east of the entrance and half the width of the sidewalk. Cops keep admonishing us to keep it that way. Hungry TV cameras, cameramen, plainclothesmen, organizers bunch near the entrance.

We try to carry the big posters but the wind does not permit. It is light now and over thirty placard-bearing women are in line. One young mother has her baby strapped to her back with a sign: "Hell no! I won't go (in 1984)." Other mothers have made emergency arrangements, brought bail money. There is a thin trickle of draftees. We wonder what and when "the action" will be.

After picketing in the cold for about an hour, a few of us retreat to the cafe across the street for warmth, nourishment, and the restroom. Inside, we're told there'll be a meeting at 7:15 around the corner.

Promptly, women huddle. Various curious males from the press and TV try to listen. "This is a women's meeting," they're told. We discuss alternatives--shall we go in, block the doorway, wait for the return of the delegation to the commanding officer? "I believe in law and order," says a woman who has lost her son. A young man comes up, asks to see her sign, takes it, cracks the wooden brace and throws it on the ground. Finally, a straw vote — who would be willing to commit civil disobedience or to be arrested? Half a dozen hands. Discussion: not enough people here, not enough raised their hands, some of us can't. Granted all that, how many would be willing? Same number raise hands. Agreement: we'll see if the delegation is allowed in: if not, at a signal, we'll all link arms, those unable to go to jail at the end.

We resume picketing, watching the doorway. Almost immediately, two women push in front of the entry, raise a banner. We surge toward them and lock arms. Police surround us. We resist but are pushed to the west of the doorway. As the momentum increases, I feel I'll be bottom woman. I brace myself against the wall and then notice the paddy wagon waiting for us. Will we be inside in a minute? We begin chanting, "Hell no! Don't go!" Someone shouts, "There's a pregnant woman here!" We make a path for her. TV cameras are trained on us. Women are interviewed. The destructive young man is given a chance to say his piece. Drowning him out, we sing "Study war no more," chant, "Hell no!" and "Thou shalt not kill!"

Slowly we are released from the police embrace. We return to the picket line. A few feel we have not seen it through. "Come down tomorrow if you want to participate in civil disobedience," says a young woman from CADRE (Chicago Area Draft Resisters).

The march to the Civic Center starts, a little ahead of schedule. A station wagon circles back to pick up latecomers, slow the advance marchers. We discuss another action.

At noon, women huddle again, are told to lower signs and go to the center of plaza, where Mayor Daley has forbidden demonstrations. Objections: without signs we'll be invisible. So, Gary Rader of CADRE stands near the sidewalk with us, is presented with a huge check for the Resistance by Pat Milligan of Women's International League for Peace and Freedom. Gary embraces her, thanks us, tells us 1200 young men have turned in their draft cards. Then people put their signs down, crowd around Gary while he is interviewed for TV. I look up at the Picasso lady, think: wouldn't it be wonderful if somebody would hang a sign on her saying, "I didn't raise my boy to be a soldier."

Later, on the five o'clock news, do we look impressive.

November 7, 1988

Saturday I completed my review of Lyttle's book, a really hard, even painful job. I got this feeling about unrecognized events which I knew of, a feeling of oppression or repression which I had to overcome in order to record them: My first witness vs. the Viet Nam war with American Friends Service Committee (AFSC), after Women's International Democratic Federation (WIDF) conference with Viet Namese women (I hope I had the chronology straight), the *Playboy* demo, Women Strike for Peace before the House Un-American Activities Committee, the reluctance of Chicago Women for Peace (WFP) to include condemnation of the war, and most important, factually, Movement for a Democratic Military (MDM). So it involved some checking of facts via *WIN*, files, etc. My problem each time is having to overcome what others will think and trusting to my judgment.

I almost decided not to include the personal recollections about the first AFSC vigil and the Viet Namese women and maybe some WSP references but in the middle of the night I told myself that this was history and should be included no matter how low my self-confidence was. Let the editor deal with it if it seemed irrelevant to her. [November 14 Ruth Benn called, liked it and said soon she'd send another book.] I also told myself that the personal reminiscence of the vigil, etc. at the beginning was how I started talks and that if it was a good opener for speaking, why not for writing? So I pounded the mattress and said I will include these things, and I did. I truly hope it enriched the review because though the work, *The Chicago Anti-Viet Nam War Movement*, is a good factual account, it mostly lacked spark and breadth and I had the tension of wanting to be faithful to the book, but could not find much to say directly, so I tried to convey this through adjectives — evenhanded, detailed, admirable, well researched etc., without actually making that criticism. So I did as other reviewers do (which I have criticized), used it more as a springboard for my recollections, but trying not to overwhelm it with these.

November 28, 1988

A week ago Friday at lunch with Bea S. at that little French place on Jackson in the Loop, two younger women who had been seated near us, on leaving, stopped and one said she couldn't help overhearing our conversation and thought we were excellent role models. Bea got very embarrassed and me not much, maybe a bit more used to it. We'd been discussing the Viet Nam War movement, my review or thoughts on Brad's book and similar things/reactions.

T. Hickey called me about the No Pasaran-Revolutionary Workers Group (RWG) takeover of the Pledge of Resistance "Global" conference November 19, furious at people from the Steering Committee and not a word of warning to people. She very much wanted my opinion and for me to be on the SC (which I'd like to do but transportation/energy is a problem).

Afterwards, shaken by split threat and my instinctive reaction to tell George about it as the only one who could truly share the implications with me. Well —

December 3, 1988

Came home from trip to Austin neighborhood on bus sponsored by groups from Oak Park and Austin: Sights of abandoned buildings — streets of them. Parts do look like a war zone, worse than I had thought, although there was much emphasis on rebuilding and community and church organizing going on. So though the sights were shockers, the fact that there were determined efforts to resist demoralization and to work for betterment was heartening. Though I do have doubts about private efforts to revitalize and though business is necessary to serve the area, really it needs massive amounts of city and federal help. Also discouraging were the drug areas and how a small shopping center they had worked for had become a drug dealing center, particularly Wendy's.

Somewhat inspiring was Tuesday night's talk by a nun from the El Salvador base community though I was put off by her opening with Bible quoting. I was genuinely moved by her/their commitment to sharing and social justice — a religious socialist vision — and also by her message to the Central America Coalition and others to do likewise here. Though I think they were more involved in sister city, material support, and protest for the Salvadorans.

I conveyed this to her through her interpreter and also my feeling that this was the real spirit of the revolution as contrasted with the casualty figures the FMLN rep. at the October 14 rally was boasting about.

I suppose if I were more genuinely hopeful I'd feel better about people's struggles. I do something to support them but there is no real movement to carry me — or I can't put total trust in one.

December 8, 1988

I'm much too absorbed in personal problems and feelings as the shock of seeing Austin neighborhood and the shock of reading Toni Morrison's *Beloved* brings home. People suffer and survive and even contribute to the well being of others (even when they are also trying to kill them to avoid slavery as with Sethe in *Beloved*). Instead of just lending my body to demonstrations, I'd like to share more of my observations and experiences which I think might be valuable. I do so when I can but not exactly how I want to do it. I'd really like a movement rap group which considers implications and broad developments, not so much historically as socially, psychologically, emotionally. Why aren't secular people more concerned with meaning? I suppose that's where the Unitarian Church works for some.

June 20, 1990

Monday, Ruth Benn called me to propose an article for *Nonviolent Activist* (NVA) on my perspective on the past, thoughts perhaps on involvement, as I see things now — all quite vague and open-ended. She referred me to Jim Bristol's article on having been a conscientious objector which people liked. I was agreeable but wanted more of a focus. I could write about feelings *re* European events but I don't want to do one of those general old-radical philosophizings. She promised to talk to Dave McReynolds about it and try to come up with something more concrete. Thinking now, I guess I could look back on various specific involvements — Camp Mercury, Mississippi, picketing with stockyard workers, going to Springfield for ERA, WFP/HUAC hearings, Arlington Heights, Rock Island, Harrisburg, 1969 DC, Canadian women's conference during Viet Nam war, Women's International Democratic Federation (WIDF) in Moscow, Rosenbergs' execution in Marseilles, Cairo, Illinois, opening housing marches, GP demos, Chicago 15 trial. My original thought was that these I was attending and supporting but took very little risk except with Arlington Heights? Mississippi? Nevada? open housing? Always felt that I never lived up to ultimate challenge? Speaking, writing, organizing, marching, theorizing, shaping a philosophy and testing it. This is just a record. How to make it significant by dwelling on one or two incidents. I'd much prefer to be interviewed. What about copy for Gray Panther paper?

July 2, 1990

Another thought: my feelings about self and writing have developed further since George's death. Maybe with him out of the way (as a burden or someone whose opinion was to be taken into account before I advanced or took a step) I saw my way a bit more clearly?

July 8, 1990

I am troubled by my reactions to my note-taking for the article. I decided to cross out the personal-political history part or to summarize it very briefly but I've been *unable to get back on track*. I thought putting ideas on cards would do it but it didn't work this time. Last night, thinking of what is sustaining me, sparked by some reference to sustenance on TV, I got a stab, an unpleasant feeling, so I guess exploring my feelings and past is quite traumatic — or is that too strong?

August 12, 1990

Moved to record following notes made during attempt to write article on "Perspectives" for NVA — a significant emotional journey which still gives me some after-shocks, having completed and sent off the article:

Is this feeling that the details don't matter so much, a long view based on experience or a disengagement? One resulting from the other? Yet I feel strongly about the ends. Maybe it's a mistake to try to put it in one neat package. After all, title is "perspectives" (plural).

Is my political past, the Communist Workers Group (CWG) in the late 30s and then nothing (i.e., no organization) years too painful? Do I feel shame at trying to exist as a group of two or three, at the sectarianism? Why? Didn't this reflect a deep commitment and a misguided attempt to carry on the vision/message? And why don't I feel better that we/I came thru it, found ways to function more effectively, tried to implement the *weltanschauung*, the Marxism (whatever that was/is), developed into a force in the movements I/we were in?

Interesting that I have reverted to *we* rather than *I*. Is this also why the past packs such a wallop? and is this partly why contemplation is so painful? What would I have done if it were only I? Well, what would he have done? So I grieve over losing that connection and the past is so full of it that it becomes doubly hard to contemplate.

And even tho I mourn its loss, can't I take pride in the fact that I continued and did so very determinedly, both as a life-saving device after his death and as a will to continue to assert my part in this union? I begin to see a big reason why going back put such a damper on my working on this article.

As for the past itself, I see no reason to relive bad moments as tho they were sins which needed confession and absolution. They are over and done with and served as experiences of how not to function and, sure, they left scars but why continue to pull the scabs away?

To others these are blips in history and what I should cherish is the fact that we/I kept going in the darkest days. And who did the research on the various papers "we" presented on issues such as the Korean war? (I still burn that George did the presentation — why not I?). i.e. who kept that intellectual/emotional spark alive and the desire to react, influence, educate, voice? Would I have done that alone? Who knows? Who cares? (Or, rather, who should care?)

So I should not hide the past as some murky, unmentionable, shameful episode but take more pride in continuing, sustaining, surviving as I'm beginning to do now in being an early Trotskyist.

I hope this helps in overcoming the block to continuing work on the article. Who suspected the depth or layers I would go thru? If it has forced me to evaluate and re-evaluate the past, our personal/political relationship, my role, and to better identify the thread of commitment/involvement; it will indeed strengthen the presentation of my view of the present and perhaps the future. I think I know what I'd like to see but I'm not even sure of that any more. If one attempt is to end in bureaucracy, accumulation for the powerful, and oppression, what is there to hope for? Is every revolution to have its Thermidor? Trotsky shrank from saying it had come but surely Stalinism represented that — the whole old guard was killed off. Yet they had to use the language of socialism.

How change is hobbled by preconceptions! How one has to *listen* to what people are saying; how rigidity inhibits this understanding; how bright or clear as one's vision seems at any one point, it is never the total vision; how one moves with the times and the new perceptions or no one listens; how to present one's vision today.

Maybe I liked Cinny's statement so much at the July Pledge convention saying the committee recommended laying aside differences on violence-nonviolence, accepting them and not continually debating them in considering future action, as a sensible grasp of what really holds the group together, tho at one time such compromise would have been anathema. Also because that is what I'm trying to do with this reevaluation of past, accept differences (or mistakes or setbacks) and try to reach a consensus on present and future?

I have an impulse to start over again, having gone thru the sustenance angle, perhaps deciding that or how I was sustained for myself, not for publication, necessarily.

Beginning to feel I have a tapestry of events and reactions to draw on for this, but unsure and queasy. Too self-revelatory? Too painful? Where to draw the line between personal, personal-political, and political?

Maybe having had the courage to examine the past, I should have the courage to look at the future which for some reason is both upsetting and invokes feelings of inadequacy in me. Who am I to project a future? Hovering over me are ghosts of my brother, Tommy, economics writers, theoreticians, Marxist scholars, politics and who am I to make predictions? Odd, since no one seems to have done an A-one job. I have been largely reactive, while carrying in my mind a vague notion of socialism. I am at sea when I look to the future — fears of depression, repression mingle with hopes of revolts, resistances, solidarity. Looking at "Great Journeys" on Channel 11, "The Silk Road," about China, I realized how large and varied and custom and culture bound people are: The Kazaks, Turkic Moslems, how do they ever become part of an urban/rural revolution?

Above is like the anatomy of writing/creating an article. What birth pangs!

Perspectives Of an Older Activist

by Ruth Dear
from *The Nonviolent Activist*, October-November 1990.

What does it feel like to work with younger people? How do you sustain it? What do you see in the world today? These three questions were posed when I was asked to write this article. At first I was delighted and stimulated, but when it came to organizing my ideas succinctly and coherently, I was flummoxed. I kept going back over a long involvement in the radical movement--an unexpectedly difficult journey--while telling myself, talk about *now!* Finally, I think I have done so. Of course, now is a distillation of then, and perhaps this is the value of sharing perspectives.

Working With Younger People

Last spring I attended the Gray Panther national convention for the first time in over five years. I found it both relaxing and empowering to be with people my age who take for granted an ability to function effectively, often in spite of physical limitations. It underlined my occasional self-consciousness with younger radicals: I feel sometimes as though I'm regarded as either a freak or a monument solely because of continued involvement and activity. A bit later, I also realized that we Gray Panthers shared events and experiences that seem prehistoric to those who came later. The Depression of the '30s was a landmark radicalizing experience for me; younger people might name the Vietnam War and '60s or Three Mile Island and the anti-nuclear power movement,

Having been active through all these crises, I often get a feeling of déjà vu at meetings, and I have to control impatience with intensely argued formulation on policy--concerns which used to passionately absorb me also. Thus at the July Pledge of Resistance convention there was considerable debate over a resolution on opposition to U.S. intervention: Should we confront it everywhere? concentrate on Central America? the Caribbean? Though favoring one version, I could have accepted any, because I knew that in the end the occasion would dictate the action.

What is frustrating and sad is the inability to convey experiences when I'm asked. What was the Great Depression like? Who were Sacco and Vanzetti? What was it like to visit Mississippi during Freedom Summer? One can give the bare facts about people sleeping in the New York subways in the '30s, the long campaign to free the two Anarchists in the '20s, or a night visit to a headquarters in Meridian, Mississippi, in the '60s. But short takes just won't do it. How does one describe the context of an event without being considered wordy or irrelevant?

On the other hand, working with younger people is refreshing, energizing, and enlightening. I'll never forget the waves of hope stimulated by the first student sit-ins for civil rights at the end of the McCarthy period, and the subsequent emergence of Students for a Democratic Society. There were radical movements which called into question perceived Marxist dogmas about the primacy of working class leadership, the inability of middle class students to effect change, and the secondary role of black and women's liberation.

In the process of supporting these new movements I had to learn a different language, to discard the rhetoric of protest, and look for the underlying radical impulse. Somewhere along the line, I also started questioning the rhetoric of revolutionary violence, partly because I had come to see nonviolent direct action as a powerful tool for resistance and change.

Perhaps the hardest adaptation has been to the growing Christian religious emphasis in peace and solidarity groups. Long accustomed to the secular peace movement, I still wince at the preponderance of crosses at anti-intervention demonstrations and reflect that in the heavily Jewish movement of the past I never saw a Star of David banner or heard an assumption that Jewish values were the good ones. This is not to gainsay the respect I have for religious co-workers with a truly radical perspective. A few years ago, I was struck by the message of a sister from a base community in El Salvador to a solidarity group in Oak Park. She asked not so much for support as for people to build like communities here. I'm not sure that message got through!

Keeping On Keeping On

Frankly, I find the question about sustaining activism annoying. The ultimate response surely is no different for an old person than for a young one. In fact, in some respects it is easier to function because one has more time, less effort is expected (rightly or wrongly), and one has less to lose. This last consideration helped me do civil disobedience around U.S. intervention in Central America. Having long supported other resisters, I felt it was time to act. When would I get another opportunity?

Seeking validation, I asked a number of local Gray Panthers and others what kept them going:

"The future."

"Anger at a situation."

"Activity."

"Concentrating on concrete issues."

"You can't *not* do it."

"Other people in the movement."

To those I would add only the urge to spread the word. Younger readers, where is the age difference?

Always Something Going On

The question about sustaining activism has an unstated clause: "... when victories are few and capitalism seems gloatingly triumphant at home and abroad." The answer to that is that there is always something going on:

liberation in South Africa; sit-ins of the homeless; people's movements in Latin America; demonstrations for choice, civil rights, better working conditions. I think of this dedication in the IWW song book, "To fan the flames of discontent." Without a strong, unified international movement, one has to look harder for the sparks, but they are there.

What's ahead? A '30s style depression? In the absence of significant radical parties where will people turn as conditions worsen? Will grassroots movements grow and coalesce? Or will there be some form of fascism? Now that one phase of overt rivalry is over, will the U.S. and U.S.S.R. ally against the third world?

Sorry, age does not give me answers. However, experience gives me the conviction that movements arise unpredictably and in unexpected places. It would be nice to have some big solid victories that stayed put, but perhaps it's not in the nature of that beast History.

From time to time, I hear women complain that what they fought for their daughters take for granted. Well, the daughters will fight for other things--and so will we.

August 26, 1990

Yesterday at Pledge regional, I said I'd be willing to fill Board vacancy for a person from Midwest. However, thinking it over, it's probably too much — four times a year — and I don't think I want the responsibility. I prefer conferences, like the regional or national, where I can meet people and exchange but the nitty-gritty of decision-making doesn't appeal. Of course, since Cinny will be the new national coordinator and conduct business from Elgin, Midwest meetings are more likely. Maybe someone with more vigor?

The other day, I went to look at Karen Horney's *New Ways in Psychoanalysis* again and scanned the chapter on Freud and femininity. I was shocked at his theories on penis-envy and the utter devaluation of the woman, the touting of the male and the regarding of woman as primarily a male *manqué*. I had been very impressed by his theory of male and female elements, the dialectics of that etc. Now, the women's movement, the whole assertion of woman's power and potential, the social discussions of patriarchy and a male dominated world, as well as the psychological implications, the assertion of woman's place in history, biology, etc. . — all made Freud's theory seem very dated, patriarchal, warped and a bit ludicrous, like some prancing, ego-tripping theory. Well, that was 60 years ago and I and we have come a long way.

I could see better why the women's movement was so bitterly opposed to Freud. Now, it's harder for me to honor his contributions. Why did I hold on so long? and feel I had to defend his major contributions? Because they *were* major, ground-breaking and should be recognized for the positive too. However that is history now, but maybe not to me because I grew up in the period of Freud's newness and because my family were so interested.

I had the same feelings about Marx and Marxism when he was faulted for some racism or sexism or adultery. I tried to hang on to the basic contributions.

Well, one does that with many things, with a tendency to excuse or play down the flaws. Why does every theory and person have to be either perfect or n.g.? I suppose it hurts me when people throw out the baby with the bath water because that is an injustice to the theory and the person, it is not the whole picture. But then neither is the positive only.

August 30, 1990

I think maybe the urge to write came as a result of thinking over the remark by Caroljean that I'm a writer and so I don't need an organizing job — hah! Well, I'm gratified but still uneasy at being so designated because I feel I didn't write that much, not full-time anyway, and so I don't deserve that distinction. And thinking over, that while George was struggling and trying to become a paid and published writer of fiction, I was being published, tho never paid, and of course not in a capitalist enterprise. But why does being called a writer make me uneasy as tho I hadn't fully earned that title? Maybe, like George, I want to be paid and recognized commercially and maybe that's why I had such strong reactions to his emphasis on tailoring his writing to be sold.

Why, also, can I not speak of myself as a writer without reference to him? I have folders of writings (and talks) and a good part of radical activity was writing, but that seemed to me nitty-gritty writing, polemical writing, not writing with a capital W. Certainly my columns for *Voices* and *WIN* were a different type of writing, reporting on experiences of another kind, and book reviewing still another. I don't think I'll ever be able to write fiction, and then I think of that 80-year-old woman who had a novel published. Well, I have no real desire (I believe) to write a novel but I would like to be able to craft a piece of fiction.

I drifted into thinking of my traumatic abortion at age 21 and having to be brought back by Ma for a repeat. A connection with aborted desires to write fiction? I guess I'll never be able to handle the emotion, the emotional content of fiction, the self-examination and revelation. Look at the trouble I had with the "Perspectives" article!

September 25, 1990

More or less recovered from severe back spasm, week of 10th to 17th. The Sunday it started I went to Third Church and, listening to Don, I had a surge of feeling that I was ready to join. I had been thinking it over, feeling uncomfortable at being on the outskirts, in a way getting benefit without commitment, finally deciding that the philosophy was acceptable and at times inspiring but still balking at that word *church*. If only it said *association*. However it is very carefully schooled so as not to give offense to radicals, atheists and Jews. Still have some demurrals: lack of consistency on my part, Jewish background, Christian atmosphere (unconscious but part of, say, Don's background).

September 27, 1990

Still conflicted about joining Third Church.

I realize that I went thru something similar on joining WRL, more or less accepting pacifism, a big step after a political lifetime of supporting the need for revolutionary violence to achieve a socialist society.

October 6, 1990

Am I being terribly inconsistent? The title Third *Church* and the phrase, "a liberal religious society" — these two words stick in my throat. I can of course learn to ignore them, much as I ignore the Pledge's statement about a faith-based organization, even tho I demurred at that. I've been going over what exactly I want or see Third Church as supplying. I think of it as a community of support — Aldine flinging her arms around me last Sunday and saying now I was part of the family with her, and, then, seeing me about to demur, saying of course we've been in many families together.

Realizing that with George I probably would never have joined because we were a support group, so to speak, and now I lack that deeply. So it will, hopefully, supply a lack.

Secondly, I feel accepted as part of something, rooted. Related to that is the opportunity to function with others in some respects and more ready, perhaps, to go to picnics? theater parties? etc. as a member rather than a hanger-on. It seems to me a human desire to be in a community. I have joined after much consideration, sitting on *desire* to do so, pitting a set of principles or attitudes aq1 it. I remember vividly agonizing over accepting the peace movement and pacifism as my area to function and did so after realizing that despite ideology, that was where I felt comfortable and where I had been *de facto* functioning. Similarly, with going to Third Church forums, staying for the service (I still stick at saying the *sermon*), eagerly taking in Don's lecture.

As to universal religious impulse, I balk at that formula. I was impressed by J. Huxley's *Religion Without Revelation*, but I must put it in other terms. To me it seems that humans have another dimension beside the day to day concerns with material existence, an ability to look beyond the immediate to general, universal concerns, to feel awe at the vastness of nature, to see humans' place in it, and to strive for things beyond the immediate. Certainly that is a premise of socialism, Marxism. Is that what's meant by religion?

October 12, 1990

I started writing this entry to deal with my fears and anxieties about accepting/not accepting religion. Certainly I'm more tolerant, certainly I understand religiously motivated people a bit better, certainly I sometimes feel a bond with them and can accept their passion for peace and social justice is like mine — or *vice versa*. And I am interested — or was — in comparative religions as a clue to how people think and see the world and the universe; hence the attraction of Tony Hillerman's description of the Navahos' world view. How we in the movement balked at comparisons with religious sects, the regarding of Communism as a religion etc., in that faith began to replace reality. I think what troubled me also was that I started to think maybe I could accept love as a valid emotion to have for others, tho I have been repelled by its use to mean solidarity, support, caring. It always seemed to me phony to say you loved people you couldn't know. How prophetic in my article for NVA was my observation that I had to learn a different language. I'm doing that now! I guess I didn't distinguish between *agape* and personal love! Why *should* this trouble me? If I could learn a different vocabulary in the movement, why not here?

October 6, 1990

Monday I spent most of the day working on a five-minute testimony on a state Universal Health Care bill (fashioned by Illinois Public Action Council) to be presented Tuesday. It was very well received by the six to eight GPs there and I was quoted at the end of a *Sun-Times* report on it the next day. I was wondering whether an all-day preparation for so short a presentation was sensible — and I sure got my answer! I seem to be very good at these short takes or at presentation in general, as long as I do my homework!

Odd how I detach feelings from their sources: Thursday a.m. I saw opthamologist who said my right eye was stable this time, maybe my sight even slightly better, and left eye still OK. Yet I attributed all my euphoria to other things.

October 10, 1990

I'm continually amazed at how bucked up I feel at becoming part of Third Church and relating it to feelings on joining the radical movement. I realized also this a.m. that talking about Sacco-Vanzetti after I had spoken on national health to the Third Church Women's Alliance picnic also helped to make me feel comfortable in joining.

October 12, 1990

I can see why I feel fiction is so hard to write. How do you represent a multi-faceted character with authenticity and conviction without making the person seem duplicitous (Mrs. Ramsey?).

Today, I drove Faith home from an overnight stay. She had come to the Women's Alliance picnic to hear Maggie Kuhn whom I introduced. It was a beautiful fall morning and afterwards, despite an impulse to contact some old friend in Hyde Park, I drove back, up Thatcher Drive and then to Thatcher Woods where I parked and walked up the path to the glade or clearing where I'd scattered George's ashes over five years ago. While in Hyde Park, I also thought of driving to see our apartment house on Oakenwald Avenue, but then decided enough of nostalgia, of trying to experience the pain that such revisiting brings.

So evidently I decided, subconsciously, to visit what I call George's grave. En route to the drive and woods, I thought of my introduction and chairing the Maggie Kuhn meeting, of the strokes I got, and I felt a sense of adequacy. At the site in Thatcher Woods, after being there a short while, I started walking on the concrete path and then turned back, feeling I had not given enough thought and time to what appeared to me at first as a ceremony of leave-taking. Going there, that is what I felt it was, but at the spot it had seemed incomplete.

So I sat on a log and had the feeling that I would take away part of Joe with me, that that was the part that was important — what was in me of him, of my life with him, of his stamp, of what remained of our fusion, so to speak. In other words, I would carry the memory, the love, *the* living together, that I would never really lose. I think perhaps I'd been afraid that if I said goodbye, I'd somehow forget him and I realized more fully, emotionally, that I never would or could.

* * *

Impressions of today's Anti-Middle East War demo at Ned Brown Forest Preserve, preparatory to a march and demo at the Army base in Arlington Heights, linger. We stood holding a sign: "Rich People Make Wars and Poor

People Fight Them," or some such, and were much photographed, including by Channel 2; but what made the news was the demo at the base. Apparently, cops, dogs, even riot hoses, were lined up all around the fence. Sorry we didn't make it to the base, but we did not want to stay any longer.

I guess I'm bothered — and maybe moved — by the long unfocused rally, beginning with a Native American religious ceremony including fire, people coming up to smudge themselves, each one in the huge circle (about 200) being given a few strands of tobacco, much talk of land, spirit, peace, Native American grievances, etc. And I felt chivvied into another ritual, remarking that had it been a church ceremony, it wouldn't have lasted (or even been tolerated) so long. Feeling I'd come to protest U.S. intervention and impatient of being plunged into another culture. Aware of grievances and oppression abstractly but resenting the initiative taken away and having to be part of something I would not have chosen. I noticed people, particularly Catholics and others, being part of it, bowing heads, holding up left hands with tobacco, etc., and I felt outside of this dedication and acceptance of spirit. It was not the spirit I was looking for. These people did not press my particular buttons — solidarity, resistance to US intervention etc.

Earlier, at Wendy's restaurant where a friend and I went for tea and coffee because we had arrived early, I was sharing with her feelings about the lack of a movement culture, a milieu of support and consensus which was broader than the few people and groups we're accustomed to in the movement today, and I felt this at the rally and reflected afterward that, lacking such a culture, others supplied it with theirs, i.e., the church, religion, etc.

The organizers had gotten Koreans, residents of Chicago Housing Authority, Palestinians, a Panamanian, and Puerto Ricans to speak — a worthwhile attempt to integrate other groups. Presented without any introduction or focus, or relation to the stated purpose of the demonstration, I felt a bit lost. I don't think the feeling was only mine. I felt people were there primarily to protest the United States-Middle East aggression and waited patiently to express this.

Am I to go on hankering for a lost movement world which has not existed for 50 years, except, perhaps, during the 60s and early 70s? Maybe Fran is right — I'm very Euro-ethnocentric and I want to push things into forms that are nonexistent here. It is depressing that class consciousness in America seems to have retrogressed and expresses itself in different single-issue movements or in ugly xenophobic or anti-tax movements. What will it take to make a movement coalesce? I doubt that just building bridges will do it because people bring their particular consciousness and grievances, but maybe I'm selling them short.

Perhaps that is why today's meeting is disturbing — like a picture of different movements touching but not really coalescing. Yet I can't expect Native Americans to look at it my way. They no doubt feel we Euro-

Americans are foisting our concerns on them. What will it take to fuse something overarching and yet with a more solid underpinning? Is it that I can't see the woods for the trees? Yet I try!

What also nags at me is this talk and notion of *deficit*. Why can't we turn it around and say, yes, there is a deficit, a deficit in health care, housing, living conditions, peace, civil rights? And ask Congress to deal with that deficit. I can't believe that no one else has thought of it. Yet I just did! To whom can I express this? GPs? OWL? WRL? Should I write a memo on this? It would be a good idea for a leaflet. Maybe use it for that sociology class at Triton in November? It's really an observation that belongs in an interview, but I'm not being interviewed!

October 13, 1990

As to *love*, wasn't I expressing some of this in my realization that people tend to bond, as with even hostages and captors at times or my roommate/companion in Moscow, Mary Boyer. Not always, of course, but the bonding was an expression of that feeling.

Went to lake front at Fullerton with Jo. I enjoyed sitting on the rocks (not the actual sitting which was not too comfortable), looking out at that vast gray, blue-green expanse of water with only the horizon ahead, and walking a bit along the water's edge. I had a mystery and Jo, a magazine (*Self!*) and a little book of psalms which she was using to meditate and to soothe or calm herself. I envied that, having a book of familiar, engaging, turmoil-easing, even poetic material. To some extent garden writing [by others] does that for me sometimes. I remember using *The Garden in Winter* at our house at 645 N. Taylor when I couldn't sleep — and I still can't believe I gave it away!

October 16, 1990

Non Violent Activist came with my article on "Perspectives" — nice picture of me that Ed Hedemann took in '78. Article seems OK, a few minor revisions. It's odd. Ruth Benn took out my reference to her name in my introduction and Pat Farran took out some specifics in my biographical statement. I don't know why people don't like such references. To me they sharpen up a piece, add info. make it more relevant. Is this a different theory of writing?

October 21, 1990

I brought my article to the fiction book group last night and everyone read it, a few even saying it was good, but I had the feeling they didn't quite know what to say. Also, *A Room of One's Own* had this special significance to me — how Woolf approached her theme, opening it out and unfolding it thru a discussion of early women writers, but the chord that had been struck the time before in the group wasn't there.

October 30, 1990

I'm moved to write that somehow *Sister Age* by M. K. Fisher, the book or author distances me. She is *observing* old people rather than *experiencing* age in these stories. I'm disappointed and keep being put off, thinking now I'll really get into it, but chafing at the *descriptions*. Somehow it is a very self-centered book, apparently written about 20 years ago. I believe she is now in her late 80s — 86, I think — so in the fifties she would have been 40 plus and even in the sixties, 50 plus, so she was looking at old people, possibly with a view to adjusting to old age — admirable and interesting perhaps, but to me, somewhat irritating. Somehow May Sarton or Florida Scott-Maxwell do it better, enter into it, because they are writing of personal experience and the details of personal appearance are not so important.

Odd that I feel better, in one sense, about my looks because people don't expect old people to be good looking, like old equals ugly. Of course there are beautiful old people — Wendy Hiller, e.g. — but people don't look for beauty in us. As with racial and other stereotypes, they often don't see beyond what they expect to see. Of course I dislike the wrinkles and the wizening and graying, tho the latter doesn't bother me so much because I am still not white haired. Somehow the pepper and salt seems more youthful, tho of course I'm getting more salty.

Being called Gran or Gram the other day by a high school kid in a group was a bit startling and unpleasant. I couldn't see any reason for it and I wonder at the impulse to do so. Friendly? Hostile? I might say, "Young man" to him but not, "Son." I dislike the familiarity and the categorization, and I managed to convey that when I passed them again by asking if one of them had done so and saying I didn't like it. Reminds me of the time that guy at some peace meeting also addressed me as Gran and I dressed him down. He asked did I want him to call me Sister, and I said yes!

Made a point to watch *Highway to Heaven* episode about a burn-scarred woman (model?) who gets renewal by being a counselor at a summer camp for blind kids so she could present or rediscover the real person behind the public facade. Somehow it clicked for me, for my feelings that in a sense I was peeling off layers and coming to terms with the real person underneath, letting it emerge more, accepting recognition and praise and feeling more worthy of it. A period of discovery!

November 4, 1990

As to Third Church, I feel I made a decision and I am not ashamed of it and even though I may not like some people's reactions, I want to stand on it. I keep being amazed at how much it meant to me to join, how liberating, in a way, as though I had arrived, and I'm still puzzled by this. Did I not realize how much I wanted to belong somewhere (always had) and I'm a little troubled by the feeling sometimes that I'm one of "them" — the other side? the Christian world? — and could answer now which church I belonged to if I wanted, but which I certainly don't want to as a means of identification.

November 28, 1990

What can I fashion for myself? This occurred to me as I thought of the cap I'm crocheting and is challenging in the sense that I decided to go with adding color to the ear pieces as in the original pattern, despite danger of it looking like a girl's helmet. I wanted that color and variety and that ability to combine and create is very satisfying and thrilling in a way. Not so different from combining parts of a talk or an article, highlighting certain things.

I feel I may be on the verge of some break-through. About what? Myself? My beliefs? Thinking early a.m. of going to Karen's for Xmas also made me feel odd, as tho I was turning my back on a life-long stance. I spend so much time and energy formulating and thinking about formulating that I should be able to express what's bothering me. Do I feel such unease at having started something new and am I afraid of where it will lead? Out of my control? Out of the control of the past? Is it a wrenching at having to abandon some old attitudes? Why is it so important to be consistent? Am I trying to hold on to a lifelong set of beliefs while I am adrift on a log, perhaps to be carried by a current out of control? Why do I *have* to hold on? What will happen if I let go? I've done so in the past, but none seem so gut-wrenching or profound. I mulled and agonized over evaluating my past. Is it that I'm coming to the end of one journey and don't know how to strike out on the next? Will my life end before I complete the next one? Did I expect joining Third to carry me along, substituting the act of commitment for the journey itself? Should I forget about the mechanics and look to where I am going? its meaning?

There are three things at work here: one, the beliefs and philosophy; two, the desire for community and fellowship and support; three, the actual joining of an institution to symbolize this, but, not, maybe, to actualize it?

December 1, 1990

Restless night. Got some stability from imagining untangling a skein of wool, following a thread through a maze, pulling on it as far as it would go, getting stuck, afraid of making an undo-able knot, winding a little more, telling myself to have patience. Thought back also to that unfortunate Juliet cap, outsize, unfit, tired of unraveling that, feeling that wool would by now be overworked, so threw it out. But was I then, too, trying to work through a maze, knitting up my life again without George? Remembered that a clue was a thread; a *clew*, a ball of string.

Do I want control or space? I do not really need Third for causes, so I should leave structure alone, regard it as one of the places to go for renewal, get some stimulation on an occasional Sunday and outing, and enjoy the community of support it can provide. It's very important to hammer out my own role, go where I can function effectively, not look for political fights, swallow some shit, and hold before me the larger goal, which is what I do in movements anyway, as with OWL.

I am accepted in many places; *it's that I don't accept myself there* or realize the acceptance by others. I've carved out a movement niche — writing, speaking, phoning, discussing, occasionally participating in an action. This gives me physical ease, space to function, and hopefully space to get on with going through and deciding on writings.

Writing here does help but I shrink a little from pouring out so much. Why? Perhaps because it's all so personal and private and is not usable for other writing? Yet my ability to do so here is a reflection of greater ease and confidence in writing in general, the urge to express myself which I follow, words and thoughts coming to me and, in a way, giving thoughts shape. I like that ability and it is reflected in my sitting down, reluctantly, to write a fund letter for the Oak Park Middle East coalition and coming up with a good introduction.

December 5, 1990

My feelings about Third go deeper than a stance on religion: I feel I'm violating my Jewishness? Well, does that bother me so? For years, I wanted to, in the sense of wanting to be part of the Christian or gentile world, although despite my efforts, I was culturally a Jew. And I have struggled with this, later trying to establish my cultural identity, distinguishing it from Jewish *religion* — a cultural Jew, not a religious one. So the Temple represents something I defined myself against. So am I violating my cultural identity rather than my (non) religious beliefs, my political stance? Have I gone over to the enemy?

Why am I going through such a crisis so late in life? Something others have agonized over and which I thought I had resolved? Is this a question of integrity?

Well I think I've gone far enough with this at this time and I should let it percolate.

It occurs to me, on re-reading, that in typical fashion, I first dealt with my *ideas* (not that feelings were uninvolved) about religion and only now am I coming to deeper *feelings* about identity as a Jew.

December 7, 1990

Reading Carolyn Heilbrun's *Writing A Woman's Life* is profoundly stirring. To me, particularly, the description of Dorothy Sayers' ugliness and how she — I was going to say "rose above it," but that wouldn't be what H. was getting at. Rather, how, by realizing her abilities, Sayers found herself and was attractive to men though she was left by the one she really loved, but managed to make a life with Fleming who, in some sense, gave her what she needed, or, she was able to take what she needed.

Even more profoundly moving was Heilbrun's description of a good marriage: the union of two people who gave each other room to do their own thing but at the same time, supported each other, so that this was not necessarily passionate love or even sex, but something more solid. Thinking back over my life with George, I realized we resembled this in some aspects. Each functioned. He supported me in many ways and I supported him in others, though jealous of his other commitments and abilities, and I believe he was sometimes jealous of mine. Both very possessive of each other. And yet such frightful fights, mostly on my part. H. acknowledges that such a union often involves bickering but she regards that as a certain level of communication and even sureness of each other. This put my view of our relationship in a better light and something to feel good about. We did have a working relationship, however stormy or thorny.

How does one ever get a real picture of a relationship? How can one? There are so many aspects, so many ups and downs and sideways, so many *items* go into living with another: daily relations and accommodations, sharing and not-sharing feelings, reactions, expectations and dashed hopes, hoping for something from the other. Yet that unspoken commitment that I realized when I was in the hospital, seeing a husband sitting with his wife, my roommate. When you build a life together, you unconsciously absorb these things, these little relationships, these relyings on the other, these incorporations of the other in one's thoughts and plans, the assumptions and mis-assumptions, the too often unexpressed affection and regard. Yet the test was my support and care of George in three, four life-threatening crises.

December 9, 1990

Yesterday, on coming home from the big Middle East demo, I felt a great sense of loss and loneliness at not having connected with Lucy or other Oak Park people to go home or to lunch with, missing George terribly as a confidante and sharer of reactions to the demo. Possibly also a reminder of my return from my first CD and the subsequent death of George early the next morning. Yes, it did resemble the other time: a feeling of elation, not this time at doing something as significant as that civil disobedience, but gratification at the turnout, the spirit, the nice weather, my giving out Pledge leaflets. I was glad to see New Jewish Agenda had a banner. Impressed also by a flyer for a largely Black ME coalition, relating conditions at home to war.

Will that headstrong idiot, Bush, feel even more inclined to strike, seeing this building opposition? This issue, even more than Central America, seems to be uniting people. Saw a woman with a banner saying, "My daughter is with Desert Shield," and, not knowing whether this was pro or anti, I said, "I'm sorry," to her and she said, "Thank you." So I decided she was part of the demonstration. The TV news gave it good, favorable coverage, saying there were thousands of people. It didn't look more than a thousand to me, but there was so much milling about it was impossible to tell. Students and others came from other Midwestern states which TV duly reported. Monica came down with her neighbor Janet and Janet's daughter.

Odd that good feelings about seeing and embracing people should be the prelude to feelings of loss and loneliness. Maybe the demonstration transports me to an earlier time, which I shared so closely with George, and then I have a rude awakening to the fact that he's no longer there beside me. Oh, I miss that very special — if often stormy — relationship!

December 11, 1990

Contributing to good feelings: Lucy asked me to edit a short paper which I really enjoyed doing and she was most receptive and appreciative. Also, good Peace Coalition meeting. 100 people from Oak Park came down to the Saturday demonstration, Mark Rogovin said, and we made a decision to vigil in Oak Park 1/14 the eve of U.S. deadline to Iraq. Also got strokes at meeting, a bit embarrassing. How do I take it gracefully without confusion and denial? Now I have to go to meet Monica for lunch. Caroljean called to invite me to a New Year's Day lunch, and yesterday a.m. news of negotiations with Iraq were cheering.

Realized also that Don Wheat's talking about *Breaking Ranks* and other social issues fulfills a real need for me to hear a social gospel (!!) reaffirmed — not his, mine! I really mean a *message*. Well, that's what gospel means (god's *word*) though I don't want it from God or an evangel thereof. Listen to my style!

December 12, 1990

After lunch with Monica yesterday, we went into Barbara's Bookstore and we each bought a paperback copy of *Writing a Woman's Life*. Will I do more with it? Or put it on a shelf and forget it as I did with *Women's Reality*? Hopefully not, since I want to propose the NOW group do it. Should I take *The Chalice and the Blade* to New York with me? OWL meeting is in January where Connie will report on it. I think I'll try to get out of being on the telephone tree since I don't want to do legislative alerts.

Have strong impulse to get wool for vest but unsure as to color combinations. Urge also to pick up house furnishings some way. Starting rearrangements, new paths, improvements?

December 13, 1990

Five and a half years to the day that George died and I am finally closing out, probably early January, grief counseling — I hope. Looking back, it seems to me that in the last year or so, I've picked up tremendously and now wince at the state I was in for so long. Recognition, of course, has played a big part, but somewhere, somehow, I was able to absorb and appreciate it. I realize joining Third was a tremendous step as was coming to terms with my past political life. Also, of course, the Middle East antiwar movement is encouraging as is U.S.'s apparently backing off. WBEZ radio reported that there are plans for a long U.S. military presence there, so we'll have a target. I am functioning more, pleased with the NOW study group. A fortunate connection but not accidental since I had thought about it and finally asked to join — and that ability to ask to join is what did it.

I dislike the fact that I turn my back on one involvement, like the Pledge, after another. But where is it written that I have to stick to the bitter end? Isn't it better to be involved with a local antiwar effort? Anyway, that's the way I've come to prefer to function — it's easier and also, in a way, more grass-rootsy. (What a horrible word!)

Saw *Weapons of the Spirit* last night on Channel 11 about Le Chambon, a village of 5000 Huguenots in southern France who hid and absorbed Jewish refugees during WWII. They were very aware of their own history of oppression, were based a lot on the Old Testament, and accepted "Israelites" as the chosen people of God. They had two dedicated pacifist pastors and others so they had a solid leadership and a solid faith. Much is made of this faith, but in the post-picture interview by Bill Moyers with Sauvage, the author, the latter stressed their character and acceptance of "goodness" or morality. I doubt that people acted without fear, as he maintained, but the important thing is that they acted, and led me to think that I maybe too readily excuse those who don't act. Sure, they're oppressed; sure, they're lied to; sure, they don't have the means. But some do anyway, anyhow. What does give people courage? Others? Knowing you're not alone? A gut feeling that this is as far as you can bear it, or that you can't do what you don't believe in? What made me decide not to plead guilty? To do CD?

That the village survived under Vichy and the Nazis is a series of fortuitous coincidences: a somewhat sympathetic Wehrmacht leader, a sympathetic prefect, a location in the at-first-unoccupied South. Another village which was a resistance headquarters was wiped out. So the continued existence of the village was, in that sense, a fluke. All this is brought out in the interview.

Interesting psychologically that the refugees, after the war, tried to forget about the period which, despite the sheltering, was a nightmare to them, and that the author's parents who came to the U.S. with him as a very young child (he was born in Le Chambon) never even told him he was Jewish. Anyway, it was heartening! What sustains me is also faith, I guess, faith in change, faith in achieving a better world, determination to work for it without, necessarily, victories or rewards. Because it's the right thing to do, as I see it?

I also watched the Hanukkah presentation again, and something Sauvage said about his wanting to discover his roots struck me as very pointed. It wasn't the religion that was important, but the history: where I came from, the culture, the customs.

Well, it's good to be celebrating and examining roots that predate George and, so to speak, validate an existence without him and add breadth or depth to revolutionary concepts, ideas of awareness, how people react and function. Is that what this is all about?

Photo Caption pg 53:
George Dear and Ruth Dear at a garage sale to raise funds for the Gray Panthers.

Chapter Two
Trying to Assess Where I Am

December 16, 1990

In one month I'll be 77! A grim age? 80 is creeping up. What will it be like after that? Will I live to see it? No reason not to but one never knows as the body gets crankier.

At the Gray Panther Board meeting, a week ago Saturday, I said I'd be willing to write a peace column for the newsletter.

Beverley says she saw War Resisters League calendar at Left Bank bookstore. Nice to hear. I wonder if Don Wheat will ever use that calendar (*A Way of Life*) or my article in a talk. (Will I ever be able to write *sermon?*)

Mentioned to L and B that despite Third not being technically *Christian*, it still seemed so to me. L pointed out that *priest* was not limited to Christians and I realized that High Priest of the Temple had been mentioned in the Bible. In the course of this, took down the Bible Dud gave us and we looked through it for some references. I had a funny feeling doing that!

Pledge of Resistance caroling was on Channel 2 last night and I realized I had forgotten completely that it was to take place that day (if I ever really knew, since I'd decided December was just too cold for me to do the open air stuff). I also keep forgetting there's a weekly Wednesday night vigil downtown against U.S. intervention in Nicaragua. Will it take outright war to move me? I do prefer functioning in Oak Park. I didn't go to bannering. Well I should do what comes easy, contribute what I can, and not wear a hair shirt about what I don't do. If I help to keep the fires burning and encourage others to do so, that's a role I can and do play. I don't have to do it all or feel I should do exactly what I did when I had more energy and stamina.

December 18, 1990

Whew! Have shingles!

December 19, 1990

I guess the visit to New York to see family showed some new strengths: survival and functioning through pain, ability to enjoy things despite it, going through all the motions of travel. Cared for and well treated by May, Vi, Peter, Karen. A little disturbed by *contretemps* about Middle East. P and K evidently feel U.S. troops there and UN actions are not altogether bad.

Apparently some people are supporting Iraq, according to them, and Cockburn, which I don't quite believe. I feel it's a difference of emphasis, a suspicion of Arabs and Palestinians by Jews and more conservative liberals or peaceniks. So we have a political difference. It explained to me why there was no comment on my button, "U.S. Troops Out of the Middle East." In a bookstore with Karen, a man liked my button and when I said this to her, no comment.

Much saddened by her description of the singles her agency represents against landlords: the poverty and hopelessness, especially of the mental cases. Talk at Xmas dinner of conditions made me realize how inadequate concentrating on peace is to deal with these conditions. Yet what can one do? How much support to give? Should I stop advocating peace in order to save a few lives here? Can one really do that? I'd like to be part of a movement that was handling all these things. Yet would that make a difference. I've been waiting for people to rise up and organize and hope that will happen, but is that a retreat? Well, I'll do what I can and try at least to provide or enhance a climate of support and awareness.

January 1, 1991

Listening to New Year's Eve Midnight Special, just before midnight, heard Mahalia Jackson singing "Down by the Riverside" and Peggy Seeger and Ewan McCall singing their drinking songs to the working class. Pleasant and encouraging. It took courage to turn it on. I eased into it, first listening to WTTW pop New Year's concert. I miss George, realizing how much a part of New Year's our listening to the Special was.

Finally finished Erikson's *The Life Cycle Completed*, much moved by his comparing two statements:

Marx (1844): "Just as all things natural must *become*, man, too, has his act of becoming — history."

Freud (1930): "I may now add that civilization is a process in the service of Eros, whose purpose is to combine single human individuals, and after that families, then races, peoples, and nations, into one greater unity, the unity of mankind."

Erikson equates this with acting as an adult "and a knowing participant in one human species-hood," overcoming "'pseudo-speciation' that provides a moral basis for hating others."

I guess what I feel good about is the connection Erikson makes between society and psychology and of a basically socialist or solidarity world view. I feel as if a link has been made that I needed. Well, this requires much further reflection and probably discussion.

January 10, 1991

Intended to write in here as a means of coming to grips with pain, a handle by which it may be borne, to quote Epictetus in *Disturbances in the Field*, but occasional reminders of this philosophy seem to upset me and I can't figure out why. Anyway, at first the pain was a challenge which I seemed to be facing, but since it has been more persistent and insistent I feel at its mercy and hate the idea of spending time lying down so it'll go away or recede. Actually, any exertion — dressing, preparing food, washing clothes (which I did yesterday) — seems to bring on pain.

El called me again yesterday to try to persuade me to come out this weekend, Bobbie will be there. Am reluctant for several reasons: pain for one; lecture on Unitarianism at 12:30 at Third on Sunday for another; plus the town meeting on the Middle East Sunday evening. Also, snow predicted for weekend.

Eager to hear Don Wheat on Unitarianism and to hear the following one on Unitarianism and Judaism as I know little about either. I'd like to get a better fix on what I joined.

I'd like to have the strength to go beyond — and resist — the pain, to have a philosophy that will enable me to do so. Or is that not possible? What do cancer patients do? Exist between morphia shots? I'm sick of keeping a stiff upper lip and waver between telling people of my sad plight and then putting a cheerful face on it. It's as though I'm saying, "Don't give me too much sympathy, don't suffer about me, and, most important, don't pity me." Will I become more resigned? Is that possible without some light at the end of the tunnel? Goddamn these nerves, nerve endings, uncontrollable pains!!

Do I feel guilty about lying on the couch, watching "Bonanza," say, as a form of self-indulgence? A waste of time? But if that is the way to deal with the pain, get distraction, then it is therapeutic. What a load I carry — not calculated to ease the pain, certainly.

In spite of all, I did manage the three calls for the Pledge telephone tree about Sunday and Monday. Which is fine, but as soon as I can't go to a meeting, e.g. like last Monday night, I feel guilty about it, not measuring up, somehow failing. Fears also about old age? Will this weaken me beyond caring for myself? After all, I'll be 77 next Wednesday. Do I feel I have to carry some banner of independence for old people? Do I use extra energy to prove something and when I don't have it, I'm falling behind?

Didn't realize how many ramifications all this has. Can't pursue this longer, some pain, not feeling too good, but hopefully some burden will be lifted. Clarification without easement is *not* what I'm looking for!

February 26, 1991

Increasingly better. So this month I have written a peace column for GPs, undertaken to do a fact sheet on women and peace for OWL's women's history potluck in March, volunteered to program GP annual meeting on theme of war's effect at home and did the De Beauvoir chapter on Lesbianism which I found very good and very glad I did it and got it out of the way.

February 28, 1991

I was able to make notes for an article for Brad Lyttle's newsletter, an expansion of my feelings about peace movement and Gulf War aftermath. At first I felt I had little to write about except some strong feelings/conclusions, but in the act I think I'm developing an article with more meat to it. I guess I underestimate the strength and depth of my conclusions and thoughts on the subject. Certainly, with some examples to flesh out my meanings, I can produce a good opinion piece. Am surprised, too, by the validity of some of my questions about the future in the conclusion of my NVA "Perspectives" article: Would U.S. and Soviet Union unite against the Third World? Would there be a more reactionary (fascist) government here?

March 2, 1991

Am surprised, thinking over how I finally came to grips with my political past while trying to write the "Perspectives" piece for NVA, that I *could* separate the political from the personal that I needed to get over that block to dealing with the past, to burying it as something to be ashamed of (yes and no!), should have showed me conclusively that I can't. As I did my emotional crash during the gulf war outbreak and buildup. Why did I clutch my political past to my bosom so? A product of being far left, revolutionary? Fear of establishment? Warnings and prejudices about my head being turned around? I still have a stubborn feeling that my political philosophy is my business and not to be discussed or reviewed with a view either to validating it or changing it.

I'm writing now because I feel a little stuck. I want to complete this article for the *Midwest Pacifist* before I start on women and peace for OWL because I feel I'll get carried away with that. I know I'll be stimulated but somehow I'm afraid of that. Why? Related to feelings of something important to me being trashed? Will I never get rid of that?

Well, only in the last several years have I come to a fuller realization of the impact of my brother Tommy's influence. What a vise it put me in, as did my family's atheism and radicalism: wanting to believe in God and country, and then interested in *The Mind in the Making*, anthropology, etc. and yet not receiving permission so to speak. So I got the message that school was a crock, ideas were a crock unless they had a revolutionary stamp of approval. No wonder I sustained little interest in studies. A painful, will-sapping conflict — better to drop out and sink myself in the movement. What would I have done otherwise? Well, that was already the Depression and I probably would have connected in some way.

Maybe I'll get ideas if I go to Congresswoman Cardiss Collins meeting tonight and can further expand my article. If not, maybe I should give it up or write a very short think piece, perhaps in the form of questions. Less pontifical and calling for fewer positive assertions?

March 17, 1991

I am moved to write in here, I'm not quite sure why, perhaps to digest the day. At Third Church, Don's sermon and readings concerned with pain and living after the fall, i.e., after the loss of health with physical well-being; how Max Lerner combated disease and pain at 78 and is still functioning at 85; how a woman nursed her husband for years through a steadily more debilitating heart condition and his and her struggle to keep him interested in former mental pursuits and her imprisonment as caretaker for lack of same for herself, especially getting books for him as I did for George (thankful myself his was not such a long-drawn out illness but rather a series of crises, so that I did not have to work so hard to keep my spirits up and I could function and continue my interests). Nevertheless a saddening thing. However, the singing of "Simple Gifts" by the choir and "Kevin Barry" by all of us were mitigating, as was the intermix with a few people. One man addressed me. We had met at a Milwaukee conference (Mobilization for Survival? Pre-Mobe?) and he remembered he had asked if I was Tommy's wife (Mrs. Stamm) and I'd said I was his sister. Also talked with Aldine some and learned she and Mina Riddle were planning an un-performance/lecture on Jane Addams with Peggy Lipschultz and Rebecca Armstrong. Interested, and said I'd let OWL (and maybe NOW) know for May 19.

Later went up to Lucy's. She read me some poetry from an anthology of Spanish works in translation, an anti-imperialist poem by Neruda and one by a woman who'd committed suicide. And she showed me some poems which the same group Ann Wheat had invited would discuss. Sounded interesting: Auden, J. Viorst, C. Heilbrun, L. Hughes etc. Mostly social commentary.

March 19, 1991

Went to hear two women historians at NOW meeting at Dole library last night. Interesting sidelights though the woman who had written a monograph on three Swahili women I found less interesting than the first one who talked about women's history and women's place in history. The second one is doing research on Women's Liberation Union, and, listening, I had the feeling that I was history, that I was part of it. I wondered how one defines history when I heard the 50s referred to as such. To me this is life, not history. How one makes a distinction, in a way, is subjective, in terms of what one has experienced in one's lifetime at any given point. So I was stimulated but didn't know how to share it until this writing. I didn't want to inject myself without some relevance. Contributing to my feeling was the job I had done on women and peace at OWL and my Viet Namese resistance bit. It occurs to me that I am using my Viet Nam women's resistance material without further publication, and it's a good use.

March 27, 1991

Beautiful day yesterday. Finally mailed *Midwest Pacifist* article to Brad Lyttle on my reactions to the peace movement's schizoid approach to supporting troops, etc. Took me a while. Had made notes for it and put these aside to work on talk on women's history in the peace movement for OWL.

I was delighted to see the overnight blooming of crocuses in many places, our front included. I still prefer the species ones; somehow the color intensity is enhanced by the yellow pollen-bearing centers. Also saw chionodoxa, dutchman's breeches, and some hyacinths! Wonder if Spring Beauties are out in Thatcher. I should call El and Rosie to go out. At Walgreen's, Tuesday, there were six seed packets for a dollar, so I bought them, probably foolishly: marigolds, dwarf zinnias, 2 coleus, alyssum, thinking I'd plant some, especially coleus, for house. Maybe, maybe! Anyway, it gave me some contact with a garden.

April 1, 1991

Worked a little on Universal Health System testimony for Wednesday but not quite satisfied. I would like to work in military spending and insurance companies more smoothly. I feel I should on both counts. Started book on unemployment, *Impatient Armies of the Poor*, for Gray Panther newsletter, but dull going — clumsyish style, figures, but somehow no real drama though he quotes a lot. Odd that some people can infuse an account with interest and grace while some don't get off the ground. I thought the material would carry it — or me — along but it doesn't and I sort of resent having to do it. Noted that at the end he has a fair account of Trotskyists in the Teamsters Union in Minneapolis.

April 2, 1991

Watching *Eyes on the Prize* again last night, running all this week, glad to be reminded of Congress of Racial Equality's role, Freedom Rides. Shocking, brutal resistance to school integration. I lived passionately through that time, if mainly vicariously, but so much was going on that outrages merged. Valuable to see them highlighted. Sad to see so many white racists mobilized against kids and teens; hysterical reaction to one Black man, Meredith, at "Ole Miss," such irrational anger and fear. What made them so angry? What makes nationalities so emotional and ready to kill other nationalities or ethnic groups? Is this a glue that holds these societies together? Is this such a strong bond or is it the scape-goating that provides the bond? There *must* be some group chemistry, but it's hard for me to translate this into something uplifting. Certainly there are other, better bonds to look for and to attempt to make or to strengthen. And how does the overlay of their religion serve them in this — a righteous cause? A feeling of effectiveness?

Those two who killed Emmet Till, were they avenging a familiarity, an insult to a woman relative? But then why deny it? Because of the law? Knowing they were observing the etiquette of the South? But why take a life for that? Why that extreme hate? Like some ancient medieval or tribal custom when life was cheaper? Certainly this was so for the poor and oppressed. Why so much sexual fear? With such inflamed people one is helpless to appeal or reason. I suppose it's the ones who stand by, don't get so inflamed, see more of the picture, who react against it — like women. Though white mothers trying to prevent Black kids from going to "their" elementary school can be just as vicious. Saw some of that in the Chicago area at Mt. Greenwood where I went to counter-demonstrate and to lend support.

I feel just as disturbed at the nationalists in Eastern Europe, scape-goating one another and the Jews as well. What prompts these mass lynchings? Why does each tribe feel it has to fight the other for existence? A shortage of the wherewithal to live? But it seems to go deeper than that. I respond to slogans like "Solidarity," and will try to help workers, etc., but why do *slogans* become *sloguns* (as I inadvertently wrote)? What is it about the flag and patriotism that moves so many people? Identification with something larger than everyday concerns? Why such emotional loyalty? I can see that part but I can't see wanting to trash everyone who doesn't come aboard. Maybe in the past, I felt more so, but I can't remember really wanting to off someone despite slogans about revolutionary force, the necessity for armed struggle.

For me, I think the best lesson is that *all* slogans change, that one cannot be frozen in one set of catchwords, but that the underlying drive and impulse is for something better, fairer, easier, richer in content, bonding people. That's why, I suppose the Third Unitarian covenant appeals to me tho I still balk at *love*. So many new approaches and meanings to learn! And I still haven't penetrated the *why* of those extreme, hateful emotional reactions of the racists. Look at the L.A. (and other) police.

Some join to kick ass but others who deal with crime are frustrated and this ends up in kicking ass too. But when you have a helpless human being in front of you, why try to exterminate him? He/she is already helpless. Exterminate all of *them*? Then what? Of course people's hereto suppressed anger gets validated by a system of police oppression and brutality, by other white racists, as in the South. And suddenly, even though you feel you are asserting yourself, you are also relieved of responsibility because everyone's doing it — it is officially or unofficially sanctioned.

So people reinforce each other and bond in a cause — hate of others in these cases or preserving some mystic purity or way of life. And this is emotionally liberating to them I suppose. But what would they really like to see? A controlled-by-them universe, country, neighborhood? Gangs would like this also. Is it intoxicating to see others squirm, plead, shrink in terror, cringe under boots, die at one's own and one's buddies' hands? Is it an attempt to keep a bewildering world, understandable, under one's control, *limited*? Hence know-nothingism. It is a frightening universe and approach to contemplate, so I suppose I'm writing out the fright or menace and trying to come to terms with it. Glad of being in a sheltered community, with all its faults, where one can reason and get angry at *political* differences but not act them out, oppressive though results might sometimes be. I guess also this is a similar reaction to *Shoah*, and why the film about Le Chambon was so uplifting, reassuring in a way. Here people went about supporting one another and the victims and assumed that was the way to be, in contrast to the assumptions of German society of that time, *e.g.* But this was a sheltered community — as is mine — and one needs these in order to continue. Fortunate, but should not be guilt-making because others don't have that opportunity. It is from such bases that one can try to do something about others, hopefully without guilt but with strength, if one doesn't grow complacent about it.

I think what this is leading up to is a message to myself not to be ashamed of joining Third, to value the community, draw what strength I can in terms of political and personal support and remember that, despite differences, we do have a yen for social justice and a shared understanding of the general way society operates. A *community*, in short. I hunger for some sort of spiritual or philosophical communion but I also hang back as with the Unitarian women's weekend which half attracts and half repels. Because of the vocabulary? Maybe by *spiritual*, philosophical-emotional, *weltanschauung* is meant? I guess also I'm afraid of pat answers, pat formulas?

April 5, 1991

Disappointed in miniseries on Arabs and Arabic culture on Channel 11. Moyers asks superficial general or picky specific questions and the answers are not very satisfactory or specific, as a result. Obviously these people think the Koran is important, but it's like saying the Bible is and though people quote the Bible a lot and frame decisions/questions in Biblical terms, that is the language and background ethos but it explains little about American society and the way individuals function in it. And in discussing adultery last night, it centered around women caught in adultery and the punishment therefore. Dr. Suleiman did not indicate emirs and rulers can or do ignore the rules. What does emerge is that the West picks one or two aspects, generalizes about them tremendously as symbols which give the impression that these are major characteristics. Discussing the headdress/veil, for women, the Egyptian woman pointed out that women function as engineers, bus drivers etc. and made headdress a matter of choice. Whether or not this is so, she and the other woman authority brought out that women function in the Arab world, realize professions, etc., etc. Also interesting was the tendency of us here to characterize Iranians, Turks, et. al. as Arabs when they're not. They also brought out that Saudi Arabia is the strictest (and worst? most oppressive? most backward in our terms?) Arab society — the U.S. ally!

* * *

Watching the late sixties program and the rise of Black power, Black pride, Black nationalism in the U.S. movement, I thought they put it in good perspective. It also brought out that Black Panthers never preached hatred of whites and had a revolutionary program, Marxist-influenced, it seemed to me. Sad how leaders were cut down, one after another, and how no new leadership has emerged. What will be the next breaking point? The Establishment, by nipping in the bud cross-national, cross-social alliances, encourages a resentment against all whites and a Black nationalism that will result in more riots. Evidently they prefer ripping the country apart in different localities and putting these fires down to confronting a class-conscious, interracial alliance. And how they demonize people! Black Panthers, Stokely, Rap Brown, etc. etc. The sight of Attica prisoners, stripped, made to crawl in mud, leaders singled out and run thru a gauntlet — how does this differ from the Nazis? From the L.A. police brutalizing a victim? Same hate, same deliberate anger, same lawlessness that is legally sanctioned in a backhanded way, same license to kill and maim.

Had to stop to file my nails — too disturbing to keep contemplating I guess.

On the up side, Greta G. calling about my moderating a panel on peace for Gray Panthers for their cable TV video program. Said she heard from someone that I was the star of the testimony show, Wednesday, (on Illinois Universal Health System). Surprised, since no legislator asked me a question except for one woman who wanted to know if I had a Medigap policy. That committee was concerned with price, not health, though the line now is to say: Of course we want health care for all *but* will this do it? Can we afford it, etc. etc. Well, I guess my testimony is a well crafted piece, doing more than using the usual statistics, asserting a larger concern, taking on the need as against military spending, putting GP support in a context of our general position. But, again, since no official said, "Good job," I felt it fell flat though a couple of people in the audience said it was a good job and a reporter from the *Southtown Economist* checked the spelling of my name. I wonder if it made it.

Obviously, the committee didn't want to take on larger issues — a disappointment since, though trepidatious (is there such a word?), I wanted to take them on for their total concern with money and taxes and ignoring of the population's health, such as the AIDS epidemic, which our health system seems totally unable to cope with. One suburban (I assume) rep raised the drug problem in terms of the poor, health and the *cost*. And one (Parks) kept insisting that polls are no good because the question of higher taxes wasn't included — not true, as a matter of fact. One small business man welcomed proposed coverage while another opposed it since he wasn't covering any employees now and would have to cover them under a UHS! A contemptible bunch! Russo made a good pitch and Anthony Young was on top of it, but it is discouraging always to pose questions in terms of affordability financially rather than affordability socially. If the *will* were there and the government was for it, it could be done. Though I can envisage, say, hanky-panky and corruption with one insurer as with many.

April 11, 1991

Intrigued by Bethesda (Lutheran) Retirement Home ad and sketch of the apartments; actually two small rooms with a small kitchen, one clothes closet and two pairs of windows to the whole apartment, sizable living room and bedroom though both are smaller than my present ones. Drapes are furnished, I believe, once a month cleaning, a coin-operated laundry room. All this for $40,000 down and $450 per month. Attached to a hospital. Also there is parking but it's unclear as to residents' or visitors'. It's the first affordable thing I've seen. Apparently all white and not in an integrated section of

Chicago! Even if I overcome reluctance/dislike to moving from Oak Park, a Lutheran home (brochure says it's open to all), squeezed quarters for me, and evidently not much of a view, that $450 per month would come to only a little more than I pay now, when figured monthly. Their pitch is to home owners to figure out their present costs and compare. I'd like to look at the actual apartment for a better idea and because arrangements intrigue me anyway. They speak of cultural activities and transportation for shopping, etc. It would be easier physically, but what would I do with my office?

April 13, 1991

As it turned out, I went to see the apartment and found it utterly unsuitable, on top of a panic spell while waiting to be shown. A very small apartment with an inadequate kitchen, half a refrigerator and, I believe, no freezer, which would require bending all the time, as would the oven. Not much thought for old folks, apparently! Parking would be $20 per month — no real bargain, that. It's disturbing and saddening as to what is barely affordable. I can see why sharing is a better option for space (and maybe even gardening?). However that would provide no care. I guess if K. Anderson can stick it out at 80+, even tho she would like to be somewhere really carefree, I should.

Today's long Board meeting of Gray Panthers was mostly about the National Executive Committee's or Board chair's recommendation essentially to disband GPs, and we registered a strong disapproval and outrage and I got to write the letter, based on four-five agreed-upon points. A marvel that we got good points, a good basis for a letter. Bob Wiebe was very good in shaping this and copies are to go out to other networks as well as Board members. A thoroughly disgusting scenario from a two-months-in-office Executive Director who was concerned about the Project Fund, legalities and lobbying and had an insulting scenario for a new group called "The Activists" which superficially resembled our activism but was really oriented on lobbying and essentially disregarded the grassroots. This is one of the few times that such a large committee, eight to ten, drafted a coherent outline so that my writing it was rather easy.

Writing this, I realize it was a good antidote to that frightening episode at Bethesda. Incidentally, when my escort there spoke of church services, I said I was Jewish and she said they had one Jewish resident (another live one?). I guess in general I picked up from hearing from Lucy, arranging a probable

Ruth Dear, seated, and Elsie Goldstein, at the Gray Panther garage sale at Henny Moore's house.

visit to the Belgian movie at the library tomorrow, and of course Maria's enthusiasm and admiration is infectious and comforting. Looks like the Gray Panther annual will be programmed adequately. She got Robbie S as moderator and I'm to give a two-minute introduction on GP background. (I can really be proud of that original brochure which I mainly wrote, now, in view of the attack on GPs from that organization-man Executive Director!)

April 14, 1991

Would like to discuss Bethesda incident/reaction and good feelings about writing that letter of outrage to National Gray Panthers which extended to feeling good about facility with words, ability to construct something on the spot, so to speak, as with letter to speakers for GP annual meeting, as well as crafting good talks and articles in a lengthier process. Maria asked me for a copy of "Perspectives" article when I mentioned it and I agreed. I feel uneasy about pushing it, but why shouldn't I? I wrote it for publication and it says a good deal of what I want to say.

Every time I think of Bethesda, an outstanding feature is the long blank halls. (An association to school? educating?) Plus an image of that cramped apartment with its minimal so-called galley kitchen — a discouragement to any real cooking. I guess it underlines that I'm certainly not ready for that. But it's also the cramped quarters: a sort of isolation or imprisonment in a cell. Feel angry at their concept of quarters for old people, as though light housekeeping means no space, a grudging "affordable" constricted living space.

Strong feeling that fright spell came from memory of attempts to find a home for Ma and the *sturm und drang* associated with that: guilt, conflict, resentment, caring, — a frightful bundle — Interrupted by phone call from Henny, *re* improving the letter and on the proposal to GPs.

I was going to say, before the interruption; plus maybe a feeling of it coming down gkhjjjlk'; on me now. A fleeting thought: What right have I got to want to die in my home if she didn't? The situation, I was going to say, is not so different, but it is. I have no children to look after me and see that I'm settled and visited. Wouldn't death be better? Intellectually, it seems so, but not emotionally.

Maybe if I get weaker and/or sicker it'll look better — but it will still be an institution. Well, I've dipped my toe in — and stubbed it! At the same time I have fantasies about a garden apartment, space, light, a place where I can still write and keep papers and files, and *be in the outside world*. Somehow, that seemed a place for shut-ins, tho I realize I'm over-reacting. One is not shut in if one goes out, but somehow the ambience is closet-like, the opposite of coming to a new place and seeing possibilities. An opening out that I crave, rather than a closing down, despite limitations. How to resolve this dilemma? I think part of it is also a fear of losing control of one's surroundings/environment, despite physical limitations which, of course, also mean a loss of control.

Meanwhile I keep thinking of a theme for my two-minute introduction to the program of GP annual, something along the lines of the violence of the status quo since the title of the panel is "The War at Home." i.e., there is a war going on, both the immediate domestic effects of the war hysteria, hype and actual costs, and the oppression and poverty and how the vulnerable parts of society naturally are the worst attacked by it.

April 18, 1991

Obviously all this churning about living quarters and furniture arrangement and plant decoration is tied in with feeling better physically, being able to take in some of my environment, looking at possibilities, stretching muscles, examining options, of a way to live despite doubts, hangups, loneliness, discouragements which, I must say, I've not had so many personally as far as recognition and expression. But war and physical problems did sandbag me. So I suppose I should lower my sights.

I feel I should volunteer at Third Church for *something*, maybe the Jane Addams thing? Somehow I've pulled back from Pledge and antiwar activities, even locally. I guess it goes in cycles. I don't feel as much that I have to go to all these things, that I'll slip and life will pass me by if I don't keep my hand in. Well, I do feel that to some extent, but the writing and GP volunteering to program the Annual, to write peace notes, etc. keep me going.

I seem to have two contradictory tendencies — to retire/withdraw and to get involved, and since I've regarded myself as mostly having the former, I've under-recognized the latter. Like I typed myself and ignored what didn't fit the stereotype, as with so many other things.

I also have rhythms which I'm learning to recognize better: how I go about writing something — the idea, letting it lie fallow for a while, the working on it, again letting it lie for a while, the final painful coming together of the ideas and the final shaping of the piece. As with the unemployment history I'm reading. I know I can mark places, that I can read and let ideas, reactions shape, and that in the end, I'll come up with something of relevance and interest, even tho the book does not really engage me.

I hope I can resolve some of my doubts about income, living arrangements, and even realize my wish to have green surroundings and even a garden of *some* kind. Or is this utopian?

Which reminds me that I was put off in the unemployment history by the way he dismissed the utopian attempts in the mid-early nineteenth century at communal societies. Certainly, if unemployed struggles needed examination, and the atmosphere in which they occurred, these communal attempts needed more recognition as part of that atmosphere and, more important, part of that movement. Well, I have one thought for a review already! I guess it's not possible for me to read something like that without reacting and creating some analysis.

April 19, 1991

I keep feeling I want to make a change but I'm not sure in which direction and in what? What are these impulses to fix up, to move, to make some other arrangement? How will I resolve this or will I just drift? Spring makes me want to spring — up? somewhere? When will I get a definite answer? Or will I? I think eventually I do take hold, but I dither and agonize so that the final action seems overwhelmed by all the preceding and preparatory emotions.

I felt good that the Chicago GP letter got a seemingly instantaneous response and that Dave Brown called from New York to report this and to reassure. Also feel good about getting a Midwest Committee for Military Counseling rep on annual meeting panel, as well as a Greenpeace rep. The MCMC rep is a male Black c.o.; hopefully we'll get a Black female nurse on child/mother health also, plus a Middle East rep and one other — a big panel if all five come, but nicely varied as to sex, race, third world. It should be a good array of concerns. Now the problem is to organize the afternoon. Workshops on the issues raised? Can we choose two or three on the themes, such as how GPs can affect or work on these issues? I'll run it past Maria. Somehow that seems better and more productive than discussing the organizational future of GPs. Can we ask these people to tell us what they need, such as how to support c.o.s and someone willing to do so?

Yesterday I called David Finke since I couldn't get a live answer from the office phone to arrange the MCMC bit. He said it was good to be working together again, or words to that effect, and that apparently stirred up a lot of emotion, remembering George's working for them.

There was another good side to calling David and that was the decision to do so. Frustrated that I couldn't raise someone at MCMC, it occurred to me that I had connections, names of others like David whom I could contact. And that feeling of being able to connect and doing so was a very positive one. I've done it before and I finally accepted that I can do so because of the groups I've been in, people I've met.

I know people writing journals always feel they'll be read, but even though it's true of me too — I visualize Karen doing it — I'm beginning to feel that this is not the point and what I write is important to me, including all these practical details, helping me to come to a conclusion on occasion.

April 20, 1991

Disturbed by *Sunset Village* play last night about an old woman in a Florida condominium who breaks her hip and refuses to let her kids put her in a home. A bit exaggerated, I thought, as she could have had a housekeeper which at first she refuses. A very stubborn, independent, ornery woman. Then, an hour later, I started watching *I Never Sang for My Father* but couldn't stand the ornery father, sweet dying mother, and the trapped son. Are these the only options? Why can't there be a good support system, pleasant, non-institutional surroundings, etc. I think that what I fear as much as unpleasant surroundings is a move away from familiar circumstances, nearby friends and neighbors, etc. Though I've found I'm not nearly so isolated as I thought I was or would be. And I suppose eventually I'd make friends or neighbors where I'd be. But I'm haunted, like Ma, by being abandoned by friends. I'm impressed by visitation of Third Churchers to the woman in the Maywood home (I don't even remember her name!), but I'm not someone whom people feel easy being neighborly to, I believe. I guess I should talk this fear out too.

April 21, 1991

Went to OWL meeting on shared housing and, as seems to be the case now, disappointed at what it really is: an old home owner renting out a room (and sometimes, separate bath) plus kitchen (and maybe parlor and garden) privileges, sometimes accepting care and chores in lieu of money, sometimes chores included in a low rent. They last about a year, the speaker said, so these are stopgaps for a home owner who wants to stay put. She also spoke of chore service which she also runs. A poorly attended meeting — not a thrilling subject apparently. Originally, I was going to skip it but I became curious after my Bethesda investigation.

I realized fully the truth of Anita's observation that there are arrangements for the poor and the rich but not the middle class. Had always resisted this feeling that that was a distortion in favor of the middle class, but yesterday I thought of my having too much in assets for Mills Tower, yet Oak Park Arms was unaffordable (even if it were desirable). I think mostly what appeals is the included cleaning and moving to a new place. The latter would probably be as rude an awakening.

April 22, 1991

I guess what stimulates me about Don Wheat is a sort of social approach plus some genuine, profound — to me — observations on life and living. He does have a great sense of humor, though, referring to the KKK burning a question mark on a Unitarian's lawn. I missed my chance to participate in the Jane Addams program which partly motivated me to go yesterday morning — a lesson to go with my impulse!

Anita M. offered to drive to the health conference at First Unitarian in Hyde Park, May 4, and I felt good about going to that church as part of the family. I tend to relate to mentions of Unitarianism and Unitarians now tho I hesitate to so identify myself — a not uncommon feeling for me on joining something which I had resisted but wanted to join in spite of rational, "principled" (rigid?) objections.

Thinking back, I keep wondering at how much I missed — and others too — by slapping labels on ideas and activities, a kind of shorthand, in a way, in our radical rhetoric but also a mental laziness in the end. Just because Marx, Engels, Lenin, Trotsky or whoever analyzed things carefully and came to conclusions should not have meant that we didn't have to do the same. Well, we did, but within an iron framework of concepts which resulted in too easily dismissing others' ideas. A valuable training in analysis in a way, but also a freezing of attitudes. I suppose some of this was important defense against co-option of ideas etc., but a recognition of the whole spectrum rather than the putting forth of only one's position on it would have been better. Of course, in a struggle this becomes difficult and I can see people so engaged sneering at ivory tower reflections, but without some reflection and assessment, and not only of strategy, one does get lost in the immediate and, in the end, to the detriment of one's principles.

Whenever I try to assess this, nagging old attitudes reproach me, so to speak: Am I rationalizing an abandonment of ideas? Becoming conservative, complacent? Well, I'm looking back, trying to assess where I am, what I believe, and since I am less able to participate streetwise, I have more time to reflect. And, also, because I'm alone now and not involved in and with a lifelong companion, I have been reflecting and evaluating. However, even when one arrives at some understanding or outlook, it is relative. Events are bound to change any complacency.

So what is solid? What is bedrock? I came to terms with my political past during the 50s and it stopped haunting me. I am a little better able to assert it even. The farther back in history it seems, the less acute are the various differences and emphases. With the Stalinoids, I do have to hold on to my vision that we are all part of a movement for social justice partly because of their m.o., and partly because of conditioning from experiences as a Trotskyist, and partly because their squelching of opposition harks back to personal squelching at home by Tommy, my brother.

I'd still like to find a niche at Third. Yesterday I sat through an awful hymn about God and God's will, Lucy telling me I had too narrow a vision which I resented because it seems to show a lack of respect for where I'm coming from. I suppose I should quietly assert some of this and not let it simmer, maybe I will! Why should I have to translate God into something meaningful for me? That's acrobatics. I can accept what some people interpret as religion but I don't *have* to speak their whole language and I feel they should respect mine. As a matter of fact, it's that requirement that chills me and would drive me out.

April 30, 1991

Next time we'll really finish De Beauvoir's *Second Sex*. Should I read her biography? Her book on aging? I really don't want to deal with her anymore. She creates a lot of unrest and anxiety in me, so she must be saying something very profound emotionally, stirring depths which I don't wish to acknowledge. It is a profound work in the sense that she tries to examine very thoroughly woman's position and I should make allowances for that and her culture. She is very passionate and contemptuous, at the same time, about older women. People last night thought it was because of her mother, because she herself was barely in her forties when she wrote that chapter. Whatever. So I should at least look at the work on aging to see how or if her attitude was modified. Considering that Gray Panthers is only twenty-plus years old and the ageism consciousness began to grow just before that, I should not be too surprised. But though she tries to strike a balance, her feelings and attitudes simply overwhelm that section and deeply shocked Anita and me, not so much the younger women. Well, we should forgive pioneers for not having the knowledge they made possible. I suppose gradually and later, I'll come to realize more clearly what's so disturbing to me — or maybe the question is too large to pinpoint.

Jean made a good point about how intelligent, brilliant women find themselves isolated and strongly reject identification with the women they see around them, to whom they can't relate because their concerns and attitudes and ideas and grasp are out of their league. So we agreed that De Beauvoir was strongly rejecting them also. One should not, because one is a feminist, therefore automatically defend all and any women because they are women and shrink from identifying the bad points of their condition.

May 9, 1991

Much moved last night, watching tribute to Marian Anderson. It brought back late 30s-50s and, of course, the effortless lovely voice as well as the discrimination angle. How tight that color barrier was!

May 17, 1991

Received a letter from a guy on death row and it's like a plea for help and I don't quite know how to answer.

Interesting that more articles are coming out now on the peace movement's "support the troops" aberration. I hope Brad uses my article; it is right in that vein.

Have started *The Women's Peace Union and the Outlawry of War* by Harriet Hyman Alonso and find it more interesting than the unemployment book but also not very well written, evidently a thesis. Interesting that what she'll date as "the twenties" is too general for me. I want to know the year so I can relate it to my chronology. Well, younger readers (and writers) don't care because that was not a time in their life. I also keep being thrown by the term *non-resistance*. Today we'd call it *resistance*. Well, that was pacifist terminology which Dellinger fought against and coined the term *non-violent direct action*.

Coming to the end of this journal. Should I close the book on it? I've written a great deal in half a year.

May 20, 1991

Acceptance ceremony at Third very nice yesterday. Despite original disclaimers, all three of us who joined together came to it. We filed up to the front platform, each of us was given a carnation, and Don read some descriptive words about each of us as we stepped forward when our name was called. Applause, and individuals welcomed us privately, too. Felt feted and maybe now I'd feel more comfortable there?

Yesterday, ran into John Poole who is still working at Eighth Day, the only lay person there. Said he's just getting the feel of the job, so it must have been an adjustment from Nicaragua! He's still in the Central America sister group too. Somehow I've drifted out — reactions to Gulf War/depression? Turned off by peace coalition in Oak Park, if it still exists. Originally I intended to stay with Sane-Freeze to connect with some antiwar activity, but the whole blood-giving bit (donating blood for the troops) basically outraged or violated something within me. I understand the attempt to anticipate (and answer) the kind of critics who mistakenly attacked Viet Nam antiwar activists as not caring for the troops. Glad I asserted my position however since now a bit more criticism is coming out. The price of leadership? But if I don't stay with it, is that leadership? Well, the assertion is a way of providing it in a specific case and I don't aspire to lead anything any longer though I suppose that in a group some elements of this occur. Am I going back to my feelings in the 60s-70s that I preferred writing about peace to being on committees, organizational ties, etc. as my basic or major contribution?

Is this good or bad? Withdrawal or reevaluation? In a way, the involvement hasn't slackened so much as the type of involvement has changed. Maybe it's because I've found a niche and am comfortable with it — -writing, speaking, reading — but I'm nagged from time to time by the feeling that I should be doing something concrete either for myself or an organization or a cause. How concrete can one get? Isn't writing very much so?

June 3, 1991

Yesterday, at Third, a memorial concert for people whose relatives had died this year, sitting between Bev and Lucy, gazing at the foliage outside, during Dvorak's slow movements, I remembered George's death, this month, which up to that moment I had not related to this concert. I realized that for me this was a memorial for him too, and slowly I began to feel sorrow and grief and wanted to communicate it and wondered if I was posing and realized from the depth of awakened feelings, that it was not (perhaps my way of approaching sorrow — sort of gingerly, from the outside, and only gradually acknowledging that I actually feel it?). I had an impulse to reach out for Bev's hand, realizing I had called on her when he died, wondering also, later, about Lucy's feelings about her mother, wondering would I have the courage to talk about it and feeling the need, that I should. When the concert ended, I did, telling each of them separately. I asked Lucy, did she respond too and she said yes, memories were more vivid now. Bev responded too. And I realized expressing sorrow and sharing it was no big deal, people accepted it without fuss, and though, in a way, I felt there should have been more fuss. I realized also that I was the only one making the fuss and making a big important thing of communicating it. Maybe I'm saying now it's not so unique and incommunicable.

June 4, 1991

Now, after an hour's call from Bev, a bit shaky and dizzy (from IBU?) because I voiced feelings about Tommy, pinpointed that Ma didn't intervene more because she didn't see it, he didn't show her that side. We touched several such spots, resonating with my experiences, so that, overall, I did more than just act as a sounding board because I shared my feelings, a bit hesitantly at first but not so much hesitation as I once had. In short, I entered into it more deliberately and I think that made it more of an exchange. Bev throws so much emotion at me that at times I'm overwhelmed and it was good to throw some back, so to speak. Glad I had something to give back and realized again that giving part of myself helps others.

June 18, 1991

June 13 passed painlessly. I wondered if the sorrow I experienced at the Third memorial concert wasn't a catharsis of some sort — not dramatic but profound, and thus a lifting or freeing from the grief. It's there all right but healed or healing.

September 14, 1991

Tomorrow afternoon, demo against Clarence Thomas, and I feel mixed about it — and him. Obviously he is a reactionary on social welfare, government responsibility, a devotee of Ayn Rand! Yet seeing him sweating it out, although I don't really trust or like what I see, I feel sorry for him in a way, distaste at these white males probing a black's attitude. Interested to hear of his apparently radical college days and I wonder if the reported feelings of some Democrats that he might be better than a white judge are correct. I'd hope that, but I doubt it. After all, he was an obedient bureaucrat to Reagan and Bush and resisted enforcing equal opportunity laws. The trouble with concentrating so on Supreme Court composition is that then one feels defeated and the outlook bleaker than it would if one were concentrating on other issues — a main drawback of trying to work thru the system.

Also, I feel slightly guilty at ignoring the Salvador demonstration today. Were it local, I think I'd attend, but the effort of going down, standing around in the heat, listening to speeches, just seems not worth it. I'm a little ashamed of that feeling but there it is.

September 16, 1991

In the evening, went to see Conspiracy 7 play with Eleanor L. driving me and I got to know her better. The play, to me, reminiscent, but of course not the real thing and at times seemed to stress the uproar and high jinks rather than the oppression and issues. Hoffman looked arbitrary and ridiculous rather than menacing. The audience was very enthusiastic, clapping and sometimes more. Though I liked seeing it, I couldn't clap; I felt the audience was applauding the sentiments expressed. I particularly didn't care for the selections from the defendants' closing statements; they somehow seemed melodramatic rather than sincere. Del Close as Dellinger was totally miscast

— too sharp-featured and not capturing the essential mildness of style. The other defendants were more convincing as to looks, but it was, in a way, looking at somewhat cardboard figures. So, though moved, I couldn't clap. Also, I was surprised at the audience's standing for the judge when they could easily have expressed sentiment by staying seated as did some people in the actual court.

September 19, 1991

I went to the Women's Alliance lecture by Shirley Ann Ranck, new minister at Universal Unitarian [Unity Temple] on "Cakes for the Queen of Heaven," where I felt somewhat uneasy at the goddess worship and the primacy she stressed, as though having a goddess or a she-God really made things different. The archeology and early history interests me, but I can't get the spiritual kick out of it that some people seem to. Well the topic *was* "Toward a Feminist Theology" or some such.

It was an interesting talk and slide show despite my misgivings, and I did relate to my partner who was stimulated by my approach and background.

Meanwhile, I have to chair 10/5 meeting of Gray Panthers and help set up a workshop at the Midwest Radical Scholars and Activists Conference, pay bills, wash clothes, etc. etc.

September 25, 1991

Went to NOW book group yesterday on *Composing a Woman's Life*.

Choices, choices. Sunday, to Feminists Against Militarism reunion and subsequent skipping of 9/30 health demonstration as I'll stay over, not wanting to drive home in the dark. I can't have it all and I should feel good that I *do* have choices. Though feelings about going to a play with Women Mobilized for Change women highlights stodginess at Third.

At the book group last night, listening to people generalize about Freudians and psychiatrists, I felt uncomfortable and had impulses to object but realized it was pointless. What is also saddening is that someone like Horney and her criticism of Freud is unknown or forgotten.

As I write, I realize how much I like formulating thoughts and putting them down, trusting to feelings and first formulations and shaping into appropriate words and expressions. I guess it's a feeling of empowerment which sometimes flows from me and, of course, sometimes doesn't. In this journal I can write as I please and as it comes to me. When I write an article or a review, it becomes a task where I have to discipline my thoughts, shape my impressions and observations into a coherent whole, and produce a finished, organized piece of writing. So there is a conflict or constraint and a self-consciousness of the impression I want to convey or create. It would be nice to discuss writing with someone! I couldn't do it with George — too tight, too jealous, too critical, too shy. I just couldn't open up to him.

The book group were talking about the marriages discussed and Bateson's theme of complementariness and her acceptance of woman's nurturing, supportive role though the subjects were four independent women. This also raised in my mind the meaning of success: achievement? money? acceptance? Discussion also illuminated for me the way a new movement like feminism thinks it has invented the world and some women tend to recognize no other women before them. Jean P. picked up on this. Donna had said that before the 70s, women, especially unmarried women, didn't contemplate or practice independent careers or look at marriage other than traditionally. I shared my insight with them — the way new movements invent the world — and hope it was valuable. It was valuable to me to express it as part of my continuing internal observation of movements — how they rise, fall, regard things, regard history.

Thinking this a.m. of the Soviet government and the corruption and bureaucratization, I realized that a centralized government was very open to this, particularly when it gave itself the task of representing a minority (the proletariat) and also a majority (the peasantry): the habit of thinking history is on one's side, the proletariat is the future and the link to socialism. Lenin perhaps tended to be aware of these things, as did Trotsky. But can one really put one's faith in a few honest, dedicated men (few women were in leadership!) to keep things right?

Theoretically, the Soviets were democratic republics, but only of the proletariat, and this soon became lost in a bureaucratic maze. It seems to me that this bureaucracy, even when acknowledged, is not something you can control from the top. After all, this was a concept on Marx's part, and the Russian Marxists, in attempting to twist it to Russian conditions, were caught in an impossible situation: a power vacuum in the wake of massive unrest and desire for a new order, and they stepped into it. Actually, these were huge radical parties representing the working class. So, to hold power, they became dictatorial and then came people without this basic understanding.

Amidst all the trashing of communist Russia, it would be nice if someone reviewed the early measures and decrees and arrangements — as with the Paris Commune — to show how progressive the society intended to be. I am uneasy at socialists trashing communism and the October Revolution and Lenin, as though the Kerensky government were the answer. And it's this and a few other attitudes that prevent me from joining the DSA (Democratic Socialists of America) though I'm powerfully attracted to the Midwest Radical Scholars and Activists conference which Gray Panthers endorsed and where I'll participate in a workshop. I've been interested in preceding years but never quite got up to doing anything about it.

September 26, 1991

Yesterday, Gert Rubin sent me another book of her poems, mostly all with nature themes, and on waking this a.m., I'm thinking over how I responded to them and how I responded to nature, surprised a bit that I never tried to express this feeling in any formal writing. When I think of how thrilled I am at Spring opening, at shoots emerging, at trees, at the graceful forms of house plants. Too close to me? Too much a private emotion and love?

October 9, 1991

Sunday, Sue Lodgen came up to me after the service and said she wanted me to take home one of the chrysanthemum pots she had brought in memory of her father, as I was an inspiration to her. I said, what a lovely gift, and she replied something about my being or bringing a gift to her. So I brought home a big, beautiful pink-with-yellow-centers plant. And I have been turning over the compliment ever since. I was truly puzzled at first, feeling how could what I am or do be so extravagantly construed. Uncomfortable but very pleased, feeling I never set out to be anyone's inspiration and do not do so now. How can just living and doing what I want to do be considered inspirational? Is it the fact of my age, longevity? But to attribute it only to that is to downplay it and I truly don't want to do that.

October 12, 1991

Very troubled by Anita Hill's accusation of Clarence Thomas, Supreme Court aspirant, of harassment and pornography. It seems too pat, too much like the Willie Horton tactic of Bush in the sense of bringing it all down to a personal, rather than a political, level, of fighting dirty. It could be true. God knows, harassment is a fact of life in the workplace as long as there are male bosses and female subordinates. And, as a commentator remarked, Thomas' defense or assertion has been on his character. But are things to be decided on the basis of kinks or marijuana? It seems an abysmally low level, a reflection of the way the Right has chosen to function and it means something is very wrong in the U.S.

It's also true that it's a heavy emotional question, one which women have been fighting to get recognized and abolished, and there is less reason to doubt her than him, and a great way of making a feminist point on the issue. But should one sink to their level? This digging up of dirt, of smearing in effect, no matter how solidly based, obscures the other issues. Of course women and others tried to discredit him on the issues and resorted to this only when it looked like he might be confirmed. Am I just accepting a male attitude that these things are not important? Is not sexual harassment a personal/political workplace problem? Something is wrong somewhere and in the heat of the emotional response, it is hard to sort out and get a clear view.

Yesterday, went down to Democratic Socialist of America forum: three Canadians on their health system with Quentin Young and Ron Sable. I have such a longing to be associated with something socialist, where the discourse assumes such a belief! All three Canadians were members of the New Democratic Party and called themselves socialists.

October 16, 1991

Thinking over last night's exchange at NOW book group, where I shared my feelings about being a role model and an "inspiration," I realize now that that's quite a trip for me. Of course, I waited for an opportunity or opening so to speak, but I don't think I was being boastful; my ambivalent feelings were and are genuine. Also, I went a bit reluctantly, sorry to miss the Dead Sea Scrolls on Channel 11 and the full condo meeting for the new residents. But I did open up despite not having the book (*Writing a Woman's life*) and when people were exchanging about women's biography and autobiography, I was able to recall quite a few. At first, we couldn't recollect reading women's autobiographies when we were younger, but then we stimulated each other. I said no one held up a model woman to me though I did learn or hear about Rosa Luxemburg and Emma Goldman, and M. remarked, "but you followed them anyway or became similar." Another stroke for me and quite unexpected.

Thinking over the stuff I sifted from my Moscow trip notes [1963], specifically the Moscow demonstration for Valentina, the first woman astronaut, I realized that to feminists it would be interesting historically, not quite sure why, but it seems my instinct was sound there. Will I ever get on with it? I laid aside the International Clearinghouse [Women Strike for Peace] notes to finish going through. I wish I could ignore them, partly because though I recognized a piece of mine, none of the material is signed, and, partly, because it occurred in a painful period of struggle in the organization over direction. WSP was action-oriented, decentralized, anti-nuclear weapons and, as a result of its activity, the House Committee on Un-American Activities (HUAC) went after some of the participants, including Dagmar Wilson. Should the Chicago group send supporters to Washington and openly support Wilson? I led the faction that openly supported WSPers under HUAC attack and we joined women from across the country who flooded the HUAC hearings and were electrified to hear Dagmar's response to a question about Communists in WSP. She replied that WSP accepted everyone, thus ending a dark era of kowtowing to a witch-hunting committee.

Yesterday, Carl Cowl called; he's here for an international socialist convention or conference. Ninety years old, still living alone, still a Marxist, still traveling around the country from time to time. Why can't I continue like that?

HUAC SUMMONS WOMEN STRIKE FOR PEACE

by Ruth Dear
April 20, 1994

Twenty members of Women Strike for Peace were subpoenaed by the House Committee on UnAmerican Activities to appear December 11-12-13, 1962. The committee was investigating Communist infiltration of women's peace groups, particularly in New York. Dagmar Wilson though a Washington DC resident was included as leader of the movement. Immediately the Washington steering committee issued a statement: "...We submit that it is not we women who should be 'investigated' but those who, with the cool logic of madness, attempt to reconcile us to complete destruction . . . . Our 'crime' is to cry aloud that nuclear war must not be permitted, and we shall continue to cry aloud with all our strength."

They issued a rallying call to all supporters to come to Washington and some 500 women answered, coming in groups, some staying for a day, some for all three days. I went with the Midwest delegation for the December 12 testimony to support Dagmar.

Getting a Chicago group together in less than a week's time required some doing! Upon getting the news, I called several others in Chicago area Women for Peace and we arranged for an emergency steering committee meeting. There was at first some confusion and resistance in our group. Some felt we were acting hastily, some that civil liberties issues should not distract from our basic aims. To this I countered that we could not possibly ignore this attack on the peace movement, and this approach and the information from Washington carried the day. This involved a discussion of tactics for there was no consensus as to procedure. Others called before HUAC had taken a variety of courses. Some invoked the First Amendment as protecting the right of free speech, press and association. Some took the Fifth Amendment, standing on their Constitutional right not to incriminate oneself. Still others were for boycotting the proceedings entirely, which was my inclination. Dagmar, however, had agreed to testify, and I felt that we had no choice but to support the women under attack, no matter what the specific tactic.

Then some women in Chicago wanted to say to the committee, "Take me too," as did other local groups. Finally, when I called DC to find out what they wanted us to do, Dagmar answered that they had decided to ask everyone to offer to testify. And about 100 women did, but the committee turned them down.

On the train to Washington, we Chicagoans were joined by WSPers from Champaign, Ann Arbor, Pittsburgh, and Detroit and it was a whirlwind trip: 20 hours on the train each way and 15 hours in Washington.

Like the other women before the committee, Dagmar was in a frightening situation. Three Congressmen and a lawyer faced her. She was also accompanied by a lawyer, but by HUAC rules he couldn't advise her unless she asked nor could he speak for her. The New York women who preceded her, I heard, had the roughest time and were in great danger from the committee as a "wrong" answer might result in suit for perjury and jail. However, Dagmar Wilson also took a dangerous course, refusing to answer questions about any person other than herself. Had the committee authorities wished, they could have made it very hard for such refusal to cooperate since she claimed no legal grounds by invoking the Constitution. "Look sweet but be tough as hell," was one instruction I heard.

The audience itself constituted a form of theater composed of mostly well dressed, lively, cheerful women, some holding babies, each wearing a white rose or a white card, hanging on every word, laughing appreciatively at some riposte, occasionally applauding. Throughout her testimony ran a thread of defiance ever so politely expressed. Her bold assertion that WSP accepted everybody. "even Communists," was electrifying and ground-breaking for a peace movement that was in part cowed by the extreme anti-Communist atmosphere created by the trials. Newspaper headlines told the story:

"Blessed are the Women for They Shall Abolish HUAC" (*New York Times*)

"Pacifist Group Leader Rejects Purge of Reds" (Chicago Sun-Times)

"A House Confounded Cannot Stand up to the Ladies" (Village Voice)

"Group Open to Reds Says Peace Leader" (Chicago Tribune)

After that day's hearing when Dagmar was showered with congratulations and hugs, we took a long cold walk to the White House to demonstrate against nuclear testing with the cops disallowing our placards, telling us to keep moving. Originally the plan was to honor the sculpture of the suffragists in the Capitol rotunda but women were barred because of "rewiring" occurring there. Back in the hotel room and on the train, we compared notes and tiredly discussed the whole experience.

Despite all the preliminary doubts and hassling over taking action, I still feel very good that we had responded immediately, rallied women in support, and were there to show our solidarity. It has remained an outstanding experience since in essence we made a strong feminist statement, defied government authority, and turned the tide of acquiescence — a truly radical act.

October 17, 1991

Yesterday, finally went over the WSP National Clearinghouse stuff and put the Moscow trip material, separately, in one of those portfolio boxes. Looking over this material, I realized how many things I've been into and maybe a chronological listing would help. Like 40s: Circle Pines Center, Washington Park Open Forum; 50s: Co-op, Credit Union, research, CORE; 60s: Women Strike for Peace, WILPF, Citizens for a Democratic Society, Moscow trip, book and play reading groups; 70s: Mississippi, Women Mobilized for Change, Toronto meeting with Indo-Chinese women, CADRE [Chicago Area Draft Resisters], WIN magazine, WRL, *Voices* peace column, Gray Panthers; 80s: Seneca women's peace encampment, Arlington Heights arrest, Metro-West Peace Coalition, Gulf War committee. Coalitions, speeches, workshops, Jane Addams bookstore, Third Unitarian — it seems to go on and on.

I guess my philosophy was involvement, more so after I kicked the notion that I had to be a Marxist theoretician/economist to be truly useful and "correct." So "activist" is an accurate appellation, but I also did some analysis, reporting, reflection. As these threads emerge, as I go through material, I feel I want to hold them all, or gather them together to see the whole picture and evaluate such a life. That sounds dangerously like autobiography which I don't really want to do. And a listing or description of activities is not autobiography anyway, more of a background of where I'm coming from. From the above, it seems no matter how discouraged or depressed or withdrawn or miserable my situation, I did keep some thread of involvement and, certainly, of interest. And when I think of the 30s — National Student League, Left Opposition, Revolutionary Workers League, Communist Workers Group, etc. — it's quite a long record.

Maybe I've learned moderation, not to quit a group when I don't totally agree, not to lay down laws for how to act or how society should be. Maybe, in railing against people's not projecting socialism, I'm railing at myself? It takes me quite a while to come to terms with something, to get an acceptable basis to join, to decide how to handle objectionable parts. And one can always voice objections and supports, as with Third Church on flag proposal.

The ghost of the past still haunts me when Carl Cowl calls and is still holding people to a standard of revolutionary Marxism. And part of me still responds to those echoes, as though I've constructed a world of ideas and attitudes which ignores them and then I realize how far I've come — compromised? — and it's like having two or more world views, as the one where I am now is inadequate and maybe even escapist. But one must construct a philosophy to live by, and the eclectic one is the one I've chosen.

There is, nevertheless, a continuing radical impulse or consciousness that will not let me rest with too many compromises. So that in the groups I'm in, I tend to be at the left edge. That's good, I believe, though not always comfortable. And even when I think of that DSA forum last Friday, on

Canadian health, where socialism was an acceptable word/concept, I know I would interpret that more purely and consistently if I were with these people and find less agreement than I thought. I think now I will join, having written some of this out, maybe coming to terms with myself about it, and to balance Third? Though I believe the thinking of some people there is probably in the same or similar grooves, supporting Democrats in elections, etc.

I should avoid, just because I've given up somewhat on Marxism, reacting to Carl Cowl's reaction when I said it was a valuable analysis or some such, thinking I should have said *the*. Now I find that attitude confining. Just as with Freud, one should keep the kernels of truth — as I see them — and use those and appreciate these contributions despite flaws or criticisms, something I struggle to do. Just as, maybe, I'm looking for kernels of personal reportage in my writings?

Sometimes I can't really believe I'm contemplating my writing assembled in book or pamphlet form. What a long way I've come, and despite discouragement, I've stuck to it so far. I can even contemplate that, once assembled, I could spend winter days typing or re-typing some of it. I don't even know a Ms form for submission! I'd like to ask Gert how she did it. I'm even contemplating adding some background or minimal info *re* these pieces or maybe threading them in some way. If I were editing someone else's work, I would know better how to do it. Doing my own is so fraught with uncertainty about value and judgment! Well, I'll try to keep on trying.

October 19, 1991

Gert replied, offering to look at some of my writings, and I should take her up on this, but I'm a little afraid to. Lying here, thinking over *Voices* column, *Hyde Park Herald* Moscow letters, *Win* column, etc., I realize I have been in print and not only in movement publications. Why does it take me so long to realize this? Why did I approach each of these as concrete, ephemeral, separated? Good, but drowned in a sea of generally poor self image? Given that internal atmosphere, it's a wonder I didn't drown completely — but I didn't. I got help, which is a plus for my survival instincts.

A Visit to the Mississippi Summer Project, Summer 1964

by Ruth Dear
Talk given on Chicago Gray Panther radio program June 1978,
based on a *WIN* article, August 1969.

The Mississippi Summer Project was launched in 1964 to register
Afro-American voters who were disenfranchised in that state. June 14 was
the first orientation session for people who had volunteered to go down
there. It was an electrifying time of appeal and hope — and terror, for one
week later, three student volunteers, Chaney, Goodman and Schwerner,
were murdered near Philadelphia, Mississippi, though their bodies were not
found for some time.

When these civil rights workers disappeared, many parents of similar
student volunteers held a press conference in New York City to express their
concern. I saw on the TV screen the sad, worried face of a woman, a
co-worker in the peace movement, and was much moved. Shortly after, at
the national conference of Women's International League for Peace and
Freedom (WILPF) in Indianapolis, I met Marjorie Collins who had been
reporting for the *National Guardian*. On impulse, Marjorie and my husband
George, who had come to meet me, decided to take our vacation time to
drive down to Mississippi, pulled by this vital movement for freedom.

We stopped at Memphis, Tennessee, where orientations were being held,
and then, ostensibly as tourists, drove down through a strange land —
Mississippi — very conscious of our Illinois license with its "Land of Lincoln"
slogan. In Greenwood, we were met at night by a young Black man who led
us to headquarters. As the situation was very tense, we were advised to go on
to Meridian where there was a bigger center and the atmosphere was not so
fraught.

At Meridian Freedom Center, we met many people, attended a rally in a
church, and a group meeting where the danger of mixed couples appearing on
the street together was discussed. Then we drove out to Philadelphia to get
the feel of the place. White people there seemed very grim and tense; by that
time they were in the country's eye as the search for the missing three was
national news.

The most upbeat aspect of our stay in Meridian was the Freedom School
and library where donated books were being assembled. In fact these Freedom
Schools were one of the most impressive aspects of that summer project.
These were free-wheeling alternative schools, usually in churches, with
volunteer teachers who were mostly Northern white college students. About
2000 Black teenagers participated. Although a curriculum had been adopted,
individual schools developed their own versions, Black History and French

being the most popular subjects. Carthage Freedom School read James Joyce. Holly Springs put on a play about Medgar Evers' death. Many mimeographed newspapers. Often teachers and students went out to register voters and then came back to discuss. Since the so-called students knew more about the community than the so-called teachers, everybody taught and learned.

Remember that all this was taking place in an atmosphere of hostility and fear. I heard Staughton Lynd, director of the project, explain how SNCC (Student Nonviolent Coordinating Committee) community workers would come in from the field, bloodied and beaten up. Some schools were burned. So all this ongoing activity reflected deep commitment on the part of students, parents, church leaders, and families who put up the volunteers.

October 22, 1991

At opthalmologist's for angiogram yesterday, I was reading *Dialogue*, a magazine for vision-impaired people. A blind woman wrote that, in addition to speaking, non-verbal communication is important. The missing of facial expressions, gestures, cues and clues, are what makes the blind sometimes seem cold or distant; they can't pick up on visual clues they can't see, so they don't respond or feel encouraged to take the initiative. I was impressed with that insight which has stayed with me, maybe because a shy person seems frozen and aloof too because of lack of courage or confidence to pick up on these clues/cues and of unsureness as to their meaning. So, as I've noticed, people think me cold or ungrateful when I don't make the effort and sometimes don't even have the know-how.

October 30, 1991

I've gotten over the worst of the grief about George and faced my political past with more equanimity, having wrestled with it for "Perspectives." I've even been able to handle pain and some disability by continuing to function — in striking contrast, it seems to me now, to when I'd become overwhelmed by it and gave in to it. I've even been able to acknowledge certain strengths, seeing the good points as well as the bad.

I wish, in writing, I could convey some of the things that were important insights or vignettes to me like the bidding for cheap labor at the New Jersey Campbell Soup factory during the Depression when George went there, or the appointing of a racist to be civil rights chair in his steel local, or the objection of union officials to having their office organized.

Since last winter's Gulf War and the shingles, I have felt I lost a good deal of a positive view. I don't really know what my ultimate philosophy is, though I still feel that unless people recognize a common interest and common struggle, there will only be repression and reaction. I feel we are in a particularly grim, discouraging period in the U.S. especially. So I feel overwhelmed by the power of reaction and the acceptance of it here.

November 10, 1991

Dissatisfied with GP workshop yesterday at Midwest Scholars etc. conference, partly due to lack of strong emotional response from attenders, partly feeling not entirely on top of it. i.e., the feelings I wanted to share were not picked up on, maybe because there were more men than women. I sensed response from women, but got more intelligent or articulate response/exchange from a teacher from Schimer College. A young man said nothing at all. I also felt ill at ease with Henny Moore's hard sell, converting it to a GP pitch where I wanted more discussion of implications, ideas, etc. I kept bringing it back to a radical outlook. Maybe I'm too used to sharing with women? A thought to bring up at the NOW book group.

Maybe the GP's strength is the *idea* rather than the *doing*, the consciousness-raising and the passing on of the feelings of empowerment and liberation. (I couldn't find the latter word and thought of *generation* instead — a valid one!) We say we advocate, but do we really? Only in the sense of propagandizing, but not really advocating for people/individuals. As we say, we don't do *for* them. Maybe that's a copout? It was empowering to be able to advocate for Faith on our return trip from Yugoslavia and in the matter of the hotel rooms, too. In another sense, too, haven't I been advocating for people all my adult life, feeling I was articulating their needs? I guess the word *advocacy* is a matter of interpretation.

If I honestly want to advocate and not just pose as a radical, I must stand behind my background or, at least, on it openly because that is what I professed. In a way, it's safely behind me (a cowardly thought) but I am that too and I owe a great deal to that education. This thought/emotion came to me as I was thinking of Don Wheat's topic today: socialism. Maybe I wish I could advocate it from a pulpit?

Thinking of my thoughts yesterday: maybe I was passing through some crisis of faith still, a continuation of last winter's utter depression about the Gulf War and the efforts against it coupled with my inability to do more because of pain from shingles.

I wish I could have a firm philosophy about Gray Panthers' continuing, how to either revive it or let it go. I want it to continue because of what it does or did for me and it's that aspect I'd like to hold on to. In some sense, it gives ageing a purpose and a perspective, so it has deep emotional roots in me. It is a living, sustaining concept and I should try to keep it alive but at this point I don't have the slightest idea how to do it.

I can visualize some of what is required, but I can't supply the energy for it, and, it seems, neither can others.

November 13, 1991

Was moved by the interview with Kathy Kelly, a sweet, dedicated, seemingly totally sincere person. In conversation afterward, she was very bitter about the Catholic Church, child molestation by priests, unthinking obedience and "owning" the ceremonies. On the other hand Kelly said, Bob Bosse — a Catholic priest — lives in an SRO place to be among the poor. In a way, these are class conscious people or, rather, poverty conscious. The difference is, I suppose, that they are there to help rather than struggle, but that's not true considering the number of times they interposed their bodies, like giving all. I suppose, I see a like dedication which I still marvel at. Marxist radicals tend to think they're the only truly dedicated people, even if they don't say it, because they have the answers. At least that was my attitude.

November 16, 1991

I guess part of my down feelings are part of the gloom and doom of the approaching holiday season, though because of the day-after-Thanksgiving reunion and the probable Thanksgiving dinner with Lucy, certainly this part of it is OK. But Christmas, of course, is waiting in the wings and fear of acute loneliness haunts me.

Well, on to tonight: A play about Nicaragua, *Brigadista* is showing at International House and Terry Burke and Scott Berman are picking me up. Tomorrow a.m. the author of *There Are No Children Here* is talking at Third and Don is sermonizing.

After reading the national Unitarian glossy magazine that is apparently sent to all members, I feel let down. I seem to be searching for some sort of emotional/spiritual/experiential exchange which I'm not getting. Either I don't understand the vocabulary or — a symposium on religious education seemed shallow and superficial or else I don't attach the same meanings to the words. I would like either a greater delving into the roots of the movement, the implications of actions and feelings, motivations, goals — I don't quite know how to say it — a yearning of sorts for the type of sharing I perhaps once got in the movement with George, the unspoken assumptions underneath the exchanges. I thought of the WMC reunion but my experience with the Feminists Against Militarism reunion was disappointing in a way. We did share some, but the other women were on this New Age wavelength and my reaction was (and is about the upcoming November 29th Women Mobilized for Change reunion) that we will briefly exchange and then resume our busy lives or they will resume their busy lives.

November 21, 1991

Reading *My Son's Story* by Nadine Gordimer, I was struck by the true descriptions of a relationship between two dedicated movement people: their feelings, the aspirations, the almost total absorption in the cause, including the maneuvering within, the dropping away of some people, the shifting of sides and positions, the strategy discussions about the activity and the committee/leadership people. And I realized I'm still grieving both for George and for me and for the lost movement involvement, together and alone.

November 25, 1991

Yesterday, I was going over the bottom file drawer and recalling and reliving the past — 60s, 70s, early 80s — and got some stuff as possibles. I now have a thick folder, including some background material, and I feel some failure of nerve. I'm impressed by newsletters, particularly those of South Side Women's International League for Peace and Freedom, and a couple of notes for introductions of speakers.

My back got to me, doing the files, so I took time off to watch *Citizen Kane* — absorbing and evocative plus interesting technique of fading back and forth. So it was not an unproductive day, particularly as I discussed some Gray Panther stuff with Agnes, particularly a January meeting with Kathy Kelly and letters to regional groups. (I should draw up the contents of a letter.)

Calm and peace I really crave but also the excitement of achievement. Impossible combo? Well, in a way, I have a little of that in the feeling or knowledge that I have recognition, have ability, have done things, have lived, at least in some aspects, a life worth living. That sounds boastful but I do feel that I have spent it on worthwhile things, trying to help, maybe with grandiose ideas when younger, but putting ahead of me a goal of betterment for society or elements thereof. I think I had an impossible ideal of absolute dedication and reproached myself for personal aspirations or attempts at gratification — that "selfish" script, I suppose. And, of course, *My Son's Story* has evoked all that, as, in a way, *The Mandarins* did.

Ruth Dear, on the far left, with other Women's International League for Peace and Freedom (WILPF) members, wearing black sashes, protesting the murders and attacks on civil rights' workers in the American South and in South Africa.

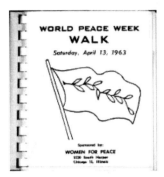

Cover for photo booklet George prepared of the World Peace Week walk in 1963 for Ruth to take to Russia.

The spring Peace Walk down Michigan Avenue, Chicago, 1984; Ruth Dear in front line on far left, Elsie Goldstein, Jim Lynch, and George Dear holding War Resisters League banner.

Ruth Dear, right, with Adele Kushner, Seneca Peace Camp, Rome, New York, July 1983.

Perspectives on Women's Resistance to Militarism in the 60s and 70s

Talk at the Opening of the Midwest Feminists Against Militarism
Conference at Circle Pines Center, Michigan
September 12, 1981
by Ruth Dear

History is a funny process. Bella Abzug gained national fame because she ran for a male-dominated Congress successfully, became a spokeswoman for women's rights and got fired by President Carter. Barbara Deming who laid her body on the line from the 50s on is largely unknown today except in feminist and pacifist circles. This demonstrates the importance of writing our own history. The Women's Pentagon Action — the weaving together — is symbolic also of the threads of our history. There are all kinds of connections between civil rights and the Viet Nam war, between civil rights and feminism, between feminism and war, between the women's peace movement and feminism, between rebellions against the prison system and anti-militarism etc.

In focusing on the last two decades, we are slighting our roots, so I want to stress the fact that there has been a women's peace movement for most of this century, dating from opposition to World War I when American women in 1916 demonstrated under the slogan, "Down with Militarism." In 1917 Russian women textile workers in Petrograd had a strike and demonstration for peace, bread and freedom on International Women's Day which snowballed into a general strike that led to the abdication of the czar. In this period, Women's International League for Peace and Freedom was founded. In the early 20s three women founded the War Resisters League as an activist radical pacifist organization.

The 60s and 70s were an incredibly exciting, active period of movements for Black liberation, student liberation, women's liberation, Native American liberation, lesbian and gay liberation and old people's liberation. It was a period of implicit rather than explicit vision — people carried out their concerns in action, banding together in communes, rap groups, community groups, acting on concrete issues, defining things by style, coming together every now and then in huge demonstrations.

The first direct actions we witnessed were in the civil rights movement starting with sit-ins by students at lunchrooms, the Montgomery bus boycott, escalating to mass demonstrations and confrontations. And just as the civil rights movement borrowed mass tactics and sit-ins from the union movement of the 30s, the anti-war movement borrowed from the civil rights movement of the 50s and 60s.

In November 1961, Dagmar Wilson, Margaret Russell, and Kay Johnson emerged from the Women's International League for Peace and Freedom to found Women Strike for Peace, an action-oriented, decentralized, anti-nuclear weapons movement. At first WSP consciously cultivated an image of middle-class white-gloved women and used that as a sort of street theater. As a result of WSP's activity, the House Committee on Un-American Activities (HUAC) went after some of the participants in New York. Women from across the country flooded the HUAC hearings and were electrified to hear Dagmar's response to a question about Communists in WSP that we accept everyone, thus ending a dark era of kowtowing to a witch-hunting committee.

The first direct action for peace that I witnessed was a year or so later at Camp Mecury, Nevada, when a WSP group went out there to demonstrate and an unaffiliated (from WSP) woman went over the fence and was arrested. This disconcerted some women as her action made the papers and eclipsed ours. Others of us were impressed however.

Women continued to be active in the resistance movement that arose in the wake of the Viet Nam War. As rage mounted, people began expressing this in direct actions from draft card burnings to trashing induction centers to demonstrating and even to self-immolation as with Alice Herz in Detroit. Each action set off another. Going over articles on these actions, one is struck by the inventiveness and determination of women, some of whom acted together as a group, some with men in a group, and some alone. I have culled over a dozen such items, mostly from the Midwest, and if some of the names seem familiar, it is because they are present at this conference.

* In 1967, in the Chicago area, Faith Bissell and Jayne Switzer sat in at an induction center. In Oakland, California, Joan Baez and her mother blocked the entrance to one.
* On May 15, 1969, the Chicago 15, including two women, raided one of the largest draft boards in the country, covering the Black community on the South Side of Chicago. They removed the 1A files, doused them with gasoline and set them afire. Then they called the press, stood around the fire, hugging and singing, "We Shall Overcome." In court, Linda Quint was one of the four defendants claiming insanity as evidenced by their lifestyle, putting the prosecution in the position of proving it was not crazy to live communally, wear long hair, etc.
* About a month and a half later, in New York City on July 2, Women Against Daddy Warbucks shredded 1A files at a Manhattan Selective Service Center, bent the "1" and the "A" keys on the typewriters and left a note to employees to think about the worse destruction occurring in Viet Nam. Next day, they rallied at John D's plaque at Rockefeller Center to demonstrate the link between oil and the military. They poured a mixture of oil, shredded files and torn dollar bills, using it as a kind of confetti. Four women were arrested and dragged to jail.

* Still in 1969, women went to the Evanston, Illinois, draft board offices and started reading out names of men killed since the start of the war, expecting it would take 24 hours. When the doors were locked, they joined hands with Northwestern University students until the police came.

* In November 1969, the Beaver 55 surfaced at a resistance conference at the time of the big demonstration in Washington DC. The group included Jane Kennedy and two other women. They had destroyed draft records in Indianapolis and magnetized tapes at Dow Chemical in Midland, Michigan. All received heavy sentences for both offenses.

* The DC 9 — 2 women and 7 men — celebrated Washington's Birthday in 1970 by another draft board raid.

* On income tax day that year, seven women blocked the IRS office for over three hours.

* Just before Christmas, in protest against army spying, Adele Halkins and Lyn Cima of North Shore (Chicago area) WILPF dubbed themselves "Ad Hoc Unit of Spy Spies," went to the 113th Military Intelligence Group in Evanston with a statement that the army was under their surveillance, dusted objects with face powder, carrying a magnifying glass, and asked for the files. Needless to say, they were refused. The police were summoned and they were arrested and fined.

* April 29, 1971, "the four of us" — Eileen Kreutz, Marybeth Lubbers, Thom Clark and Johnny Baranski — poured blood on Evanston 1A files.

* In October 1973, Fran Holzman, Dolores Robbins and three men blocked a train carrying bombs for the Cambodian front.

* A year after, November 11, 1973, Joan Cavanagh and two others were convicted for bloodying files at the Viet Nam Overseas Procurement Office because Food for Peace was being channeled into the Saigon military, police and prison systems. When they were sentenced to probation plus one day a week at a voluntary agency serving Americans, Joan, together with Hank Skyjack, refused to comply.

* March 20, 1975, Beulah Sander of National Welfare Rights Organization and Anurta Rodriquez, a Puerto Rican activist, joined a group sitting in at Senator Javitz' office for 23 hours to protest his vote for military aid to Cambodia.

* That summer, a group of women stole counter-insurgency plans against the Boston population to be used in the event of martial law. Jill Raymond wrote from a Kentucky prison: "I intend to fight in every way, as a Lesbian, a feminist and an Amazon."

There were individual acts of resistance too:

* Susan Schnall, a nurse in the Navy, refused to serve.

* Eartha Kitt at a White House luncheon confronted Ladybird Johnson on the war in Viet Nam.

* Martha Tranquilli refused to pay war taxes, was assessed $5439 on a

monthly Social Security check of $256 and wrote from federal prison: "In two months I'll be out recidivating."

* Pat Arrowsmith distributed antiwar leaflets to British soldiers and received a sentence of 18 months in Holloway Prison in England in 1974.

* Sareta Dobbs was the first woman conscientious objector. A Black woman of 20, she was a clerk in the First Armored Division of the US Army in Ansbach, Germany. Her doubts crystallized on hearing officers talk about how they got hardened to killing to the point of enjoying it. She refused a quiet discharge "to be true to myself as well as pave the road for those who might follow." She finally won a discharge early in 1975.

Women were also in the role of supporters of resisters and opponents of the war:

* In 1966, three GIs refused to go to Viet Nam — the Fort Hood Three. Mrs. Samas, wife of David Samas, and Grace Mora Newman, sister of Dennis Mora, spoke at meetings of protest when the men were court-martialled.

* Also speaking out were Karen McGregor from Detroit whose fiancé was killed in Viet Nam in November 1968; Chris Cheatham whose husband was jailed for refusal to go; and Jean Willette whose son was killed by a U.S. sergeant in Viet Nam.

* Naomi Wall and other women in the Toronto Antidraft Program pressured the Canadian government to let deserters come in openly.

* After the mass arrests in Washington DC of the May 1971 resisters, Mary Trendwell of Pride helped to organize support of 52 community groups in Washington for the prisoners: "We were the wave of the 60s . . . . We don't want them to think that the wave of the 60s has turned them down."

* Chicago area North Shore women organized Help for Imprisoned War Objectors.

What of the relationship between feminists and anti-militarism? The first stirrings of the new feminism occurred in the Student Non-Violent Coordinating Committee where women raised the issue of their position in the movement. Black women were in the front lines of the civil rights struggle and were often beaten but at headquarters (quaintly called "freedom house") they did the shit work and were never the public spokespersons. In the Spring of 1964 they rebelled and collaborated on a paper on the lack of sex equality in the movement. This was presented at a November conference. The position paper said that the source of the problem was the "assumption of male superiority . . . as widespread and deep rooted and every much as crippling to the women as the assumption of white superiority is to the Negro." So they translated beliefs in freedom, equality and community into sisterhood.

This consciousness grew into the women's liberation movement as women in Students for A Democratic Society raised the issues and began to act on it. By the time of the sit-in at the University of Chicago, women in the Students Against The Rank made as a condition of participation, the sharing of tasks and responsibilities.

Though feminist consciousness was high in the women's peace movement and among women resisters, the same can't be said for all of the peace movement. In 1970 there was a picket line at the Playboy Club where, believe it or not, the Viet Nam Moratorium Committee had scheduled a fund-raiser after an anti-war demonstration. At that demonstration, Chicago Women's Liberation Union had distributed a flyer calling for protest "against this humiliating and degrading event . . . . In this century women have always been the backbone of the peace movement. We have been its secretaries and shit workers. And women have had their own peace organizations." The peace establishment was angry at us, but a Bunny gave us a raised fist salute from one of the windows.

As Bea Stuart of Women Mobilized for Change remarked in an interview in 1973, "It could be said that it all began with my agony over the Viet Namese and ended with the beginning of the understanding of my own oppression."

Let us also not forget the resistance of Joan Little, Inez Garcia and Angela Davis to the prison system which is part of the oppressive system, a military system in its own right. Jean Little defended herself against a rapist guard. As Andrea Dworkin remarked in an interview, "We will diminish violence by refusing to be violated."

A word now on international contact among women in wartime:

Visits to Viet Nam were made by Grace Paley and Norma Becker of War Resisters League, Cora Weiss of Women Strike for Peace, Kay Campf of WILPF, and others. My first knowledge of the size of US military involvement came from Viet Namese women at a Women's Democratic Federation conference in Moscow in 1963. They told a WSP delegation that 10,000 American troops were massed in their country.

Eight bloody years later, when US involvement was no longer hidden, a group of Indo-Chinese women visited Vancouver and then Toronto accompanied by Malvina Reynolds and hosted by the Voice of Women. At Toronto, between 300 and 400 US and Canadian women came to express solidarity and discuss ways of ending the war. It is interesting to note that some women criticized our American delegations for being overwhelmingly white, middle class, and not very radical. Thinking about this, I realized that with the exception of the word "white," this characterized the women from Indochina — three teachers, one professor, one doctor and one housewife — who were expressing patriotic and nationalist sentiments. The radical act was the meeting in wartime to express our being at peace with one another and our determination to end the conflict, which, in time, we did.

The 70s also saw the rise of anti-nuke protests and direct actions on a scale larger than those of the Viet Nam war — Seabrook and Rocky Flats, for example — in which women were extremely active. Then came the whole issue of the draft and the drafting of women. Having been opposed to the drafting of men, radical women could not understand the logic of the claim that for true equality we should be cannon fodder too. That is equality in death. It is noteworthy that though this was a vital issue, the anti-draft movement (CARD) seemed slow to pick up on it, so we put it on the agenda.

Now the Reagan administration has put militarism on the agenda and linked it with a sweeping attack on women and poor people in general and has givenuipooooooopiuupoi us El Salvador and a dozen other outrages to protest. However, we are verging on the contemporary, so I'll stop, with a few last words of course.

Many women in this room have lived the history we have been reviewing. We have started the 80s with radical action and a radical consciousness — the Women's Pentagon Action and the Unity Statement. At this conference we will plan further action, enriched by the experiences of our sisters and in turn enriching the history of the next decade.

December 6, 1991

A very pleasant weekend. Thanksgiving, so-so, though we four women at Juanita's had a long discussion afterwards. Better was the WMC reunion, 11/29, from 11 am to 6 pm, reminiscing, being videoed, giving some material to Gert, hearing Yoriko Hohri's fascinating account of the redress trials for Japanese-Americans interned during WWII. Nicest of all, was on 11/30. Nancy and David Finke picked me up, we met Jim Lynch at O'Hare and over supper did a lot of exchanging and afterward, on the way home, stopped at Peterson's at David's suggestion for hot fudge sundaes.

The exchanges were good, satisfying and interesting rather than nostalgic, though there was a touch of that, and, afterwards, memories of George. Night before last, I awoke, thinking about something and then thought I'd discuss or show it to George. It seems to me this was only the second time this occurred. The first was early on, waking and thinking George was in the bathroom because he wasn't there beside me.

December 9, 1991

Awoke, gratefully out of a dream about feelings and decisions about the nonviolent route, the path of persuasion, the attempt to come to terms with a radical past which gave us sympathy and empathy for impatient radical acts, or, rather, the mind set that produced them. Actually, such stupid, provocative acts were never in our history. I thought of some Pledge people's reactions to U.S. intervention in Nicaragua, wanting to trash windows, etc., which seemed to me childish, but I was reluctant to condemn them.

So I think the dream was a sorting out of these feelings, a drawing of the line, an opting for one way which did not necessarily mean other ways were not valid for their proponents. I've gone through this before *re* WRL, pacifism, etc., but up to now I've had a sneaking respect and sympathy for the other, more violent ways and now I realized I could acknowledge their existence, not read them out of the movement, accept, but demarcate myself more fully and clearly from them. All this after seeing *Weapons of the Spirit* again about people in Le Chambon who sheltered Jews during World War II and the German occupation of France. I was troubled and intrigued by the role their religious beliefs played in their actions, trying to sort out how to approach the religious belief question and their attitude and psychology. Pierre Sauvage, the author and producer, called them extremely healthy and referred to the enthusiastic reception of the film at the American Psychiatric Association meeting. So, what sustained them? What sustains me?

They seemed solid, determined, unpretentious certainly or un-selfconscious, but what caused that solidarity, that fusion of wills that enabled them to stand up to authority? Living in community? A community of faith? In a way, isn't that what the Pledge of Resistance called itself? Isn't that what the radical movement was to me and others? A community of belief? Isn't that what sustains one during arrests and confrontations? I don't quite buy the interpretation that they did this so solidly in the sense that they had no doubts, fears or second thoughts. They may have presented a matter-of-fact front, but that is what one also has to do against authority, if one is subverting it.

Anyway, I think I'm searching for the qualities that enable people to resist and act, and, in the process, create a community of solidarity. And in a sense, it does not matter what the specific beliefs are — it is more the will to do so that encompasses a community. These people did it very quietly, as they had to, but others may do it more noisily via picket lines while they quietly inside resist hunger and doubt.

I think I keep looking for this spirit that sustained me early in the movement or for the manifestations thereof. But it seems to need some unifying purpose, action, not a church institution but a system of beliefs in confrontation with a situation requiring unusual effort. Why does it seem to require tragedy or threat to evoke it? Well, it's good to know it's there. Does one strive daily to experience it and not succeed? Does it lurk there and emerge in crisis?

Somehow I've lost faith in this, but does it not exist in such daily strivings, in concern for the poor and oppressed, in rancor against injustice? I guess I do things and wait for the emergence, and maybe experience it in small actions like getting arrested. And maybe it would help to be more expressive about it, but, thinking of the people at Le Chambon, they did not seem expressive except, perhaps, in their religious observances and this opportunity or occasion to do so is what reinforced them.

Did I not experience something at church Sunday when singing the Hanukkah hymn and the special reaction to the phrase about the prophets that touched me — a pipeline to them, some roots — as well as in the Mozart concert, in the seeing and greeting people? Even in Petrakas' story/sermon/lecture? And did I not get a special thrill from seeing Terry Burke, knowing that she had joined recently, feeling I was welcoming her, even encouraged by learning that Scott was still skeptical when I remarked the word *church* had been a big barrier to me. Somehow I was glad another Pledge supporter/ Nicaragua Solidarity Committee supporter had joined Third, as though to reinforce my joining.

It's also a question of accepting one's own beliefs, despite the fact that revolutionary Marxist doctrine holds that violence is necessary for effectiveness. It's a question of saying that may be so, but I don't like it and I choose not to follow it. Does that mean one impedes a revolution? I don't see that violence per se has a long-run effectiveness either. It may accomplish an immediate change, or a defense against other oppressive violence, but in the long run, peaceniks will be needed too. Certainly, if workers etc. seize power and struggle to maintain it, I could not oppose that and would seek to support it in other ways. And I don't think I'd go around preaching it — or against it, either. Of course, in a struggle, which side are you on? is posed sharply, but if it is a genuine struggle for better conditions or a better society, cannot one support the idea without actively engaging in it? It seems to me that I felt the need to be arrested because others were doing it and I could not just stand by all the time. I had to show support concretely and to the authorities. As for reaching that point, I guess the struggle or the issue is what decides that. Something that seems impossible or fearful becomes do-able if divested of its abstract-issue quality and becomes a step to take, as with pleading not guilty rather than dealing.

I think what I'm concerned with here is the integrity of my beliefs and being comfortable with them despite former training, echoes, acceptance of one particular truth or way. How to hold to present beliefs without betraying former ones? Or, rather, changing beliefs without feeling one has betrayed one's past. It seems to me that the past *has* gone into what I believe but I have modified along the way and come out here, at nonviolence and fellowship and ameliorating conditions rather than a straight revolutionary path (which, anyway, *seemed* straight) since that path and that focus were inadequate to the conditions and later feelings/events.

I *don't* want to lose the focus on being with the oppressed against oppression, on being for social justice. I just don't know the particular form such a society would take, none of the models, mostly social democratic, that I see being terribly appealing. But then is it incumbent on me to decide this? I can only work for what I see immediately, with a vision, of course, but I do not have the responsibility to present or establish a model, a responsibility which in the sectarian movement I was in, was inherent: a vanguard etc. I do think that enlightened or more aware people provide the leaven and the insight and sometimes the will, but only as part of huge, dynamic motions and changes. And without the milieu from which they arose, they often falter, become inadequate, lose their roots. Certainly, if that is the way things go, change in their role is inevitable and one must constantly look elsewhere, but not dishonor *their* contributions.

What has bothered me is that we radicals were so sneering about any other path, closing off other people's ways of coping, other people's beliefs, as inimical and weakening — an adversarial position that was ideologically isolating and was, to some extent, born of ignorance and sectarianism. Working with religious people has given me some such insights as well as working with other people of good will.

Also, my tendency was to dismiss people who did not fully accept my views and to assume they were totally in disagreement, further to the right than they were in actuality. It was an absolutist approach which assumed people were either for or against, whereas, actually, they were somewhere on the way or on the spectrum. Thus, I was somewhat surprised, from time to time, to hear of their involvement in civil rights or even peace-related issues. Of course, our style of operating was always to expose the hypocrisy or weakness or basic acceptance of the system, which tended to exclude, even though we did not say so, any gray areas or similar areas of concern. It is the way of liberals to be apologists, etc. but at times their concerns ran parallel to ours. I think it was a matter of acceptance, too. I did not feel accepted because of non-mainstream views, although sometimes I've been respected for them. So of course I should respect my view more as well as respect others! I'm afraid it was a very black and white universe to me for a while, particularly since so much energy went into it.

Which raises the question of *dedication*. I found this in the movement and have lived with this need ever since. Is this what sometimes impresses people? It *is* a trait, and I don't think I can live comfortably without contemplating it in some way. Look how depressed I was when I lost hope last winter. The bottom seemed to fall out of my beliefs. Am I now regaining some of that with these considerations, reflections, spiritual experiences, looking back?

December 12, 1991

Much taken with *The Plague* by Camus which I got from the library Tuesday and have been reading with a view to insights on the people and actions at Le Chambon. I am impressed with observations on sorrow, ordinary behavior in the face of enormous threat, coming to grips with a situation, or not doing so, as the case may be. It speaks to me of stages of grief and loss. But I was also looking for the key to people's dedication: What keeps the Dr. Rieux' going, helping, treating? They have come to the point where people decide to do something — the clerk, the observer, and even the journalist Rambert. Faced with a universal calamity, they decide to do *something*, to organize themselves and others to help. A profound work which speaks to me more now than when I read it before.

Realized yesterday or the day before that my profound reaction to the plaintiff's testimony and interrogation in the Kennedy Smith rape case was in part a reaction to vulnerability and probing. But I really am troubled by the merciless way in which a rape claimant is dissected and, really, attacked, for proof. Surely there should be a better way, an agreed-on set of criteria, and certainly not this horrible glare of TV publicity. It becomes an indecent show, like watching an Inquisition. Who would ever try to testify, seeing how Anita Hill and this woman were savaged?

Thinking over *The Plague*, I realized the chief doctors are all men. Camus seems to inhabit a male universe.

I do feel I'm in the midst of something, that this question of courage, dedication, steadfastness keeps recurring. I feel it has something to do with writing/reluctance/desire for publication and the feeling that if I make up my mind to make a presentation a grim road of persistence lies ahead.

Maybe my dream about our steadily asserting where we stood and the conviction that it would have some effect was a renewal of — I hate to use the word *faith* — belief, a coming to grips with where I do stand. This, of course, has been a constant, ongoing internal dialogue, and sometimes an external one, and maybe it will never end both because of the nature of my belief in struggle and change and because of my unsureness.

Is this what Christians or religious people have called a testing of belief? Sometimes it seems to me that in my dislike of revenge and vengeance, I have absorbed Christian beliefs, more so, apparently, than many Christians. What a complex web of beliefs, reactions, experiences, learnings go into a philosophy! Is it right to pick apart these strands — to what end? If I remark on this Christian element, I feel guilty that it *is* Christian and that I have absorbed or assimilated (!) this without acknowledging it, as though I practiced some deception on myself and others.

Well, I keep feeling on the verge of some break-through or realization, as though I've reached some conclusion perhaps but am not yet able to express or realize it fully.

So, am I shopping around? Certainly, if examining different options and approaches and philosophies can be called shopping around. So the stew will probably continue to bubble! Am I sorry? Not really. I feel that anything that opens up a path or a new way of looking at things is beneficial and certainly mind-expanding. And it does something for my spirit as well.

December 15, 1991

Finished *The Plague*. Much struck and also moved by this work, including the way different characters faced it and ultimately participated in the effort to alleviate it. But struck even more by the maleness: no central woman character, no woman personally emerges, no one is even named except Mme. Rieux and Jeanne, Grant's obsession, but she's not an actor. Tarrou even prefers his self-effacing mother, and such a woman is to him ideal! Did Camus inhabit a solely male world with women as background servants? The doctor's mother comes to take his wife's place as housekeeper. Surely, in such a situation, allegorical or not, women play a leading role as caretakers, as organizers of help, etc.

One of the most striking characters, Paneloux, the priest, is most agonizingly drawn: his revulsion at the suffering and his wrestling with God's will in this situation. A profound work emotionally, and, though, it in a way celebrates humanitarian spirit, it is also careful to distinguish it from heroics. People do what they have to do, are somewhat changed, but not basically. An existentialist approach?

Right now it's snowing on and off and I wonder if we'll make it to the Gray Panther winter solstice party at Maria's.

December 20, 1991

Went down to Gray Panther steering committee meeting yesterday and found it quite pleasant. I did say I would edit the newsletter if I could get someone available to work with, and now I have the name of Renée Buecker in Oak Park to approach. I do want to do it since a lot of creativity is involved — shaping an issue, highlighting, etc., etc., expressing, using material.

Yesterday morning I looked for my written piece on Camp Mercury and couldn't find it. Again! Going through the file of selected stuff, I realized how much would have to be done and had a sinking feeling about it. I should approach it piece by piece and type out what I have selected from longer stuff and do, finally, the nitty-gritty of backgrounding it. Maybe the urge to organize a newsletter should go into this more serious, to me, stuff.

December 24, 1991

Yesterday, went over the box of writings again to select another to type up and came on some good ones, particularly women's resistance during the Viet Nam war, and I thought of the possibility of using that as a main piece since it summarized some longer pieces: the *Playboy* club demo, Alice Herz's immolation, even the Chicago 15 reporting. I also liked the Barbara Deming tribute, saw possibilities in the cosmonaut Valentina piece by using a paragraph from a letter to George to begin it. Wondered about Arms Bazaar (historical, mostly) and about the Jane Kennedy hearing, though quoting her may be what makes it relevant.

Will I calm down after Xmas? Will I find a niche? It occurred to me that I could have gone to the social action committee to propose sending valentines to prisoners of conscience. Well, I'm doing that through Gray Panthers. Maybe I should put in the newsletter an account of sending them and suggest others do it for Easter? That's ending this entry on a more positive note, and that is a cranny or a nook, if not an actual niche.

Chapter Three
There Is No Writing Out Real Grie

January 1, 1992

What would I like in the New Year? To complete the writings I've started to edit and to have the firm possibility of publication. To keep a measure of good health and good spirits. To keep and improve relationships with people I'm close to. To have some peace *re* Third Unitarian, to resolve some of the ambivalences. I could also wish for the moon, like equanimity, control under all or most circumstances, recognition for publication, etc. But I'm trying to be practical or pragmatic.

January 2, 1992

Pleasantly surprised last evening at the play, "A Very British Coup," concerning a Socialist Prime Minister and his cabinet, elected by a landslide, and the subsequent efforts of the Establishment, via civil service and secret service, to bring him down. He actually refused to call an emergency and bring in troops when the power union held out, the implication being that the leader was bought. He stood up to the U.S. and insisted on dismantling the nuclear arsenal and getting U.S. bases out of Britain.

I had watched in apprehension, fearing that he would be brought down, but despite attempts to create a scandal, he outfoxed them by a surprise revelation on TV about this plot, calling for a general election as well as an investigation. At one point, near the end, there was a face-off between the top hush-hush man, an aristocrat, and a Tory, and the PM who said he also had ancestors. So we're left with the feeling that he would pull it off.

Afterwards, it occurred to me it was based somewhat on Nicaragua. I am so used to material about failed socialism, failed idealism, that I expected the *coup* to succeed and was very glad at the outcome and the message. Somewhere in the story is a message of how to deal with this, but, of course, there was in this projection, a Soviet Union which came up with the money when IMF, under U.S. influence, was making conditions about armaments. Maybe it was about Cuba too.

But what chance now do these events have in the real world? People will strive and maybe create something better for a while, but will it survive? I still feel a study of early Soviet attempts to change things, to mold a society, should be made, to see what influence this had. I'd like to see more hopeful things, to revive a faith in what can be done, to give the daily struggle some coherence and light, to open up and discuss possibilities instead of chewing over old formulas.

The weather has been gray for almost a week, the sun would help too. I so want to see some positive, good victories, regardless of how they develop afterwards, to recapture the feeling of accomplishment and encouragement.

Though, come to think of it, I've always been in a movement fighting defensively and only on very rare occasions has there been such a feeling. Of course, the excitement of the 1930s can't be duplicated — or can it?

A sobering thought is that the U.S. got out of the Depression by tooling up for war. Is this inevitable? You would think that people would learn, but U.S. entered World War II only 20 years after the World War I armistice and was already supporting Britain only 21 years after. Listening to Bush talk to Frost last year about the Gulf War as if it was a crusade made the American representatives portrayed in "Coup," seem very authentic. Such idiocy and egocentricity and posturing!

January 4, 1992

Just finished working on two pieces — a rewrite of the Valya Piece (first woman cosmonaut) and an introduction to the interview with the Chinese women and the interview itself and feel much set up by this. I also reread my notes of the trip to the WIDF conference in Moscow: interesting to relive and be reminded of it.

An on-the-whole pleasant memory in contrast to the one I had yesterday watching the British film, *Mandy*, about a deaf-mute little girl and her isolation, particularly her pressing her face against the window or the wire fence, looking at other kids playing, wanting to take part but unable to do so. It brought back such a sense of desolation and loneliness, a memory of the unhappiness that engulfed me at the lack of friends, the wish to have them or to have the courage to participate, to make a move to them.

I find it hard to realize now how many years I was in that unhappy condition and also to wonder that though it was a source of distress to Mama, nothing was done about it. I suppose that since she herself did not have the skills, she could not teach me either by example or instruction, and play groups, if any, would have been prohibitively costly. Yet, yet, yet, I suppose that sort of regret is useless but painful. Why was there so much concern about my body and so little about my psyche? She did apologize later for her ignorance or the ignorance of the times. Yet how can she read so much Freud and not apply it — or did she to herself?

Well, there is a whole different atmosphere today. Counseling is common and even exists in schools, but if it had then, it probably would have looked only like another institutional appurtenance to be opposed or feared or ignored. I can't imagine her in a PTA though that came a bit later.

To return to today, I'm a bit surprised at the elation I feel at working on those two things. Yesterday, I decided I was in the midst of a block, particularly about the Russian experience and wondered when it would end. And early this a.m. I decided I would work on the material, no matter what the outcome, and I feel now that if I can assemble it and theme it, I'll have accomplished a little summing up of my life in the last 30 years. Of course, if it never sees the light of day, I'll be frustrated but at least I'll have worked to bring some coherence. Next, I hope to tackle the Mississippi write-up. So much depends on the framework which, if it is good, can sustain a lighter piece, if well worked in.

Today I should shop and try to type up at least one of the two things I've worked on. I also think the *Hyde Park Herald* editing of my Moscow letters was good and I wonder how it could be used again.

January 6, 1992

Borrowed *Final Exit* from Connie Wilhelm which is mainly about doctor-assisted suicide. It seems only prescription pills will do the trick. The author advises stockpiling them and lists which pills and also recommends a plastic bag! Somehow that turned me off, and I realized that this was for people in extreme physical pain to whom this would be a welcome release, whereas I think I am more concerned with emotional pain or despair. Troubled also by his emphasis on talking it over with an MD and finding out his/her attitude — a no-no I'm afraid, but it did bring me out of the notion that there was a fast, easy way to go.

I wondered if the 90s will see another upsurge like the 60s which were thirty years after the Depression upsurge. Superstitious? The 30s came ten years after World War I ended, but the 60s came in the midst of a war. So did the Russian Revolution, come to think of it. Does that mean another war? Will that be Bush's "solution" too — or that of his followers? Of course, nothing is ever certain, personally, politically, but it would be nice to be lifted up again on a wave of hope and growing struggle. Well, I can't hold it back — ageing, I mean — it would certainly gladden and probably energize me to some extent.

January 7, 1992

The piece about Russian cosmonaut, Valya which I typed yesterday, and I started revising a bit, tightening up, and by now I think it's acceptable.

Called NVA editor Ruth Benn yesterday about the June Middle East Walk for Peace to update the interview with Kathy Kelly but mainly to broach the subject of publication. She gave me the phone number of their contact at New Society Publishers and when I asked who does War Resisters League literature in general, she implied that they did and offered to submit my stuff for the February WRL budget meeting. I demurred because I'm nowhere near ready.

I'm amazed that I'm pursuing this retrospective of my involvements but I suppose it's just the summing up process of old age which Everett Koop referred to. It's odd, though, that activities which seemed so discrete and not particularly strenuous or time-consuming except in spurts, seem to make a record of steady involvement, no matter how episodic at the time. And, in a sense, there was continuous emotional and intellectual involvement — the air I breathed and still do. Thinking how we/I just went to things as a matter of course, I couldn't understand people's respect for that. I hope my memory does not deteriorate to the extent that I can't remember the history of things, actions, feelings, events. That is one big reason to do it now, regardless.

January 9, 1992

I have to arrange a proper list of prisoners of conscience to write to. Since we can only send about twenty, which is what I expect at the Gray Panther meeting, I should pick out the longer-term prisoners as some may be out or getting out very soon. The more I read about these prisoners, the angrier I get at the "support the troops" syndrome. These people *are* giving blood and are being ignored here, by and large.

It's becoming clear to me that the stamina necessary to keep the apartment in reasonably good shape is not there. I haven't vacuumed for over a month, relying on the lighter sweeper and the duster. It would be nice to know again that it had a basic cleaning. I become more conscious of it when people are due to come and I do a surface job, but my Puritanical self insists that's not good enough. When I think of all the bending and pushing, I pale, and there's no use kidding myself that I'll get to it. Energy conservation becomes particularly important because I want to have it for typing and other things.

January 10, 1992

I decided to attend Third Unitarian Church Social Action Committee to propose writing to prisoners, if I have the list ready.

How to define the limits of the Gray Panther Steering Committee? Decisions on nitty-gritty functioning but not broad policy? The Steering Committee seems to have decided to have speakers at all meetings though they dubbed alternate ones for program and business. Things really seem to be moving, due mainly to new members in the last few years and partly to new conveners, including Maria Bartlett and me, though Henny, the third co-convener is somewhat absorbed with moving. We have new people on the Health Committee, a new Membership Committee and Treasurer and new editors. It would be a boon if Colorado GPs would come through on hosting a regional meeting and other chapters agreed to come. Now remains the task of organizing a fund raiser. I hope Maria does not get too absorbed in her engagement to be so active.

Well, a lot about GPs. I must see, though, that I continue the editing/typing/getting a theme for my stuff. I hope a book review request doesn't come too soon in the midst of all this. Now if only Gert Rubin would return my stuff with a favorable opinion! I hate to jog her as this is a big favor she's doing.

January 13, 1992

Went to see *JFK* with Peter and Fran Bender. If Stone researched the material, why are MacNamara and John Kennedy presented so favorably? MacNamara was a hawk whom we cursed and opposed. We saw no signs of their easing up on Viet Nam. Robert Kennedy was a union buster, so where does this liberal aura come from? Why do people have to make heroes of others just because they agree with them on certain things or because they are attacked by people farther to the right? Why can't one just recognize and label elements without taking sides when there are really no good sides? How imprecise and distorted history, so-called, is!

January 21, 1992

Aroused by Martin Luther King Jr. observance yesterday, watching and reliving the King's civil rights demonstrations and movement, including Chicago, remembering Gage Park, etc., thinking how much easier it was going to a demonstration with George.

Today, I hope to take the Gage Park, King-led march write-up to the Oak Park River Forest High School history department head in answer to the notice in the *Wednesday Journal* that they wanted recollections of civil rights events for Black History month. For a presentation?

I reached 78 years of age and am appalled when I think about it, at how near 80 I am. As with 70, it seems now the ultimate? penultimate? crossing. 90, I can't even contemplate and I don't know whether I'll live another decade or so or whether I want to if I lose more energy and have to decide about living quarters, lifestyle, etc.

What It Feels Like To Demonstrate
for Open Occupancy in Gage Park

Friday, August 5, 1966
by Ruth Dear

We drove up, intending to look over the demonstration, see where the picketing at 63rd Street was, and express our solidarity by joining it for a while. Workers coming into the evening shift at my husband's place of work had told him that the police were not letting cars through along Marquette Road (67th Street). So, thinking to get around this, we drove down California Avenue with the intention of turning off onto Marquette Road and into the park. As we approached we saw blue-helmeted policemen lining California Avenue. A cop was directing traffic. When we tried to turn left onto Marquette Road we were motioned ahead — no turns.

By this time we could see white people milling all around. A glance into the park showed whites strung out in a sort of circle around a few people in a little hollow carrying a sign. It was impossible to identify it.

Excitement mounting, we drove to 60th Street, circling around in order to come down Marquette from the west. A huge American flag and a Confederate flag, carried together, appeared. At first I did not take it in. For some reason I thought the Confederate flag was the Union Jack. Then I remembered where we had seen it so flaunted before — in Mississippi, July 4, 1964, right after the Civil Rights act was passed. An open car containing two young couples passed us. A blond girl was sitting on the top of the back seat wildly waving a Confederate flag, enjoying the excitement with the others.

Unable to find an approach to the park we finally drove to Mozart and Francisco, parked in front of the only apartment house on the block, and left, hoping it would be intact when we returned. I recalled how, in 1964, in Greenwood, Miss. we drove downtown, parked the car on a side street, and in the dark went to meet a young man who would take us to SNCC headquarters.

We cut through the park at California and 67th, not walking too fast because the crowd was now shouting and holding up pro-Wallace signs. I was puzzled. Henry Wallace? I still could not connect Alabama's George Wallace with a group of Northern whites.

Then I took this in too, but I still had the dazed feeling that this couldn't be. Even though I heard the continuous chanting, the roar every time a cherry bomb went off, the screaming, taunting girls, the pop bottles being flung.

Because we had cut across the part we came first to the head of the now forming line of demonstrators. We were told to form four abreast, then eight. Everyone was quiet and nervous except for the marshals.

Then came a great roar from the mob. King had arrived. Bam! Roar! Applause for the bam!

We stood for half an hour under this barrage while passage was negotiated and finally, finally we started off. Listening to the roar of the crowd, I thought, they are doing what a crowd of enthusiastic supporters would do — accompanying us with applause and shouting. If this were only a sound track people would think we were being cheered on.

But we saw the faces. And I began to feel I had seen them before too, on TV as Negro mothers led children to a white school amid a barrage of abuse and threats or as Negroes demonstrated in the South for freedom. But this isn't the South, I kept saying to myself.

Then someone called, "Watch it!" and another missile landed nearby. We had been advised not to duck because someone else would be hit in our stead. But this was impossible. One ducked before one thought.

Marching eight abreast on the right side of the roadway with a line of policemen holding back the crowd on each side, we were constantly admonished to look ahead, keep our heads up. A ninth person got into our line and we would get raggedy. "Keep your line straight," would come an injunction from the line behind. This constant alertness was very supportive. After a missile, it helped us to re-form our line, keep discipline, and get on with the march.

The mob preceded and escorted us all the way. For our march north the American and Confederate flags were held before us. When we got to 63rd Street, however, two large flags with the end-the-slums symbol were brought up as part of a little ceremony of kneeling in front of Halvorsen's real estate office, praying and singing. This was the only time that there was a real hush in the mob, as if they were uncertain how to handle this more traditional aspect. Then we rose, proceeded like a silent, dogged army and the mob roared again.

We returned to 67th, our starting point, and to waiting buses. Tension mounted as we wondered how we would get out of there. The police directed the first group of women to the bus, obviously fearing a rush by the crowd. We were crowded in, told to sit three to each double seat, to fill the aisles, and to close the windows. We did so and took off. Immediately singing started, a wonderful release of tension. As we passed through the park, some waved to the Negro policemen. Almost all responded. One threw us a kiss.

The bus grew unbearably hot and a few women insisted on opening windows. People on street corners glared at us. Only one man, however, did anything overt — he threw his cigarette at us.

So we were returned to the Action Center at the church to talk about it, and to wait anxiously for the return of the men.

January 26, 1992

Despite fatigue, I brought in both accounts of civil rights experiences: Gage Park (1966), Mississippi (1964) to Ferguson, head of OPRF history department. He wants to put me on the program in February. I felt good about having the material and using it. Also received encouragement from Gert Rubin who finally returned *Awarenesses* and *Ladies' Day at the Induction Center*. I also feel good that I organized and reproduced conscientious objector lists for Gray Panther February 1 meeting.

Listened to Frost/Mailer interview where Mailer was stressing quality production as one answer to the U.S. general condition(?). He panned advertising, the packaging of everything, something I've reflected on, watching TV and seeing how much went into logos, promos, intros to a program, i.e., the packaging versus the substance which is often poor and shoddy. Even Channel 11 seems to feel the need to make this kind of announcement. I later reflected that he was in a way a publicity hound. I just remembered his autobiography that George was so fascinated with: *Advertisements for Myself.*

Mailer came across to me as a weirdo who now believes in an imperfect god and reincarnation and attacked Ms. for lacking any substance and being solely concerned with piety. There is some truth in the reference to piety, but he's such an egotist that he can't see any value in the feminist point of view though he's learned to say "he or she" about god.

He explained better his concern with violence and his appreciation of its buildup in people, as with gangs. But somehow I had the feeling that he was still advertising himself, though more moderately. He feels both capitalism and communism have failed and that society should provide a floor of health care, housing, food, etc. and would progressively tax businesses on the amount of advertising in order to abolish it and get 'em to produce quality. A serious idea? Or still the *enfant terrible?*

January 31, 1992

Went to Social Action Committee of Third Unitarian Monday night and proposed the letter-writing to conscientious objectors and now, with Ron Chew's help, I'm to set it up a week from this Sunday. I have to get the valentines and lists. Don Wheat will provide the stamps and *Nation* article. And tomorrow I have to do the same for the Gray Panther meeting.

Monday morning I met Renee Buecker at the GP office, went to the printer's, and spent about four hours there, editing, finally, the newsletter. Exhausting because we had to wait on Jeff who *was* providing the time and the repro copy for us. Hopefully, Renee will provide more of this work, though I do like the gathering of material and placing it.

Maria Bartlett called to say she'd be in West Virginia for an engagement party on June 6, the GP annual meeting date, which means I'd have to handle it as Henny will probably be gone by then and, in any case, would be out of local involvement. Looks like the luncheon/fund-raiser is looking up.

Robbie Skeist knows Ann Sathers restaurant owner and thinks he can get us a good deal. That would be a relief. Then our main concern, aside from the menu, would be deciding on price and sponsorships and program. It looks doubly good because Judy Burrell called last week to say she'd try to interest the Roslyn group and others where she has contacts. Hope we handle it well.

The Third Unitarian Social Action Committee meeting was better than I'd thought, though, essentially, they seem to endorse things rather than initiate them, much like GPs a while ago. Two young men came and raised the issue of censorship of Rock N' Roll lyrics — a new aspect to some of us older ones, and others, and there was quite a discussion of this.

My tutee, Margaret, did not come, being sick with the flu and then a cold, so maybe we'll meet next week. Fran Bender came over for an early lunch yesterday, eager to share an experience with an Oak Park Temple group of parents where a woman referred to atheists etc. as "them," resulting in her feeling shut out, just as I did when Beverly exploded at me about my reactions to the Third Unitarian Christmas service. Fran said she'd spoken to Rabbi Gerson about her atheism before joining and he's said there was room for her there. So these liberal? churches make room for people; in the case of the Temple, for Jews and in the case of Third Unitarian, for all sorts of beliefs. Is this a case of people turning to these institutions because there aren't others to fill the need?

Finished Nadine Gordimer's short story collection, *Crimes of Conscience*, a sad, discouraging book of people living under oppression and how they reacted to it. Also, the story of a guerrilla leader who led a military victory and then, in the new government which negotiated with the whites to unify the armed forces, among other things, there was no place for him. He was given a Sport and Recreation cabinet position but it was really token and the new Minister of Defense was white. The P.M. knew the country's debt to the guerilla leader but felt he couldn't do more about it as he was a rough, controversial person. Gordimer is extraordinarily sensitive to all these nuances, both personal and political.

February 5, 1992

Last night, went to the Wheats', on Lucy's suggestion, to hear someone talk about Kierkegaard. Enjoyed the discussion, something I'd been hoping for and wish there was more of, either spontaneous or more structured. I was a little uncomfortable at Don's saying that Unitarianism was a religion but was interested in where people were coming from. Surprisingly, I was the only Jew there, all apparently having some religious Christian background, ten of us altogether, including 5 or 6 Catholics.

Kierkegaard appears to me a sour mystic, concerned only with the individual, a lifelong member of the Lutheran Church, and a royalist. I sometimes wonder at people who keep groping for meaning, try to analyze mystical feelings, who, on the surface, seem not to produce a very coherent philosophy and profoundly influence others. I kept thinking of Jung's early experiences, mysticism etc. Somehow the mysticism makes me uncomfortable though I respect a sincere search, but how distinguish what is within from what the world is? Do I want to fully understand my mental/emotional processes? Do I not rather want a better grasp on the world and its processes so that I can place myself within it and know best how to function? . . . thinking over what some people said about early training and observation and indoctrination in Catholicism remaining with them in some form, how could I not be and remain influenced by Marxist training and indoctrination and, earlier, a radical, secular Jewish background?

February 7, 1992

Not feeling well, I called off attending Ted Koppel's town meeting on health at Mandel Hall but I viewed it all on TV and noted that mainly the old people who got to speak related personal horror stories. No Gray Panther apparently got the floor. Felt a little bad about that and wondered if I could have, but I doubt it. Those things are choreographed to a great extent.

Have been quite busy with last Saturday's GP program meeting, doing the introducing, and bringing, and urging, sending the valentines to conscientious objectors, planning for this Saturday's Board meeting. I did type up the "Take Back the Night" speech and, of course, the newsletter.

February 13, 1992

Considering it's the 13th (George died, 6/13), I'm not feeling badly, though I had an impulse to open this book and read the last entry and I picked up the pen automatically. Last evening I called Jenny Knauss and Judy Burrell and got their agreement to co-facilitate the April 4 Gray Panther re-charge and finally reached Renée too and set up a meeting for Friday on the newsletter. I also had the impulse to retype "Awarenesses" today, fearing that I was neglecting this project. Odd how reaching people and settling a few details gives me ease and release. Also, Henny called me and I settled that we'd produce labels, but I still have to send (and write out) copy for the postcard and I have to check with Henny how many I should tell Peter to reproduce — annoying little tasks which may stand in the way of doing "Awarenesses." I also have to deposit and mail out condo checks in my role as assistant treasurer.

February 18, 1992

Philip Agee spoke at Third Unitarian Sunday and underlined — and made more ominous to me — the U.S. trend. His point was that the Establishment people, worried about the economy after World War II, decided to militarize as a way of avoiding joblessness, poor production etc. So it underlined what others have said, that we're living in a military or quasi-military dictatorship.

Do I have to wait forever for some hopeful uprising, rebellion, awakening to a feeling of frustration and/or power on the part of the oppressed somewhere? Will I see something hopeful before I die? Will I even see my stuff published, or is that a pipe dream? I think not, about both. And meanwhile I struggle with my private handicaps.

Spring will be here in one and a half months or less. Already I saw a willow from the El with those long yellow strings. Several weeks ago, when the weather was warm, I saw daffodil shoots in front. A bittersweet time when I think of the thrill of finding growth in our garden. Both geraniums are budding in the house — at last!

Take Back the Night

Talk by Ruth Dear

(Chicago Gray Panther Rally, Daley Plaza, Chicago, September 1979)

I am tired of hearing the advice authorities give to old people — and to others — to stay home, lock the doors, don't talk to strangers. I burn with resentment every time I hear this and I ask myself:

Is this the kind of society offered to us? Is fear always to motivate our actions?

When I hear people repeating this advice as a reason for not going out at night or for not going to meetings, I ask again:

Are we to accept this paralysis?

Why is society presented as such a jungle? Why are people regarded as "'natural victims" if they are perceived as weak or old? An old man may be killed for a bicycle; an old woman, mugged for a few dollars — and sometimes raped as well.

I'm staggered by the viciousness of preying on seemingly defenseless people and, I must confess, I am also staggered by the economic and psychological desperation these acts represent. In a jungle society, we are all victims.

Gray Panthers regard this demonstration as a liberating step out of that paralysis I mentioned--an assertion of our right to the streets and of our determination to support one another so that no one is regarded as helpless. We hope that out of this will come concrete steps for mutual support and protection.

In the words of Andrea Dworkin, speaking to the first Take Back the Night rally in San Francisco a year ago: "Tonight, with every breath and every step, we must commit ourselves to transforming this earth on which we walk, from prison and tomb into our rightful and joyous home."

February 19, 1992

Yesterday, after typing up "Ladies' Day at the Induction Center," I counted the number of pieces in Grace Paley's collection, *Long Walks and Intimate Talks* — about 36-38, counting poems, all mostly short. I think I have eight so far plus "Women's Resistance to the Viet Nam War," which is longer. And at the moment, can't think of others. The rape letter to *WIN*? Arlington jail? The Arms Bazaar? These seem less important and less pertinent. I'm sure I'm blocking others. Oh, yes, tributes to Barbara Deming and Alice Herz. That sets the juices flowing again!

Last night at NOW book group, Anita had a tape of May Sarton speaking and reading two of the poems we were supposed to read for discussion. "Sisters" and "Medusa." I was moved by these poems, sensual, burning with fire to create, to assert her womanhood, her creativity and delight and bitterness. It's hard for me to read poetry, feeling I miss much, and, sure enough, "Medusa" was addressed to a friend (not a lover, she said) which never occurred to me. But no one really discussed the content. Shying away from the emotion?

Anita stopped the tape at the point where Sarton started to discuss how she created a poem. I was disappointed but I didn't want to insist. That creative, manufacturing process is fascinating to me: the word usage and manipulation in order to express ideas, emotions, moods, relationships. I always have in the back of my mind the feeling that what I do is related and involved in this creativity but not to the extent of writing poetry or fiction. Yet, in reporting something, don't I try to create a mood, mirror feelings, even sketch relationships? It seems to me that "Ladies' Day" does that, as does any good piece of reporting.

I was upset at Bea's remarking, during the tape, that Sarton must be childless, so much absorption with self, and I felt, in a way, put down and also stymied. The rendering and expression of feelings, it seems to me, is a rare gift and very communicative, and if this absorption and freedom from family responsibilities permits this, that should be recognized as contributive, not something to sniff at.

February 29, 1992

"For twenty years, he's been my biggest supporter, my biggest critic, my best friend. One doesn't throw that over simply because life gets a little inconvenient now and again." (*Payment in Blood* by Elizabeth George, p. 94)

This passage moved me powerfully a couple of days ago and my first reaction was to shut the book and put it aside. But I picked it up again, put it in my lap, and forced myself to deal with the pain this evoked. I pounded my fist on my thigh, telling myself to face it, to experience the pain this evoked. I did just finish the book, not wanting it to end, as I usually feel near the end of a mystery, but which was perhaps also due to that passage and to my reaction. I am so reluctant to say I conquered something. (I note that the writing is flowing very smoothly, as though I'm carried along on a river of expression, the words and formulations coming easily and rightly, the very opposite of a writer's block. But I haven't been able to resume typing my stuff, including the GP newsletter, because of back pain. Though I had a few bad days, my spirits were up and I'm much better though any prolonged exertion becomes painful and weakening. I do hope this goes away. As with George, I want to get through a bad spell and have it all become again the way it was.)

Speaking of George reminds me that when I was asserting and allowing or inviting the emotional pain to surface, I also said to myself, "Remember how it was with Joe, not the George I'd created since his death." And that makes me uncomfortably aware that I *was* creating a somewhat idealized image even though I thought I was on guard against that. I guess it is more comforting and comfortable to do so. Is this still another stage on the ladder of overcoming grief, or at least, coming to terms with it?

March 15, 1992

I should write of good things: the cotton jersey outfit I ordered; the Monet poster and the William Morris note cards I just ordered from the Metropolitan Museum; the crocuses which flourished out front over a week ago; the Dutchman's Breeches I saw in Austin Gardens — the first spring wildflowers; my interview with Kathy Kelly in the *Nonviolent Activist* which finally appeared. (Ruth Benn wrote she's received two inquiries about this June Walk for Peace in the Middle East); printer Jeff Golden's praise of Renée's learning ability and the appearance and layout of the newsletter; the invitation to the fund-raiser luncheon for Henry Moore which Maria Bartlett and Madelyn Armbruster drew up. I am oppressed by Maria's leaving this summer and the ending of a good working relationship but I do have the newsletter, and several committees are functioning, and I'm organizing the theme for the April 4 GP recharge. All this in spite of back troubles. And I still have my writings to reproduce and assemble as well as the War Resisters League conference in Dexter, Oregon, at the end of July, beginning of August, which I hope to attend. There's also the prospect of a motor coach trip with Faith Bissell.

Can these counterbalance the pain, the insecurities, the emotional turmoil, the need to decide about the future? God knows, I don't, and since "he" doesn't exist as far as I'm concerned, nobody knows. Then it's up to me to know, but that is such a godawful (!) decision. I guess behind it, lurks the fear of death, of ultimate disposal.

March 17, 1992

I don't really know how to confront the future. Part of me would like to have it settled some way, but when I think what I'd have to give up, considering what I can afford, it is grim and prison-like. How can one write and be cheerful in an apartment like the ones at Bethesda? Where could I afford to be that would at least be attractive and offer some space?

I *am* able to function; it's slower and harder, but look at my cousin Vi at almost 88, look at Katherine Anderson at almost 89. What frightens me is the idea of having to give up everything that makes life meaningful for me. How can I exist without some impact on the outside world, or the attempt to have such impact?

How would I arrange a suicide? There is, too, the fear of not being successful at it. Also, a double-crostic I just solved was a quote from Bruno Bettelheim about holocausts — a double whammy since the word *holocausts* in the puzzle gave me a feeling of unease and fright and the realization that no matter how one might try to deny it, as a Jew, it would always be a fearful thing to one. And when I'd solved the author's name, I thought of the way someone said he'd died — with a plastic bag over his head. Still, the idea of stockpiling pills is repugnant to me, even if I were to go that way. So, the spirit to live and survive is still there. I saw this morning the first coleus seedling in the west window planter, and, later, this early evening, another.

Maybe, too, I'm influenced by the NOW women's history commemoration last night where Terri Moon spoke on women buried at Waldheim Cemetery — Emma Goldman, Lucy Parsons, Elizabeth Gurley Flynn — and told her comrades, before the meeting, that we were on the same side at the Feminists Against Militarism Conference. She talked about the Anarchist movement, mentioning Emma Goldman, Johann Most, Alexander Berkman, and then about Raya Dunayevskaya as Trotsky's secretary and affirmed a Trotskyist world view before the Stalin-Hitler pact. She referred somewhat slightingly to Trotskyists telling couples to get legally married to avoid trouble with the law. I tried to murmur a different approach: one less thing to be thrown at us. Odd how one generation can't fully understand the ambiance, where people were at, unless they want to do so in order to glorify or excuse someone. On the other hand, I was able to explain a little about anarchism when someone asked. After the meeting, Jean Peterman came up to me and said she wanted to hear more about my mother.

April 4, 1992

The strait-jacket in last night's dream of course represents the way I've been feeling about finding an affordable place with services, aggravated by Lucy's and my viewing Holley Court Terrace. This time, unlike the previous one, we viewed the finished ninth floor lounges, greenhouse, restaurant, all very attractive, and the second floor with library, commissary and coffee shop, craft and exercise rooms, etc. etc. The apartments still did not seem that impressive or roomy, but from the eighth and seventh floors, there were nice panoramas. I began to realize that anywhere I go, I'll have to compromise on space, even if sharing a house.

I'd been thinking off and on about my future, not very constructively, more in the nature of fantasizing about Oak Park Arms or Holley Court Terrace. Well, maybe some constructiveness, realizing I'd have to pare down possessions: books, desks, maybe the dining room table, one sofa, not to mention kitchenware. Why don't I begin? I thought of tossing topical paperbacks and things I never consult: biographies, garden books, as well as valises, and, a lot more.

What struck me this time, in addition to continual thought about my future living arrangements, was going though former speeches in preparation for my address to first year medical students at the University of Illinois. My view of the capacities of the elderly then, stands in contrast to those views now. I was very quick to discount handicaps, etc. and now, nearly recovered from a sprained ankle after a bout with my back, I realize how serious they can be and I dread not being able to function, to go out when I wish, to be involved with others.

Good feeling about my reception by some 175 students and the feeling that maybe I'd planted a few seeds. One older person said he'd like to join Gray Panthers.

I can move a lecture hall of students to laughter, even get a broad smile from a woman student as Dean Brody, who followed me, droned on about defects of the aged, technological devices, surgery, and other medical interventions, extending life a few years, etc. etc. I had the audience's attention throughout, it seemed, and when he spoke, they were restless and maybe a bit bored — I certainly was. Why don't I feel this as positive affirmation of ability, functioning, etc., rather than something which I won't be able to hold on to for long?

April 6, 1992

I finally decided to go to the Third Church Easter service and found it quite enjoyable. Reminiscences of Easter by Lucy, Mary Lou Shadle, Evelyn Apple and Larry Craig were amusing. Right before, Don Wheat asked me if the seder had brought back memories and I told him how Uncle Joe's rendering of the *Haggadah* got shorter every year as he got tipsier. Somehow, that made me feel more at ease and when we sat in a circle to hear the panel, it was pleasant, informal, Jonathan Reich adding a very amusing reminiscence. Later, the music was nice, Don's sermon interesting. I realized I don't have to agree with every single thing; it should be enough to be engaged, stimulated, even disturbed. I realized also how hard Don works to involve people and integrate them, especially when the spirit moves him.

That word, *spirit*, is something he dealt with later: *inspiration, respiration, conspiration* etc. and I thought of the times we in the movement referred to spirit in *our* context, and yet, somehow, in a religious context, I jump when people speak of it. I think, maybe in our isolation in the movement, we did not recognize, or refused to recognize, that there was a similar impulse and feeling in religious people, who also wanted to achieve a better world here.

I have begun to realize, also, speaking of spirit, a dimension the union movement brought which is lacking today as it is weakened: a spirit of sharing, of solidarity, of social conscience. I think this was mentioned in the *Nation* or *In These Times*, and I have thought about it. In a sense, it was almost the only large-sharing spirit in this individualistic, greed-based society. Or, rather, it mobilized that spirit, encouraged, educated, gave services etc. in its best form. Business unionism seems the opposite, as do sweetheart contracts, easily giving in to save jobs in one plant or industry. Where is the sense of workers' strength, power achievement?

I guess perhaps the student movement of the 60s was in the lead because it expressed a sharing vision. So, instead of decrying student leadership, the best way is to instill the vision of such a movement into a workers' movement. My feeling has been to follow the vision/spirit wherever it appears instead of saying it isn't according to Marxist formula. What has been depressing for me is losing sight of that vision at times, suppressing it at others, and always accepting something less.

Maybe, in concentrating so much on *my* future, I have substituted tunnel vision. How much spirit/vision is connected with *seeing*? Is that, too, bugging me in the background? I don't mean to decry the importance to me of my future; one has to look outside too to balance the situation. I think, maybe writing about it has restored the balance a bit, and obviously, I was inspired yesterday.

In decrying New York City Mayor LaGuardia and his supporters as leading people down a false and inadequate path, what were we offering in its place? A visible path? Or just the words/ideas for a different path? Radicals were fearful of being led astray or leading others astray, but what could we possibly offer in its place? Education, surely. Exhortation, twice as surely. A new vision, surely. But how to counter-pose that to an election unless we have a candidate to embody that?

It seems to me that pressing for people to be able to vote "None of the above (NOTA)" is a confession of despair. Sure, people have the right to do so, but can't we get something better than a zero? It *is* a way to register dissatisfaction, but it is also a very barren outlook.

(I wish I had a column; I want a wider audience.)

Seems to me that these thoughts were sparked by seeing that Roberta Lynch is supporting Clinton in *In These Times* and also an article on the German rightwing. I recall thinking this morning that as the U.S. economy and power decline, fascism would be their solution as with Germany over 60 years ago. This idea is reinforced by references to corporate and government controls on library books, the environment, history, etc. How can one ever get out of that network?

Dorothy Samachson called this morning. She has books for me and is recovering from an awful fall on her face. She asked me how I had made out for food and said friends had helped her. Then, talking about the future, she said she didn't even want to think about it. So I'm not the only one into denial. We agreed that old age is not for sissies. And now I remember an *In These Times* editorial about the Chicago flood being a symbol of national neglect of the infrastructure — an image of neglect and disaster.

May 4, 1992

Looking out at the treetops in Austin Gardens, a little disappointed that all were already in leaf with two light green ones in front and that this precious first opening of fresh, tender light green leaves would soon be over. Driving around, I saw many trees in this first stage. It has been such a reluctant spring and today it will be in the low fifties again. Why can't I summon the energy to plant caladium bulbs, pot nephthytis which is well rooted, feed the coleus seedlings?

Yesterday, going to the NAACP rally with Kathy Jeans was a welcome opportunity to bear witness against the horrible not guilty verdict on Rodney King's police beating and the subsequent rage erupting mostly in Los Angeles but also in other cities, though not the three biggest one: Detroit, New York, Chicago. I realized that it was directed at property in the African-American neighborhood but it extended farther than the ghetto. Even President Bush had to switch, apparently, from approving the verdict to supporting a Justice Department investigation. It was a pleasure to hear the young people at the rally, especially one white teen who was very emphatic and who concluded with a raised fist.

The emphasis was on the races' getting along. This is also what Don Wheat emphasized in his sermon at Third Unitarian, quoting from *Race*, Stud Terkel's latest. I felt he dealt too much on racism among all peoples and too little, if any, on anger.

I had thought about the violence, the calling out of the military in L.A. etc., but during the first days, I realized the power these angry people had, eventually to paralyze a city if they would, as the police were powerless for a time. Excited by that, I wished the revolt were better organized and more political, though, in a sense, it was. Anger at exploitation, high prices, unemployment, oppression expressed itself in attacks on property and, unfortunately, on individuals.

Though I disliked the random burning and looting, I decided I'd prefer this to passivity. What will be the last straw in other cities?

I wished also that Jaslin Salmon of the NAACP at the rally had expressed more support than discouragement, but he did say he was encouraged by the reactions of young people, and so was I. I don't know why I had such a reaction to the stress on integration and getting along. Am I not for that? Guess I want more militancy, too, and an appreciation of the potential. But communities like Oak Park feel threatened and this was, in a way, a good showing. The president of the Oak Park Board of Trustees spoke as well as three, four other trustees, which made me feel good about Oak Park after all the Salmon and NAACP bashing in the local newspaper's Letters To The Editor.

Gray Panther demonstration, Chicago, early 1970s.

May 28, 1992

Reflection on experience and feelings about my talk yesterday to people at a Chicago senior center: The social worker/student of Maria Bartlett had asked me to speak to a group which she said had been formed for personal empowerment and support, so I crafted a Gray Panther talk along those lines. But the talk missed the boat, I thought. This was a group of about forty elderly black people in a lunchroom where they paid only $1.25 for a meal, were given numbers, and came up for a plate when called. I had, of course, a negative reaction to this and then realized it was better than standing in a long line, and Renée Buecker, who accompanied me, pointed out that you take a number in a store and don't feel processed or dehumanized by that. So much for my prejudices!

The social worker confided to me that by getting a speaker during lunch time, we had a captive audience. I think much of what I said was too abstract. I made an assumption that they knew what a national health system was. They mostly listened and reacted to descriptions of our guerilla theater actions at the American Medical Association convention and "Santa Claus Is Too Old To Work on State Street." Before and after, Delores Crockett, a director, had exhorted them to be healthy, happy, to shun bad news and to do things ala my prescription. Hearing that they were into support and empowerment, I assumed they were like more articulate groups I had met with and took off from there.

It would have been better to take something like a national health service, talk about their experiences with the medical bureaucracy and how health care was handled in Canada, especially since someone told me they were concerned about the effect of national service on Medicare (and probably Medicaid).

May 31, 1992

Memories of Barbara Deming are ready for photocopying, but I've been consumed by doubt again as to publishability. I feel they really need more of a framework. It would be nice to have an introduction by someone else and illustrations. It could be a nice memoir that way. Dream on! Well, if I don't nothing will be accomplished. It's so much easier to conceive of this for someone else's work because decisions and judgments do not affect me to the core in the same way.

Barbara Deming: A Memoir and Tribute

A talk at Women and Children First bookstore, Chicago, Illinois,
October 23, 1984
by Ruth Dear

Tonight we'd like mainly to share our memories and feelings about
Barbara Deming, but we'd like to do so in the context of her work and
history. Tributes have been slowly coming in: mainly I've seen those from
peace groups, but there are also in women's movement publications, I am
sure.

In putting Barbara Deming's life in focus, we are greatly indebted to Jan
Meyerding's anthology of her work, *We Are All Part of One Another*. There is
an excellent chronology of Barbara's involvement which reads like a precis of
the period and each selection has an introductory explanation. This selection
of her writings makes a tremendous canvas of her thoughts and actions from
early literary criticism in the fifties to involvement in CNVA (Committee for
Non Violent Action) as well as actions before and during the Viet Nam War,
for civil rights, against poverty, for women's freedom and for lesbian and gay
rights in the sixties — all of it illuminated by insight, sensitivity, empathy
and integrity.

In fact, to read her writing of the sixties is to relive very intimately a half-
buried history. One feels the immediacy and the outrage again, and then one
becomes overwhelmed by the realization of how many things she did and on
how many fronts she did them. "On Anger" was a tremendous breakthrough
for her and for others in the feminist movement, especially her statement of
the need "to confront our own most seemingly personal angers" and translate
them into "the disciplined anger of the search for change."

I first met Barbara Deming at the second national conference of Women
Strike for Peace in Urbana, Illinois, June 1963, where we found ourselves on
the Working Committee together with Bella Abzug, Mickey Flacks and
others. Resolutions on support for the Civil Rights movement and opposition
to U.S. involvement in Viet Nam were introduced to considerable opposition
from those who maintained that WSP should remain solely an anti-nuke
action group. As debate heated up, Barbara urged me to speak once again on
the issues — she who a month ago had been in jail in Birmingham! Either
she was too shy or too unsure of her persuasive powers. We finally did
persuade the convention to adopt the civil rights resolution but were unable
to get consensus on Viet Nam, had to be content with a statement signed by
individual WSPers.

Afterwards, walking back to where we were staying (both shy, not
included in the inevitable partying) she asked me what the Depression of the
thirties had been like, "confessing" that in her teens she had been unaware of

its impact. Later reading of her involvement in the Poor Peoples Campaign and her stay at Resurrection City outside the White House during the summer of '68 (see "mud City" in the anthology), I thought she really had set out to find out.

We next met by accident in the Chicago Federal Building where she had come to support her friend and comrade, David Dellinger, who was on trial as one of the Conspiracy Seven for their involvement in the mass demonstrations at the 1968 Democratic convention. Suffering from flu, she came home with George and me but first wanted to see the site of the '68 actions which she had missed. That evening we discussed writing, particularly fiction (her short story collection, *Wash Us and Comb Us*, was not published till 1972) and the guts it took to write. After reviewing her writings now, I realize that she approached everything with that kind of guts — self-examination, sharing of herself, integrity to herself.

I remember another exchange we had, probably at a conference, about the frustrated and frustrating Jeanette Rankin Brigade. Sparked by the congresswoman, this was to be a sit-in at Congress until a vote was taken to stop the U.S. war with Viet Nam. As a result of some bureaucratic peace establishment maneuvering, it became a polite, open-air demonstration, causing many women who had come prepared for action to hold an angry caucus meeting. Barbara said she had pleaded with the demonstration organizers to at least announce that some women would engage in direct action but was turned down flat.

After her terrible auto accident while en route to keynote the September 1971 War Resisters League conference with a talk on feminism and anger, I visited her in a New York City hospital. She could hardly talk but she managed. That was the last time I saw her. However, I continued to feel a connection and still do. In the September/October *WRL News*, Grace Paley has put it better:

" . . . The fact of Barbara's death from this world on August first is only a companion fact to her continuing life in all of us. For me, and many others it's real, a settling in the bones and a continuing conversation — about how to maintain fidelity to your deepest thoughts and move with respect and a voracious ear towards the deepest thinking and longing of others . . . . 'I'm dying, but I'm very well,' she said to me on the phone. 'Everyone's here and I'm well.'"

June 12, 1992

Odd how one slides into a mood, depression, without recognizing its gravity, and then even the request for help, the getting of it, seems questionable. Odd that when one is in it, one's judgment is also clouded and, as a result, life seems or is hard and harder. I wish I could express some of this in poetry instead of straight prose. Symbols, especially nature-based symbols, coat and beautify the emotions somehow, so that instead of saying, "I hurt," one weaves the pain into a more universal form. But I suppose that would require looking at nature more and oneself less? It is also nice to be able to forge out of pain something of beauty so that the pain is not always so stark? so individual? so all-consuming? so self-conscious? Am I saying that my writings would partly justify whatever pain and defeat and depression I suffered?

June 13, 1992

Seven years after!

The Gray Panther convenership seems to be working out with Debbie and Agnes willing, and though not ideal, it is progress. We may see more progress at the Board meeting. I was glad to read that the national statement of priorities adopted all those I opted for, so there is indeed a basic agreement that cements the movement, and one should not be afraid of change. Chicago GPs came to realize, albeit reluctantly, the need for weekend meetings, opening up etc., to attract younger people.

This made me think of Robin and others on the Pledge steering committee disapproving Kathy Kelly's doing civil disobedience at a missile silo as taking energy from Pledge work, as well as Robin's patronizing attitude to a GP demo I cited. What bothered me was the lack of respect for other people and movements — a self-righteous, self-centered, arrogant attitude which, alas, I shared for so long and am angered and distressed to see it in others. How self-defeating and how it contradicts all the talk about outreach! Maybe born-again people refer to their realization of a new outlook, but for us it is not being born again, it is a widening and growth, not starting out naked and helpless, but, on the contrary, building on one's strength and experience instead of shedding them.

June 21, 1992

The packet for the War Resisters League conference came with a written greeting from Ruth Benn, *Nonviolent Activist* editor, and a note that she won't be there — a dash of my hopes for presentation of my material to her at this conference. I wondered, should I try David MacReynolds? Would Grace Paley be there? Someone from New Society Publishers? Well, at least I can keep trying and I'm not totally zapped.

At the Older Women's League meeting yesterday there was a presentation by the Live Poets Society: older women presenting their own and others' poetry. I was most impressed by a tall woman who said she'd been in a deep depression. They performed her poem, originally part of a Mardi

Gras program featuring the seven deadly sins. It was most imaginative and sharp, about lusting for Ken and trying to be a Barbie doll. June Heimrich had originated this group, encouraging them in her poetry class. A mixed bag (no pun intended!) but stimulating.

June 23, 1992

I should begin to think about my presentation on patriotism for Third Unitarian Church forum on July 5. Ideas: internationalist background, Russian background — outsiders to America, in a way, radical and peace background, feeling for working people and the oppressed in whatever country, solidarity feelings extending to and beyond strikers and liberationists anywhere and everywhere. Patriotism as an easy and facile expression that infected the movement, such as American flags even during the Gulf War. Those who want to go back to the American dream should remember the class composition of the time — landholders and entrepreneurs and slave owners — and should reach far beyond that, especially when we see the ethnic hatreds. Perhaps there will always be distrust of those with different ways or philosophies but to raise one's culture and country to an absolute virtue is a trap. Even those who love the physical beauty of America are seeing an international environmental concern for one globe, one earth. The highest moments for me were and still are meeting people from all over the globe and finding common interests and values. Whereas patriotism exalts only one's own culture and nationality. Those who say they are patriotic, meaning love of country and the good things they have in mind, are really taking an unpleasant reality, the American scene and life, and transforming it. I'd rather proclaim a love of humanity than a love of a nation-state.

There, I've written out the elements of a talk!

June 27, 1992

I'd like to put on Mozart or Beethoven to exercise by, but somehow I'm inhibited, as though I still can't let myself enjoy it — after seven years! I'll probably settle for WNIB or WFMT. Less trouble but also less committing? Why don't I indulge or honor my desire for that music? As with other things, it takes me a long time to resume some aspects of the old life. Too painful? Yet I did it to some extent with the condo garden, but, of course, that's not so personal as my own backyard though the interest is there.

June 30, 1992

I typed out the House Un-American Activities Committee inquisition of Women Strike for Peace leader Dagmar Wilson, and I realized that it needs explanation: the atmosphere of the time and particularly the accomplishment of defying the committee. I have about five pieces on Civil Rights, quite a few on WISP, the Viet Nam war, on philosophy and background and feminism. So it is shaping up, and I do feel it will make a pattern of activity and belief.

July 1, 1992

I did get the WSP HUAC hearing reproduced and I feel it is significant and wonder how I can convey that: A short notation on how this was the first time someone stood up to the committee regarding admission of communists and broke the consensus of "Of course, *I'm* not a communist" — a radical step and done by a woman!

Hope I can sleep some. I had to get up, after tossing and not being able to relax and rest. I readied personal laundry, did a double-crostic, and now probably will do accounts — an urge to do something so that I will be able to feel accomplishment and, then, maybe relax. I went to bed last night, feeling I hadn't done much yesterday aside from accounts, getting HUAC material xeroxed, a couple of phone calls about Gray Panthers, and, of course, the two-hour lunch and conversation with Monica which, till this minute, I had dismissed; but I realize now that it is a valuable exchange and part of accomplishing things: testing ideas, relating, learning, etc.

July 4, 1992

Today I have to type up an agenda for the Gray Panther Board meeting tomorrow, and maybe, maybe I'll begin on *Women's Resistance to the Viet Nam War*. Even if I don't, I think that's the way to go because it represents original research as well as personal experience. So it now seems good and significant, and I did write it up after the original speech at the opening of Feminists Against Militarism conference in 1981 because of the many requests for it.

July 8, 1992

After jotting down ideas on Gray Panther structure, I felt on the verge of some break-through but afraid to pursue it. I finally broke one barrier, putting on the phonograph Mozart's piano concerto No. 21. Have wanted to do that for my morning exercise because, often, radio programs are unsatisfactory. But I couldn't somehow until today.

I think what agitated me was the thought of consulting Renée and Debbie, bouncing ideas off them in preparation for the GP Board meeting, maybe building a leadership base in Oak Park with which I could function. I feel it is important to exchange these ideas as now I have no one to bounce them off on with Henny and Maria gone. Maybe their newness will add something. Henny called yesterday from Maine and I think that goosed me too, feeling that she was now out of it.

I think I recoiled from the idea of breaking new ground, taking the initiative.

Listening to music, wonder why I denied myself this — still mourning? Feeling I shouldn't or couldn't enjoy? The last time I tried to put on Beethoven's Sixth Symphony, the machine didn't work. That was two, three years ago and I had it fixed a year or more ago!

The talk on Patriotism at Third Unitarian went very well. After, I was surprised that I hadn't mentioned flag-waving during the Gulf War since this was such a receptive audience — about 30 people despite it being the July

Fourth weekend. All three speakers had basically the same approach. So what was I nervous about? I still carry a fear of Stalinists from the Thirties and beyond. I was surprised and gratified to hear that Bernie and Agnes's daughter was running on the Socialist Workers Party platform in another state. When they introduced me to her, I identified myself as having been in the original (Trotskyist) Left Opposition but received no response. Too ancient history? I think I tend to lump Trots and Stalinists together because style and rhetoric are often similar.

July 18, 1992

Yesterday I picked up a bunch of coral carnations. The reds, yellows, whites didn't appeal to me, and then I saw this lone beautifully colored bunch and bought it. Sitting in the aqua pottery vase in the center of the coffee table, they gladden my heart. How I do react to color!

August 15, 1992

Haunted by "I'll Fly Away" series on TV. Do I wish to fly away? Yes, to a new apartment setup and to Europe. Am I trapped as are the people in the series, to some extent? Will I get liberation? I'm annoyed with the series because it's so partial and gentle with the South and the condition of the blacks. A liberal district attorney in the South, enforcing the law? The writers want to have it all!

Last year, I succeeded in staying away from the Gray Panther office, but of course there were two other responsible people. Henny undertook so much and I'm left with no full grasp of the procedures. I think I've bought more than I bargained for. It's annoying: so little planning unless one pushes for it. I think I should try to be firm if we ever have a steering committee meeting, when Agnes returns, and delegate tasks.

August 26, 1992

Last week, I did take the material from George's memorial plus other mementos and snaps and put them in the file box with the tutoring materials. I felt relieved that at least it wasn't on the closet shelves, waiting for me to put stuff in the scrapbook. I don't think I'll ever do it, unless I'm moved at some future time. I guess it's still too painful.

I did also write to Lackey, the prisoner on death row (he may have been executed as I haven't heard from him), and to the Nigerian correspondent who wanted me to sponsor his coming here and I intended to ask what that involved, but never did. I should also call May tonight. Vi called last night to say the hurricane did not hit in May's area though she's near Miami.

August 27, 1992

Unable to sleep last night, I thought again of the realization I'd had recently that I no longer felt I had to keep living up to someone's expressed good opinion and I became sure that this was so — a marked contrast to my complaints that I didn't want to be a role model because I'd felt I had to keep living up to that or let people down if I didn't. It was a good feeling, a feeling that I was OK, worth something, deserving of respect, or, at least, respected for what I am. I guess my reception at the WRL conference confirmed that.

August 30, 1992

Well, I listened to Bradshaw for two hours yesterday about homecoming, i.e., to the hurt child within, and wondered about several things that did or did not fit into his mold: a loving family but a mother who used me as a confidante; having to measure up or fill someone's ideal as well as a jealous male sibling; the trauma of Grandma's presence when she came to live with us; the trauma of Papa's death; Bradshaw's observations that what he termed abused children are hyper-reactive, i.e., very nervous and easily startled.

September 14, 1992

Charlotte Holenia died last week, apparently peacefully. Though I disliked her and couldn't bring myself to send her a card, partly out of inertia and partly out of a feeling that I couldn't genuinely extend a hand, it is hard to see someone I've worked with passing, and in Gray Panthers now, I feel pretty alone and too much the bearer of the banner. I don't want to be totally absorbed in this worthy group that can't seem to pull itself up by its bootstraps. Last year looked good, but we lost two extremely valuable, contributing people — Maria and Henny — and though Debbie is willing and so is Agnes, there is a danger of getting in over my head.

Last night, going through my bag of tricks to relax and bring sleep, I again thought of my fantasy of a young girl going out from her home on a road through mountains with the horizon opening up and I felt I had a story inside, but when I tried to think of my early life as a beginning to it, the unhappiness of it disturbed me. I didn't want to write about that. So it's like I want to set out on a journey but I don't go anywhere. I must want to create something, to write a story. Is this related to my feelings about autobiography and a reluctance to provide a framework for my writings?

And I have made a breakthrough concerning the framework for the writing. Up to now, I was afraid to consider it, afraid of the job of constructing it, and this is the first concrete step, a starting to formulate it. I think I can go on from there, turning around how to build on it, alter it, recast it, etc. The key is the stimulation. From a cloud overhanging it has become an opener of possibilities and for that I'm grateful. What felt good about having completed the WRL conference article was taking a mass of notes, sifting, discarding, including, whipping it into shape, dealing with the two major themes as I saw them, fitting the other points in, and getting a whole that flows.

September 23, 1992

In the evening, went to the social action committee of Third Unitarian and brought the "Prisoners of Conscience" list and article and agreed to be at the table with Terry Burke on Sunday. Looks like this is a more willing-to-work-and-to-listen committee though some people confused service and action. Got two near strokes: Dorothy Wilz who remembered my talk on patriotism this summer and another woman who came up to shake my hand after the meeting. I'm getting more used to this, but I'm still a little surprised and self-conscious when it occurs, still feeling I made contributions as they occurred to me, though I acknowledge I provided a little perspective.

September 26, 1992

One should value the socialist vision for a better world of Stalinists, Socialists, etc. Can one have an organization that is tolerant of others, not fiercely competitive? Who knows? Maybe these thoughts are inspired by the looming attendance at Charlotte Holenia's memorial today. She was the archetype of the dogmatist who, in the name of knowing the right way, was sometimes cruel to others. I suppose that's partly or mostly the personality as well as the party line. How someone uses the latter and even adapts it to one's personality!

When the Democratic Socialists (DSA) newsletter comes, I'm drawn to it, almost to the point of joining, and then I draw back, repelled by some position. At least I learned of several movements for a third party so there seems to be a stirring and restlessness with the Gore/Clinton ilk. Is the electoral position the only one that repels me? People know they're being manipulated but they choose to believe otherwise, sometimes even believing they're doing the manipulating. I tend to let up on people I know who support Clinton but I don't believe I should, as part of an educational process and, of course, the assertion of a valid point of view.

What disturbs me, tho, is the hopelessness about the future which I feel from time to time, a new stage of my political outlook, discouraged by the defeats and the steadily rightward trend in general. I keep hoping that there will be another outbreak of resistance and rebellion and things will stir again so that one is less a voice crying in the wilderness.

October 9, 1992

Am beginning to rethink my role in Gray Panthers. It seems a shame that the newsletter which I really enjoy doing should be done in such haste, and, despite efforts, no fixed schedule. I think I should cut my involvement, not assume so much emotional responsibility, and not worry so. If this is an unresponsive group, then why spin my wheels trying to make it so? I don't have to prove anything to anybody, including myself. I should mark out my role more clearly and keep to it. If there is no other proper leadership, so be it.

October 24, 1992

Yesterday was a big emotional day. I learned that a friend was to go for a mastectomy and it had a powerful effect on me. Thursday, having lunch with Fran Bender at Cozy Corner, I talked some about this and almost said *colostomy* when I meant *mastectomy*. So once again I over-empathized, feeling shook up and saddened. It brought back memories/feelings about George's operation and came to a head yesterday, the day of her operation, before I called to find out if she was OK. In fact, I dreaded calling: too much like other pre- and post-operative anxieties with George.

After my haircut at 11, I thought I'd go for a drive along Thatcher Woods. What drew me were fall colors and restlessness. Driving along Lake Street and up Thatcher Avenue, I decided to look at the woods and also George's resting place, so to speak. What was really drawing me was the urge to be with or near him, my memories of this grove. I did look at it briefly but decided to follow the trail to First Avenue, and as I came uphill and got a glimpse of the stream bordered by colorful and green trees, I came the closest to a prayer I think I've ever been. I kept saying, "Trees, help me. Water, help me." And throughout the walk, I was agitated and suffering and when I came to the grassy, park like, flat area, near the bridge, I felt a powerful surge of emotion. So I acknowledged — or tried to — the depth of feeling. Before that, I asked myself, Why do I have to suffer both traumas — the colostomy and his death? Why wasn't one enough?

I went home then, after resting a while before the return trek, and gradually began to feel better. I called the hospital and got no answer, twice, so I called her house on the chance a relative would be there and was told she was fine and would be coming home in a few days. So I felt much better.

* * *

Thinking about history and my personal history, reinforced by the epilogue to A Thousand Acres, how many moments or longer periods in time are totally lost. What one has lived and lived so intensely is gone when one's mind and body are gone. That's why one should get experiences down, although one can never adequately convey the whole of an experience. As a result, one gets facets, slants, vignettes which may flesh it out a little. Maybe I'm telling myself to get back to my writings.

October 25, 1992

I went to West Suburban Hospital with Kathy Jeans this afternoon to see our friend with considerable trepidation and misgivings, and after, I said I didn't feel like going home, so K. obligingly drove around Thatcher Avenue and the woods which are beautiful. And I thought that that was out of the way, came home, did a puzzle, made supper; but underneath, apparently, feelings were bubbling. I went to wash the dishes, and in the process, also wiped the place mat on the table and began to have a disoriented deja vu feeling of reliving the experience and the grief of George's death, somewhat similar to my feelings at the end of the Thatcher Woods trail yesterday. I think that whole hospital bit with the I. V. and the blood drainage bag, etc., triggered subliminal memories/reactions.

My restlessness and anxiety mounted. I felt I couldn't settle and started a jigsaw puzzle, a Toulouse-Lautrec scene which I'd done some time ago. I finally went to bed and lay there, in the dark, only a little and decided to try to write some of this angst and grief out. Only, there is no writing out real grief and I'm beginning to feel that all my "progress" in the grieving process is like a house of cards and the life I so painstakingly built up is threatened.

October 29, 1992

The business with C also struck a nerve about my shingles nearly two years ago, recalling the pain and how I dealt with it, contrasting it with hers. Mine was not the same raw pain and not so unremitting — or was it? I do remember getting maybe two hours of relief in the four-hour period after taking a pill. So I guess that went into the pot too, as though all the emotional, physical, personal pain and George's pain made a nasty stew. It's discomforting not to be able to give help without suffering for it! I remember how I wanted to take care of George after his colostomy, to be of use, of service, and I had a similar feeling this time — until I got there.

November 1, 1992

Thinking over my reactions yesterday, I realized that the various spells of caretaking with George must have been quite traumatic but suppressed. The feeling I had at the time was that each was temporary and not a prolonged stint. I didn't really — or couldn't — deal with emotions about it or face the implications of continued nursing care. Waiting with C. for the doctor to call, my telling her to wait for this before deciding on the type of home care, was like my telling George in his last illness to call the doctor when he sat up on the couch in the dining room and said he had chest pains, not knowing what else to do. Now I wonder if my negative, angry reaction to his calling me a trump or a brick was a denial of the care required and being given.

November 7, 1992

This wrestling with my handwriting interests me. It's as though I keep mourning the loss of a nice one and although I feel I know how to write more legibly, I somehow don't or can't. When I re-read entries, I deplore the appearance and feel, in a way, diminished by it. Has this some relationship to creative writing? To deplore the messy process? To want to make things clear?

* * *

Is language power? In a way.

It occurs to me that Wayne's encouraging me to keep a journal has served a double purpose: to write out and examine my feelings and problems and, just, to write! Dealing with the one has certainly helped to open up the other, and to proceed with more confidence. Whereas before, I received most satisfaction from speaking well, and especially from the audience response, I'm getting as much or more from writing, particularly as I am not so active and less actively seek speaking opportunities. It is very good to elicit a warm response from an audience, but spoken words evaporate, vanish, but written words are *there*.

I seem to have come to a good stopping place!

November 16, 1992

Shaken, disoriented, miserable, frustrated — all these describe my dark feelings last week. Yet I co-edited the GP newsletter, lunched with Monica, went to Third Unitarian and the banquet, called Faith, reassured Agnes, etc.

November 25, 1992

I became so obsessed with plans and preparations for the Gray Panther get-together here that I couldn't sleep last night. I got up and made all kinds of lists. I am putting much too much into this!

I guess the business about the December 6 get-together is a long suppressed desire to do something decorative and festive. Well, I hope we can get 20 or more people. Should I bring up at the December 13 Board meeting the need for cooperation or else we'll fold?

November 26, 1992

This Thanksgiving feels a lot like the year's end and is related to my ending this notebook, as though nearing closing the book on the year although there's a whole calendar month to 1993 still. It's been a mixed year. I feel a bit stuck in Gray Panthers for all the reasons I've listed, and despite all the talk about a Democratic change, I think it'll be smoke and mirrors. Well, some people like to smoke it and I suppose that's what keeps them going just as my hopes do for me, but Jesus, God, there should be some victories, some real hope, some upsurge of struggle. I'd like to see one more before I die.

My cousin Vi called from New York this morning and I was glad to hear from her. She received the WRL calendar. Sister-in-law May broke her hip and was in the hospital and maybe a nursing home, and now someone has to be with her 24 hours or she won't be able to stay in her apartment! Karen has been with her; at least May has her daughter. But what a perspective: she gets a nice place, loves it, but is there on the condition of being ambulatory. Considering what it costs, they have a nerve. When you get a place with services that make life easier, you're really there only on sufferance and you are never secure despite having money. I guess this outlook would be easier to bear were the world situation easier to bear.

November 27, 1992

Watching a TV program on New England from the air, thinking of how much as a New Yorker, New England was special to me, to us, I thought of history and how one's sense of it is shaped by where one is born. Why does New England seem special to me — is it the same to a Westerner? to a Southerner? to a Midwesterner?

And so I'm led to think of my own history and how it has shaped my present consciousness and former actions and how, in turn, they have shaped my history. Whatever I have reported or described, experienced, is part of my odyssey as a radical and a woman and though mostly these are descriptions of discrete events, they are also part of the pattern of my life — woven into it and weaving it in turn.

Thus all through the revolutionary/Trotskyist years, the hope generated during the despair of the Depression, the almost-silent war years, the

McCarthy period when hope — and action — went underground, to the reviving of the 50s' Black liberation struggles, the burgeoning and growth of the 60s with people popping up everywhere once again to once again express aloud the hopes and struggles for a new society, the interconnections, the whole opening up of oppressed people in one section after another, the peace movement which took on a new meaning — all of this I lived through, sometimes vicariously through reports of other people's activities, sometimes actively participating, but always feeling a part of the radical impulse, the radical confrontation with society, the hope for basic change. So these vignettes, pieces of action, impressions really reflect my observations and experiences and, I hope, growth.

November 30, 1992

Saturday, we distributed a Third Unitarian flyer on war toys, which I had pushed, and afterwards had hot drinks and talk at a coffee house. Debbie had come too after I'd mentioned it on the phone that morning and I felt good about bringing someone along. So I am feeling upbeat again about this event, the GP party next Sunday, blind and apartment cleaning, storm windows in, the newsletter came looking great and a week ahead of time, my starting to work on writings.

Thinking over in bed, this morning, the lift the distribution gave me and the others, the socializing afterwards, I realized that Gray Panthers do not do these things such as socializing, except for a few small cliques, and open air activities visible to the public at large. It is run by a smaller and smaller group and even last year, when we achieved more involvement, that was an internal affair. The annual garage sale was perhaps an exception. So how is more such activity to be achieved? Why not a more recent retreat/Board meeting? Why wait till April which leaves only two more months till we stop meeting for the summer? Why not at least at July or August action or meeting when outdoor activity would be easiest, such as distribution on health? Why not ask the health committee to brainstorm something like that?

It felt so good to be out distributing and interacting with the public and fellow-activists although I went reluctantly, out of duty, and because it was at the corner of First Chicago bank, convenient to my house.

December 2, 1992

Woke up to a surge of anxiety, partly the effect of last night's movie, "Glengary, Glen Ross" those deadbeat salesmen in a deadbeat office, frustrated, striving, going up and down with their sales prospects, scheming, conning, contriving, wheedling, not having the stamina to stand up to the boss from downtown who talks to them like a drill sergeant.

Seeing Jack Lemmon change from a wheeler-dealer, nasty backbiter when he thinks he's on top, to a broken-down man was a phony.

I guess I'll always be sensitive to these things, get ructions and suffer about them. The important thing is not to let them distort reality or become self-fulfilling prophesies.

December 7, 1992

Pearl Harbor day!

The Gray Panther party was very successful. Rosie, El and Bobbi came and I was very glad to see them. Deb remarked that without my friends it would have been a poor GP party as only seven other members came, including a poor showing from local GPs. It was good to feel I'd helped to make it a success and that my efforts at creating a festive atmosphere paid off. But I learned also my limitations: Were I to do this again, I would not undertake a soup and maybe not even something like the mulled cider.

People mixed nicely, gathering around the coffee table, an unplanned event, while some sat on the black sofa. Dining room chairs had to be brought in, etc. Twenty people would really have been capacity!

I hope I can serve out the term with GPs. After June, if it continues, I'd like to stick to the newsletter, though, of course, if something interesting develops, I'll probably get involved. But as a co-convener, having tried various things with no result, or, rather, suggested them, with little or no result, I don't see why I should waste effort. Anyway, this fall Third Unitarian Social Action Committee looks promising and somewhat of a vehicle for action, so I don't feel without outlets.

December 10, 1992

Reluctant to write down all my feelings about *Anxiety Disease* by Dr. David Sheehan (1982) since they've bounced up and down. Reading and finishing it yesterday, I was moved at several points to make notes about reactions/memories/questions it stimulated and was, in a way, seduced by his presentation of the need for permanent medication. Then I read "Acknowledgements" at the beginning of the book and was made uneasy by his thanking Upjohn colleagues and going on to extol the benefits of a continuing cooperation of the medical industry and academia; in fact, not liking this at all. That afternoon, *Health Letter* came with a long article from August/September *Nation* on Upjohn's pushing of Xanax as the remedy for panic. This of course was very disturbing and sobering. I began to wonder about Sheehan's enthusiasm for panic medication. Later, calmer, I re-read the article and wondered some more, especially since Upjohn has funded the Anxiety Disorders Association, American Psychiatric Association, etc.

I do realize that advocates of honesty — the "good" guys — are sometimes sweeping in their denunciations and wondered about addiction, dependence, maintenance medication. It is true that in this society — and with me — *dependence* is a dirty word whether applied to welfare recipients, co-dependency, or medication. Sheehan's example of lifelong taking of insulin by diabetics is a good one. So the question is whether the drug works as hyped rather than "addiction."

The best that can be said for researchers, etc. financed by Upjohn is that they are genuinely scientifically contributing in an area that Upjohn can profit from and thus Upjohn funds them, much as corporations fund special programs for PBS rather than supporting PBS in general.

This, on top of all my other feelings about the new diagnosis of anxiety/panic attacks has me confused, puzzled and kind of stuck. It's one thing to make notes when one is in tune with the book and to feel one is learning something, opening up possibilities. It's another to have it tied to a few pills. I should remind myself that I asked for a tranquilizer and Xanax was given to me as also being an anti-panic pill and no one has yet suggested that I be on it for life. If it works for me, I should accept it . . . . It would be so nice to have everything work out, to accept unquestioningly what one is given — by mouth or mind.

December 16, 1992

It was a pleasant party at the Wheats, including a talk with old friend, Aldine Gunn, and ended with a performance by Ann Wheat's pupils doing short bits from Xmas songs and then we all joined in for four or five at the end.

I've been wondering about going to church this Sunday. The program doesn't especially appeal to me, but, on the other hand, I don't want to be alone. Now is when I miss a different sort of support group, like War Resisters League, where I can be with like-minded people at Xmas time.

December 18, 1992

Larry Gara wrote at the end of his Christmas letter that he'll edit the War Resisters League calendar commemorating fifty years of the bomb and asked for an entry on local action. My first thought was of the Camp Mercury, Nevada test site demonstration with Women Strike for Peace, but that isn't local. I don't recall a local action, though I guess I could ferret one out of the Chicago Women for Peace newsletter.

Terry Burke said the *Wednesday Journal* gave the war toys distribution a nice write-up. Maybe I'll go to church to see it at the Social Action table though the idea of a "Victorian Christmas" program is not very appealing. My spirits soared yesterday also because Fran Bender invited me to a Hanukkah celebration at her house on Sunday, December 20 and asked me to bring the Womenorah Elsie Goldstein sculpted.

December 27, 1992

Today is Tommy's birthday as Vi reminded me on the phone this evening.

This morning Kathy Jeans called to ask if I was going to the Kwanza celebration at Third Unitarian whose housekeeping preparations she was in charge of. I said yes, finally, thinking it is better to go out and see people. Glad I did! Helped with decorating fruit bowl and made little bowls, eight of them, each with an orange and evergreen sprigs, for the tables. It is a harvest festival to which people brought oodles of fruit, nuts and other things. The seven candles and seven principles were explained by a Ghanaian, ex-member of Congress of Racial Equality (CORE), Black Panthers and now with the National Black United Front.

Yesterday, a card came from my niece Karen shortly after I'd called and left a message. Her mother May has Alzheimer's, she wrote. Strongly affected by that, wondering why I hadn't realized it myself since the last two times I called May, she didn't know me until I made a lengthy attempt at identification. Vi, this evening, said she doubts it, but I think that's just denial. Karen referred to a ten-year period ahead, but I wonder. Though a friend at TUC seems to be surviving, even commenting on the fact that her memory is going.

Also, in a holiday note, another friend said her daughter-in-law had a mastectomy. Today, Agnes called to report on good results from calling Gray Panther Board members and then described her daughter's epilepsy.

On the good side, I've been to celebrations all month, including New Year's Eve probably.

December 30, 1992

Had a long conversation with Karen who called back to tell me about provisions for May. I empathized with her feelings about May's not recognizing her initially, told her of my anxiety/panic diagnosis and almost told her about joining Third Unitarian, but didn't, figuring enough revelation was enough. But I do feel more solid ground there and more acceptance — by me, really, since other people readily accepted me from the beginning.

All this and hearing of other people's troubles, as I approach 79, almost 80, raises thoughts and fears of ability retention, both mental and physical. On the other hand, I was encouraged while addressing a GP newsletter to Kathryn Anderson. Over 90, she has joined a peace group in Peoria despite living in a "racist, rich, Republican" dwelling. Encouraged, too, by the Christmas letter from Adlaide and Katherine Dear, George's cousins, who are into so many things in Jersey City — church, school board, directorships. Since I am also so connected, why do I need this reassurance?

Give Us This Day Our Daley Bread

by Ruth Dear
Written November 1974

"Look out for Granny! She's joinin' the Gray Panthers.
No damn bureaucrat can take her for a ride.
In her sturdy shoes and shawl
She'll go march on City Hall
And they'll listen or she's apt to tan their hide!"
Chorus of the Gray Panther song © 1974, Sandy Heller

As a new phenomenon--old people taking action for old people--Gray Panthers has captured imagination and attention. In Chicago it has become a good subject for the media and it begins to look as if another movement has "arrived." The desire for action is based on impatience with "senior citizen" groups, resentment at segregation by age, and indignation at callous and irresponsible employers and agencies. Yet, as always, the message gets distorted, pruned and polished. Thus the latest action, a November 26 demonstration for automatic issuance of food stamps, evoked a patronizing smile from local ABC newscaster Joel Daly despite the deadly serious theme of hunger.

In fact, 100 stomping, chanting, milling old folks with placards ("Give Us This Day Our Daley Bread," "More Buns, Less Guns," "We Can't Cinch Our Belts Any Tighter," etc.) dramatized their plight opposite the Federal Building. Encircled by a red cloth symbolizing bureaucratic red tape, people vainly grabbed at sandwich boarded "Food Stamps." Finally a Gray Panther cut the tape which was then folded up. They crowded into the building to present it to Senator Adlai Stevenson with a request for immediate legislation.

Hoping to get the most from this meeting, the Gray Panthers had dropped from their new theme song a stanza referring to politicians as the aphids on a rose. A pity, since the response of Stevenson aide John Terman had a mad hatter quality. While $270 million of federal funds are waiting to be used for this purpose, he spoke of increasing funds for outreach. To the question, "How does the senator feel about tightening your belt when some people have no belts to tighten?" Terman replied idiotically, "He agrees with you."

Indeed, unaware of the GP emphasis on all, he kept referring to "senior citizens," "the elderly," etc. This prompted spokesperson Alice Adler to take the podium again to stress concern "for the hundreds of thousands of people of all ages, including children, who do not have enough food."

At the end, as he was presented with the red tape, cries arose from the Gray Panthers, "What are you going to do with it?" Terman promised, "Your red tape will be presented to Senator Stevenson."

What will happen when these modest demands are ignored or met only with more promises? Will other increasingly hungry unemployed people raise their voices too?

Ruth Dear is a local Gray Panther. (Journal photo by Andrew Lisec.)

The Gray Panthers:
Old people who got angry

This photo of Ruth appeared on the front page of Oak Park's *Wednesday Journal*, July 13, 1983, accompanying an interview by Aaron Lisec. Re-printed with permission from the *Wednesday Journal*.

Chapter Four
There Will Always Be Things I Struggle With

January 3, 1993

I realize that for me there will always be things I struggle with, despite my desire not to have to, to be free of the need to struggle. Odd, in a way, after I remarked this morning at the Third Church forum with the new youth minister that I had been with a group in high school that felt the need to struggle against bad conditions.

But this is internal struggle which takes so much time, saps so much energy, though at times when I do get an insight, I am energized. So this struggle, too, has its ups and downs. I am tired, tired of struggling socially. There is so much injustice and so little apparent remedying of it. Yet just to accept injustice is as painful and certainly more discouraging than to struggle against it.

January 17, 1993

I suppose these down feelings now are also due to U.S. attacks on Iraq again: the anger, frustration, helplessness, not being in a strong network to protest though Henry (Maine) and Margaret (Oregon) called to share some of this, and I called friends here.

I had dreaded somewhat my birthday yesterday, but people called, took me to dinner. Well, I've talked myself into a better mood and am ready for bed.

January 18, 1993

Frustrated, stirred, angry, aggravated by this militarist society and government. The ultimate irony: celebrating Martin Luther King's birthday today with not one mention of nonviolence. During the civil rights struggles, the establishment was glad enough to support that aspect, at least verbally. Not only is Bush trying to set policy still, but he's also raining on Clinton's inaugural parade in the spirit of his Willie Horton campaign. Agnes, too, recognized this — the consistent meanness of spirit, the nasty undercut.

My frustration stems partly from being out of touch, exasperated with peace networks which don't call, and inability to do anything like demonstrating at this point. A local vigil I might be able to support or even one downtown. There does, of course, exist an informal network — Henny and Maggie calling.

How can people accept this stuff? Is there no code of honor, no ethical code that when one bombs a hotel where an Islamic meeting is occurring, no apology even? And the assumptions of that panel on the McNeil-Lehrer Report that one has to get Hussein by bombing his country, the outright assertion that we're the leaders in the Middle East and that this will continue.

And the Coast Guard firing on the Haitians! I looked for some sign of different emphasis in Clinton's speeches today and could find only an assertion of policy and maybe, maybe, I could infer a slight difference. But am I doing what all the apologists are doing? Looking for content in empty words? In a way, Clinton was talking like Bush at the beginning of his term about a gentler, kinder nation.

The international situation, the U.S. aggression, makes my personal problems seem puny but I think my feelings about both are of a piece.

January 26, 1993

A nice thing happened yesterday morning: Lillian Hayward called. She'd gotten our Gray Panther newsletter from a friend in California, liked it very much, was impressed with it and wanted to come to meetings since they're now on Saturday. Another contributor to national GPs of whom we were never informed! Felt good about the newsletter, about insisting we send it to all networks, and about Saturday meetings — all of which was largely due to my work and input. Called co-editor Renée to tell her. I said I knew this was a labor of love but it was nice to be loved back!

Lorie Rosenblum also called back and will try to get someone on women's health and history for our March meetings. Seeing Agnes's anxiety over details and telling her not to fret about how things should go, I realized I had come a long way. Formerly, I would have stewed about Lorie's calling back, but this time I was able to tell myself I'd done as asked, and, sure enough, in time Lorie responded. I hadn't wasted forty-eight hours fretting over this. Recognizing boundaries again!

Thinking of boundaries with my mother and my refusal or inability to express concern or sympathy when she returned from visiting Aunt Fanny, now blind. I guess I'd hardened myself against my former over-empathy. Similarly with my distancing myself in the last year or so she lived with us. Painful to think how harshly I did it. A survival tactic perhaps, but not a nice one.

Writing about Lillian H., I realized how important it is to include good things here as they round out the picture, balance negative, disturbing reactions.

January 28, 1993

I'm still mulling over the housing meeting at the Wheats'. Two different agendas: Diana, the nurse, wanted a home where she could give help with a common dining room, joint meal-making, and individual private rooms. This, no one or nearly no one, was really ready for, the overwhelming majority opting for private apartments. But that raised the question of why form a co-op since most seemed to want to reproduce what they had. In theory, it would be nice to have a club-like atmosphere with stimulating people, but what if people were not all that stimulating?

What do I want? Really, something more along the lines of Holley Court Terrace in terms of cleaning, care, but a friendlier, more stimulating, age-integrated group.

And could six couples and singles get along? A plus might be a nice back yard, a library/lounge, a common dining room on occasion. Maybe the excitement for me was the challenge of something new. Were I disabled, I might opt for a more communal setup, but I don't think I'd like the rules and responsibilities and small private living quarters. No kitchen? No study? Just a big bedroom? Yuk!

January 29, 1993

Will I ever have the courage to write about my changed attitude to religion, my better understanding of it, its place for others, what others mean by the word? These socially aware people's outlook is not so very different from what I mean by *weltanschauung*, world view, internationalism, solidarity, a decent society. What a big taboo that word *religion* represented, something to be shunned, scorned, fought.

I remember the rush of pleasure right after I joined Third Unitarian and then I excoriated myself for being happy at joining a Christian world, but now I realize more clearly that it was the feeling of belonging that was basic. I had the feeling in the movement when I first joined, but splits and isolation ensued, I was always on the minority, on the radical fringe. Even earlier, actually on the fringe with no or almost no friends, always dissenting or distrustful of school learning, I got great satisfaction from having a mate: I belonged to someone. Then George's death exacerbated all the old feelings and I very much wanted a community of support. Now I feel I've found it, at least for the present.

Odd that Gentiles in the movement barely react to my being in a church, except maybe old friends or comrades, while Jews have stronger reactions. Well, I was so outspoken against religion, objecting to the Christian emphasis, especially in the Solidarity movement, while, at the same time, admiring their dedication, the Catholic liberation movement, the Quakers I knew. Well, that has been a long journey and I'm still on it. I feel I can look back on a life spent in some kind of service though it was/is so much a part of me that it didn't seem noteworthy. Now I seem to be more in the role of consultant and opinion expresser as with book reviewing and editing. A sort of conduit of others' journeys?

February 2, 1993

"May I never lose
that terror
that keeps me brave." (Audre Lord, "Solstice," *Nation* review 2/1/93)

February 3, 1993

Inspired by *Point of View* on Channel 11 last night about three nuns, one of whom was very familiar, the head of a Catholic Religious Women's organization. She's shown at an El Salvador demonstration, speaking out. I thought I might see others I knew or heard of, maybe someone from Eighth Day Center, but I didn't. Their dedication to social change was articulated particularly well by a professor, an old woman, who counterposed to a philosophy of lifetime service to the poor, getting rid of poverty. One woman had left the church because of racism and sexism and another is suing because the church violated a contract to hire her. All obviously have been victimized and/or censured and refused to go along. I felt at one with their spirit and intelligence and grasp of social issues, though living the Gospel according to Christ's teachings seemed irrelevant to me, but, of course, it doesn't have to have relevance for me. It's their statement of philosophy, just as mine is Marxian socialism. Like them, I've had to come to terms with what I believe, alter it. I have profound respect for these militants really struggling within an organization and hierarchy, holding fast to their beliefs and insisting on carrying them out. Their religious rituals, though altered to suit their awarenesses, seem odd to me, but then my procedures — or lack of them — may seem odd to them. So once again I confront the underlying content and find much common ground — more than that: a shared spirituality, though I prefer to phrase it as sharing of the spirit and of course, the goals. What a road they have traveled.

February 8, 1993

Ambivalent reaction to *Eleanor Roosevelt* biography. She attracts and repels me. These talented upper class women who did things were powerful women who worked *for* the poor, aside from helping the Women's Trade Union League, but had the arrogance of being born well-to-do. I should be feeling more admiration for her and I am impressed by her accomplishments before Franklin Roosevelt became president which I knew nothing about. Yet despite her expression of affection for FDR, his mother Sara, and others, I feel a coldness. She never comes across to me as a loving woman, concerned and devoted one. She is of course the product of her time and class. Yet thinking now of the three nuns on the "Point of View" program, I feel a devotion and passion there much more to my liking, a simplicity if you will. Of course, they do not have the trappings of family and class that Eleanor had and two of them were racially oppressed as well as by class. Maybe her twittery style is an attempt to cover up this lack.

Just finished the book, devoting practically the whole evening to it. Impressed by her determination and passion after all, her triumph over emotional neglect, her many facets and accomplishments. Odd how she dressed down in the daytime and apparently shone at evening formal affairs, demonstrating her social graces. I'm appalled at the limits put upon her. She advised against depending on Moskowitz when FDR became governor of New York. Here was a very capable political woman like herself, whom she sacrificed to her husband in a sense because she would take over the office and run it. A bit jealous perhaps?

February 16, 1993

I seem to be inching toward some integration, some culmination, but I can't quite make it.

Talking about *Eleanor Roosevelt* Tuesday, I realized many points of resemblance — ugliness, organizing ability, dedication, urge to self-expression and to make a difference. Positive feelings, also, as regards growth and understanding.

February 24, 1993

Watched for one-and a half hours *Healing and the Mind* on Channel 11 and wondered about the stress-reduction techniques and process, I found that soothing and a technique to avoid anxiety, consciously directing myself to return to the breathing process/exercise. This is called meditation, but to me, it's the opposite since meditation involves thinking, meditating on something. Impressed also by a psychiatrist's remarks that giving and caring for others in the cancer group was somewhat healing or helpful.

The program also brought thoughts of death, remaining years, how to live them more fully in the sense of appreciating things and maybe even unbending a little to be closer with people. Why should I feel surprised that someone seemed very grateful and that my helping has brought us closer? Of course, the program presents, in a sense, a cosmetic view minus the physical pain, discomfort, unpleasantnesses and difficulty of daily living.

Looking for a place to hold a Gray Panther meeting featuring State Rep. Alice Palmer, went to Lutheran Theological School with Debbie. I'm sick of the whole subject, the enormous outlay of money and effort required, and dealing with people's closet racist reactions to different places on the South Side. I can't fully understand the depth of this reaction. If something seemed inaccessible to me, I just wouldn't go instead of making an issue of it.

February 26, 1993

Does anyone ever sit down, in my circles, and ask themselves and each other what they'd like to see? Extrapolate the future society? Experience together the largeness of vision, the possibilities, the emotions of solidarity, the bonding in common struggle? When all this is only implicit, one's concerns become the specifics of organization, the day to day struggle to keep an organization alive. Yet what fuels the will to do this is surely the all-too-often-unexpressed vision. And I think that's what I'm looking for though I do little sharing of this myself. How to get others to share? Well, isn't the writing, the prospect of a book, a way to do exactly that?

How inextricably wound up are the emotions, the creativity, the vision, the expression! Reading *Malcolm X* and seeing how empowering his vision was, I am also repelled by his hustling and egotism. Well, Islam was to him what Marxism was to me and encompassed real, justifiable anger at how things are/were and impatience with others' failure to realize and an arrogance and contempt for them. Anger and hatred certainly fuel rebellions and revolutions of whatever kind but they are no substitute for bonding and common struggle. Vanguardism is valuable for leadership but not as a way of life now or in the future. Well, these are difficult philosophical questions for me and I need to think more about them and how they fit into an attempt to make something from my life.

March 6, 1993

Reading *Autobiography of Malcolm X*, where he expresses such relief and elation at being accepted everywhere alerted me to a fact of life for blacks: the constant need in the U.S. to be on guard against harassment, rejection, and outright murder. This reminded me of Joan Brown's saying she experienced fear, driving in Michigan with another black woman, at the thought that they could be attacked and killed by some white racist. Then I thought of a neighbor's being harassed by Oak Park police as he was coming home late at night from his job or gig. Which led me to compare this with fears, expressed by a couple of Gray Panthers, of the South Side, not realizing what blacks still experience daily, going into white neighborhoods. We should really have a consciousness raising session of some kind.

At first, I understood where their fears were coming from — media, society's racism, etc. I too am somewhat fearful at times, but I don't say it because I realize its source and I feel I should try to conquer it instead of adding to it. So I felt these people were teetering on the edge of racism without knowing it. However, thinking it over, seeing the other side and the bitterness these attitudes engender, it becomes clearer to me that it *is* racism. A person may think this fear or "discomfort," as someone called it, applies to all new neighborhoods, and maybe it does, but I don't really believe it. I believe these are the same fears I wrestle with.

However, I truly don't know how to approach the question without creating an ugly division which might ultimately repel our black members. I guess one way would be to have a small private session to thrash this out only among the people immediately concerned. And I'm beginning to think we should go to the Lutheran School of Theology or the Harris YWCA just to make a point. It's true that old people, especially women, are at a greater risk as they are easy prey and are often attacked. But with a group event, I don't see this happening. And if we are not prepared to risk a little discomfort and inconvenience, when will we ever break or overcome barriers?

Similarly, I've been thinking that Third Unitarian Social Action Committee should have some black members, make a deliberate effort to do so, and come to grips with a project for reaching out in Austin. What a commentary, to have a social action committee with no blacks who are usually most active in social action! This last is a reflection of reading *World*, the Unitarian Universalist journal, which is devoted to increasing diversity and the interviews/remarks of black members regarding comfort level, commitment, etc. The expressed need is to work at it all the time, no matter what percentage of programs and members is achieved. It's something we took for granted in Gray Panthers, until now. Comfort level indeed! This is an expression of prejudice disguised as honesty! How to share these insights and painful truths without hurting and alienating? ("Without hurting" is an oxymoron in regard to "painful truths"!) How to do this without being self-righteous?

Well, if we can't do a fund-raiser on the South Side and can't get full white participation if we do, where are we going? We are falling apart minus an infrastructure and strong voices like Henny, Charlotte Holenia, Ruth Lind.

March 8, 1993

Yesterday, Sunday, made a display at the Social Action table at Third Unitarian: women's peace treaty petitions, archival pictures and an article from *Nonviolent Activist*, two buttons, two mounted copies of Prisoner Millett's letter, and several *Nations*. I announced this at the forum with an introduction on the International Women's Day demonstration in Russia in 1917 out of which grew the February revolution.

Still worrying about GPs, racism, falling apart, not wanting it to happen while I was co-convener, but really disgusted, disaffected and pained at this development and the feeling of not being able to convey the basic racism properly.

March 10, 1993

What has been staying with me and yet disturbing me about *The Autobiography of Malcolm X* is the fiery, even in its way, revolutionary rhetoric as against the slowly dawning realization while reading the book that it *was* rhetoric while Student Nonviolent Coordinating Committee and others were out there acting, doing, educating, and with their bodies opposing oppression, something which Malcolm X came to realize through criticisms of the Muslims for being all talk. What finally clicked for me was the similarity to my own revolutionary preachings and my final realization that this had been all rhetoric also and my turning to being involved on a more pragmatic level. That clarified a reason the autobiography resonated so with me.

I don't mean to condemn all rhetoric, mine or his, as it is educational, and I do value the radical, noncompromising insight into the actual forces of oppression. It is just that revolutionary or radical or militant rhetoric is not enough. Sooner or later, one has to come to terms with what one professes.

March 11, 1993

Received a note from sister-in-law May today — a prompt reply. She writes sadly that the doctor told her she would not regain complete health again. At eighty-seven, she really hoped for that? I see no sign of Alzheimer's except, maybe, that childish expectation. It saddened me because I think I've given up that hope too. She ends, "I never thought I would reach such a way to conduct my life" — that is, with a companion. Anyway, she seems to like hearing from me and I'll respond. Reminds me of faithfully writing to Ma full accounts of various activities when, perhaps, she could not take it in. I was trying to keep her image as I knew her when younger.

March 14, 1993

Bob Wiebe called and we discussed termination of Gray Panthers, the lack of forces to carry on, having no money even for a $500 computer, no plans for April or May or for the membership meeting. However, after talking with him, I thought, "I don't want to preside over another folding," though Bob suggested maybe merging with another group like the National Council of Senior Citizens, which is union supported. Not such a bad idea but nationally would seem the way to do it. What about White Crane? Eighth Day Center? Would they be interested?

He also said that whatever we do, we should, afterwards, try to keep in touch with one another. Nevertheless, I feel somewhat down and want to be rid of the whole problem. Why did I get so involved? We did blaze a trail but we cannot apparently continue. Yet, I keep hoping for a miracle!

March 21, 1993

Woke up about 4:30 a.m. and started worrying about Gray Panthers. The realization grew that the whole situation was a very big one for me emotionally and I should acknowledge that and try to deal with it. I definitely do not want the organization to die now and feel we should make an effort or consider the suggested possibilities. I've had in the back of my mind that maybe we could get desk room at American Friends Service Committee? Share office space there? Or with Coalition for New Priorities?

I also thought over past functioning and decided this was no sudden collapse. For years, the group was run by a small clique, with one person doing a very great deal in a style that was certainly one of non-involvement of others and non-outreach. As a matter of fact, that's why I left and returned only when there was a concerted effort to get out of a rut. But maybe by that time it was too late. The enlarged board helped but the small steering committee continued to meet and handle the day-to-day concerns. My conception of a well-functioning organization is one composed of individuals and committees having well-defined areas and working on them, as with the Health Committee or newsletter editing. However, for years membership was neglected and now we're suffering the results.

So what are our strengths as well as weaknesses? Vision, context, radicalism, issues. Are we struggling to keep an organization going on that alone? If we are indeed not an organization but a movement, as we claimed, has the movement gone elsewhere? Even as I write this and think how important it would be to consider these issues together, I realize, sickeningly: who is there to consider these with?

Tonight's meeting of the three co-conveners and Bob will probably be more oriented to nuts and bolts. In any case, any arrangement, to me, would be better than just folding. A project like the history of GPs? Certainly, issues of age and ageism are not going to go away and one-issue groups are not going to deal with them adequately. Should we set ourselves a GP history project and try to fund that? Could we interest the Chicago Women's History Collective since we are mostly women? I would hate to see us wind down without at least summing up, similar to my attempts to do so for myself? Who would be interested? What paraphernalia would be needed? Even the oral history project has gone sour. As usual, this needs able-bodied people to do the basic organizing and setting up. Am I letting my interest in history overwhelm an objective evaluation of the possibilities? But it would be a more orderly way of quitting.

Reading *The Journey of Life* by Thomas Cole and its descriptions and concepts of old age, there seems to be no conception of empowerment so far. This seems to be a unique contribution of GPs, a reaffirmation of a life force, maybe expressed a little differently.

March 22, 1993

Much disturbed by last night's decision to wrap up Gray Panthers at the annual meeting if the Board agrees. If it does not, we'd try for another year. Since it was my turn to chair the Board meeting, I made a face, Debbie offered to chair and I agreed, feeling I didn't want to be in the position of ushering in the demise. I was relieved, but feeling grew this a.m. that this is cowardly and I should face up to it, particularly as I had voiced concerns about our future two Board meetings ago.

This is a profound change and loss. For 20 years this has been part of the rhythm of my life as well as at times a support, an empowerment, and a medium of expression. I tried to imagine life without it, like some anchor being removed. It is very hard to say goodbye because it is also an acknowledgement of my limitations due to age, something I'm also very reluctant to accept. Too old for GPs! An oxymoron?

March 23, 1993

What can I write now, on the eve of GPs apparently folding? This crisis has shaken me out of my concern with winding up or evaluating a personal life, like the ending of a marriage. Re-read the journal again, liking what I wrote and noted a few places to be used for April 14 in a class at the University of Illinois on women and ageing and for a possible talk at the GP annual meeting.

In opting to fold Chicago Gray Panthers, do I feel as if I were also betraying George? He came in through me and was a leader, so who owes whom? It was a vital part of both our lives, so am I also saying goodbye again to him?

March 25, 1993

Finishing Thomas Cole's *Journey of Life* and think he has a point about the insistence of experts and anti-ageists on a normal, "healthy" old age instead of seeing it dialectically (my word) as a period of spiritual — I would say mental and psychological — growth accompanied by the infirmities of old age. Isn't this paralleling my experience? Viz. my talk about ten years ago expressing confidence in abilities and mobility and the gradual mounting, in this last decade, of infirmities and general nuisances which from time to time impair functioning.

So I find Cole not the sneaky Callahan tool I'd feared, but I do feel, in his reference to the elderly organizing, as just demanding material improvements, an ignorance of the empowerment angle: a valuing of experience during one's lifetime and a marshaling of abilities. One certainly can't transcend the physical barriers but one can certainly develop other abilities or hone the present ones as the journals of May Sarton and Florida Scott-Maxwell demonstrate. I've been searching for meaning and my attempts to sum up and distill experiences is a form of creativity. What Cole's dissertation lacks is a more profound examination of the significance of old people's movements, their liberation struggle along with the other liberation struggles. I'm afraid he can't see the implications of such organizations for the spirit, the morale, etc. A 40-year old academician rather than a movement person.

March 28, 1993

Reflecting on experiences, emotions, ideas, actions, reactions, ways of coping in whatever fashion, is like swimming in a tide and sometimes calling up one thing floating along and sometimes another, and sometimes they flow by too fast to catch, and sometimes they sink down to where they can't be reached and sometimes one gets very tired and fears drowning or inability to stay afloat or to catch up with the current. Yet this tide is taking me some place though I visualize it as going on and on and maybe out to sea. More reflections of Cole and Erik Erikson I guess! How do I keep going, stay on top, or find a friendly, gentle flow and at least locate myself by objects along the bank. Milestones? Anchors reaching out but ungraspable? Pleasant scenes or places which I'd like to stay in but can't for long? Up to now, I thought I'd arrive somewhere and in some instances I have but I'd like surer footing and not to feel vulnerable to slipping on the slippery bank.

April 11, 1993

Larry Gara finally asked me for a piece on Women Strike for Peace, not over 500 words and my write-up is only 325. I guess I can conjure up something from the files, newsletters, etc. Surely, I've written more about it somewhere.

Heard Cinny Poppen today at Third Unitarian on Haiti. Very moving, especially readings from Aristide, deposed president and liberation priest. At the end of one reading he refers to the city of hope, Esperancia, which to me rang a little hollow, sort of pie in the sky. Am overwhelmed at such times by the misery in the world and the utter logic of the need for fixing it and the utter impossibility of my doing anything about it. Sometimes I'm encouraged by doing some little thing, but I guess right now I'm reflecting the closing down of the Chicago Religious Task Force which Cinny worked for and which at one time paid for staff person for the Pledge of Resistance, now also defunct.

April 12, 1993

How does anyone exist without replenishment somewhere? Do I get some from Third Church? Occasionally, but I have to put up with trappings like hymns, and I seem to need to search for political correctness. So it's a mixed bag. I'm finding several good things there: companionship, belonging, expression and respect. I am continually surprised at the warmth, the stimulation from time to time, as with Cinny on Haiti yesterday and from Don's better sermons.

Am I asking of myself not to need such nourishment? Why not? I try to give it in little ways to other people because I'm so delighted when it's done to me.

Maybe there is no whole cloth to stand on, maybe just a garment to take with me that ravels here and there and that I try to mend from time to time. Not a Persian carpet, which Henry James told monologist Ruth Draper to stand on, but, I hope, not a sleazy garment either. Perhaps I can think of a better, handsomer cloak.

Troubled by someone's reference to Marx's projection of a "Messianic" utopia as a reflection of his Judaism. It is flip, simplistic and reductionist. I don't know how much a Jewish background, particularly his, was influential anymore than a Christian view influenced capitalist theoreticians. I still find the term *utopia* offensive as Marx and Engels insisted on the term "scientific socialism" as opposed to utopianism. Marxism was a complex, analytical, revolutionary response to a capitalist, acquisitive society, a projection of action as well as analysis and his and Engels' evolution of theory was far from messianic but, rather, a tool for oppressed peoples. The subtleties of their analysis, the profundity of it, the combination of analysis and usefulness for liberation were unique. Not for all time perhaps, not 100 percent accurate, not for some of today's complexities and developments, not able to go, in many respects, beyond their time and culture, but rooted in the reality they knew. I respect that profoundly and learned from it profoundly the impulse to change the world, not merely to interpret it.

April 15, 1993

My education in Marxism gave a foundation to radical impulses and stance and, in a way, a framework to live by via the Marxist movements. Shattering when the movements shattered, but it is still an underpinning though I am certainly not concerned today to apply it as a slide-rule.

Yesterday speaking to Susan Reed's class on women and aging at the University of Illinois, I shared feelings about the loss of George and how it affected my actions and outlook. A representative of Older Women's League had led off with her background in detail and I fell into that too and gave more of a biography than I intended. Well, maybe that's what the four students, youngish women, wanted. They certainly didn't ask questions and I feel we may have overwhelmed them.

April 18, 1993

I suppose I'm still wrestling with my feelings about Marxism. How could a man like the one interviewed by Mike Wallace not analyze, or try to, what he was up against if he was a sincere convert? Of course, a good deal of the time as a Trotskyist I spent rationalizing Soviet deeds, though at least I was critical. And I realize the need to hold on to something you believe in as long as you can. It's hard to maintain faith when the seeming embodiment of an ideal crumbles, but is that a reason to abandon the ideal? How can anyone settle for this miserable society, this miserable world, as the embodiment of anything worth struggling for? If the forces of capitalism are global and the loyalties of the class are to greed and profitability, where are we going? Who will set the terms of the debate?

In seeking a like-minded community, one tries to nourish one's socialist aspirations. In trying to act or expose the system, one seeks to express them. Dare one hope, then, to change the system? Who will do the organizing? How does one fit one's actions into the larger vision? How to continually stretch the horizons?

At the OWL meeting, Saturday, I had the oddest feeling at the discussion on availability of housing for seniors. Of course, we wouldn't like to see mobile homes in Oak Park, someone said, and everyone agreed it's a shame there isn't more affordable housing and what can we do about it? I raised the idea of federal subsidy for new and affordable housing because I marveled that we were discussing this without relating it to general homelessness, as though that were not our problem. The assumption was that we were discussing elders living in private houses and their problems only. Why don't other people bring in the larger issue?

Of course one should be concerned with local problems because they are part of the fabric of daily life and, after all, I did move to a pleasant suburb. But if we can't solve 'em all, I prefer to look beyond. It's not that these people don't consider themselves fortunate and know there is poverty out there. There just seems to be no way to deal with these larger issues. Because there is no loud voice trumpeting solutions, people fall back on dealing with their immediate concerns. So maybe by considering these problems together we are at least making a beginning? But I want more, more, more!

Is my philosophy to remain a quiet, dead one? As an old woman is that all I can do: to try to figure it out for myself? but how will that help or affect anyone else? Will raising an issue every now and then do it for me? "All my life I would have talked on street corners to scorning men," (Bartolomeo Vanzetti)! Except that I'm not experiencing scorn but acceptance. Well, maybe that's a contribution.

146

April 23, 1993

Concerned with Gray Panthers. People just don't get the situation or can't really move to a crisis mode, viz. my painful indecision and sense of responsibility and dread of the future. I wish I were rid of the whole damn problem, but that would be like deserting a sinking ship. I might come to that if it looks too insoluble and too painful. The trouble is that we want it to continue, so I build impossible scenarios of a new committee taking over and solving it. This is particularly hard now to deal with as it will not let me deal with the internal problems and insights in a less cluttered fashion, though of course this is part of my life and my emotions and reactions are the way I live it in general. How far should I go? Should I assume responsibility for a decent appeal? Interrupted this to draft an opening!

April 24, 1993

Restless due to travail *re* GPs. Earlier, had the impulse to dig in, not wait for meeting here tomorrow night, set out what I think should be done and assert it firmly. But why should GPs' fate depend on me? I feel we — the Board — have set in motion a contradiction: moving and yet having no real drive to leadership. On the one hand, Bob wants fun and games and on the other, to die with dignity. But who is to organize the fun and games? And why would that get more money than straight contributions? I feel lost in the world of finances and have deliberately set myself apart. So why should I undertake it now?

What do I really want aside from magical deliverance? Why have I run out of steam? Is it because the organization has run out of steam? Odd how an organization has so much baggage! Suppose National GP dissolved, would Chicago GPs survive as a group of like-minded friends meeting occasionally? Hardly! Individual interests do not coincide. We're somewhat of an empty shell with a reputation and a set of habits of functioning. People seem to be working without clear goals. I want out and I don't know how to do it gracefully and responsibly, so I feel trapped. Was I wrong to accept the co-convenership again? What happened to that working Board? Did Board members who dropped away see the decay before I did? Can I stick it through June, no matter what happens?

Whatever I got from GPs, I will carry with me and I hope I have educated others. Loyalty to organizations goes only so far. Beyond a certain point it becomes either mechanical or fanatical. And I'm trying to tell myself this in regard to Third Unitarian Social Action Committee: that I can sit back and let others raise their issues and I don't have to participate in those any more than they do in mine. We each have our *schtick*.

As to GPs, I have, in a way, helped and encouraged Renée to do the newsletter and of course she's trained herself and learned from Mac My Day. So this gives me some feeling of accomplishment! But how to get over the June hump?

Well, I suppose some life situations are not clear and one gets through them as best one can and I can't always run from unpleasantness. On the other hand, I've learned one has to say enough when it is enough and not excoriate oneself for acknowledging this or for not being able to hang on longer. Early sectarianism taught me, very painfully and at great cost, that living a role or a fantasy of leadership is also useless objectively. Commitment and loyalty are fine and admirable but they must nourish one as well.

April 25, 1993

The GP stuff was resolved for me, emotionally, in a way, by our Saturday night meeting and pizza supper here. Some agreement was reached on conveying the need to face the money crisis, to reflect that in the meeting and a letter, and to give advice about specifics if asked. Members of the special committee will be called.

On the whole, a nice day, quite nice. Went to Third Unitarian forum to hear a Peace NOW representative, but disappointed somewhat in his approach and lack of detail about Peace NOW's opposition to the Israeli government. He sees an opening through the election of Rabin. Then heard a sermon by a Belgian minister on the Holocaust and the role of religion which to me did not put the "event" in full context: I. e., reasons for the rise of Nazism, other victims of the Nazis.

Had a pleasant luncheon with Kathy Jeans and her granddaughter Jennifer and then drove to Thatcher Woods and we walked on the side north of Chicago Avenue (the south side was flooded), identifying wild flowers — spring beauties, yellow violets, trout lilies. This stimulated me to see what guide books I had on flowers, trees, birds for our projected trip to Florida. Found only one that might apply, *Tropical Blossoms*, that deals with the Caribbean. Also, much to our mutual relief, I believe, we settled on separate rooms throughout the trip.

Yesterday I did pot caladium bulbs and thought of potting morning glory seeds but realized they need 24-hour soaking to germinate. Looked at a pamphlet on container gardening and realized that I work with house plants more than I think, moving them around, "housing" them properly, etc., till I like the effects.

Oh, yes, at the forum's end I questioned the Peace Now rep. He spoke of people wanting security and safety, specifying Palestinians and Israelis and said they'd settle for that — a pragmatic approach. I said the people in the Warsaw ghetto uprising didn't look at it pragmatically and that the people of the *Intifada* were concerned with justice which was not mentioned. Well, he didn't like the analogy at all and proceeded to make a big distinction: the Jews had been exterminated by that time, had their backs to the wall etc. Discouraging in a way.

He was very interesting, came from the Warsaw ghetto or his parents had. I wasn't sure I had a valid criticism, but as I listened further, the conviction grew on me that an important spiritual, if you will, element had been omitted and decided to express this feeling. It's possible he soft-pedaled differences with Israeli policy because of the composition of the audience.

April 26, 1993

Learned from War Resisters League key list packet that the National Pledge of Resistance is folding. In some ways, relief as well as sadness and sort of a "justification" of Chicago Gray Panthers doing so. Repelled by approach of the New Party publication enclosed. The approach is unclear, fuzzy, and defining itself at the beginning in terms of electoral participation, under what conditions it would do so. Heavily concerned with method, though I may be wrong as I didn't pursue it further.

May 1, 1993

George's brother Dud called from Arizona to say he won't be home in North Fort Myers as his daughter Diane is very ill with cancer, a nine-year bout, and this may be the end. I was quite shaken and depressed. I even feel a bit guilty that our predictions about effects of radiation at Oak Ridge, Tennessee, where her late husband worked, came true. I wonder about her children.

May 23, 1993

Very pleasant Saturday going to Frank's Nursery with a neighbor and choosing plants for the condo and me and, after lunch with her, supervising their planting. Lucy came down and helped and later invited me to supper.

I do feel this Gray Panther business is a stretched out ordeal and much as I'd like to shuck the responsibility, I cannot fully do so. I have come to the end of my resources on this. Yet I feel if I don't keep at something, I'll be lost, without a base.

Interesting that the two most pleasant days were Tuesday at the Arboretum and Saturday with the plant selection and the relationships. Now I have a whole flat of plants for the balcony. Decided to get marigolds too and may even mix 'em with the petunias. Since I did not get the lush pinks that usually send me, but some rose, cherry, and purple, it'll be a challenge to make a nice mix.

May 27, 1993

Thinking more about school and how I subsumed all the bad experiences under the phrase, "I hate school," remembering the strait-jacket (that iron vest in my dream!) feeling of having to go daily to a place I was unhappy in, the corridors, the stairs, etc. These are, rather, impressions from movies than actual remembered feelings. The actuality is more the trapped feeling of being in an institution. I see more clearly how Jill Conway's *The Road From Corrain* unlocked something.

It occurred to me sometime today, after writing about the dream of the grid-like iron vest, that it really was the brace I wore that I was referring to, a contraption with a rigid waist and straps that came over the shoulders, designed to hold them back. I remember it was a heavy, clumsy instrument which I hated and shortly got rid of by telling Ma it made me feel funny on the way home from school, a feeling I later identified as hunger. Ma obviously didn't really believe me but assented to my not wearing it. And what of the stretcher at the Hospital for Joint Diseases, headed by Dr. Frauenthal? I haven't thought about that name for years. Talking to a friend yesterday, I compared the measures taken to deal with my back to her parents' taking her to the University of Chicago for her heart and being out of school for one year. Now I wonder how much school I missed. This is a so-far-unplaced part of my history and illuminated part of the whole miserable burden from childhood to adolescence: always under some stricture to be where I didn't want to be, including Aunt Mary's on Saturdays.

May 30, 1993

Last night, watched a two-hour *Letters from Viet Nam* on Channel 11 and was much moved by it: the actual war scenes, the terrain, the wounded, the misery and loneliness. It ended with scenes from World Wars I and II, the Korean War, and even the Gulf War. A fitting memorial to a very ugly business. Discouraged at the continual repetition of wars, thinking that it must run contrary to humanity's basic instinct to live and survive. Yet the tendency of historians to assume it as part of humankind's development. I also wondered whether there wasn't validity to women's nurturing urge and their greater opposition to war.

May 31, 1993

Nice day! Slept late, Claire called to invite me to see *Like Water for Chocolate*, a Spanish-language tragicomedy set in pre-World War I Mexico, and then we had a one-and-a-half hour session at Java Jones coffee shop — a good exchange. After which I walked around Austin Gardens and came home.

June 3, 1993

I did think today that I should type out almost everything I wrote, such as the 1969 D.C. anti-war demonstration which was both a personal experience and an historical event, particularly when I see how cursorily "Letters from Viet Nam" dealt with the antiwar movement. Am I leaking away my talent on personal turmoil? Why can't I convert this *sturm und drang* to a written experience, blending in with the rest? In a sense I've done so in my journal which I should type up since it's neat to have ready copy as with the contribution to the WRL calendar.

How does one ever write an autobiography? There are so many facets and experiences. I'm haunted by the question of how others remember their childhood and adolescence. Is it more continuous than mine or are there just more remembered episodes? I suppose people construct a history out of these episodes, something I seem, so far, unable to do. And obviously unwilling also? I do thread together playing with the tailor's daughter, Rachel, waiting for Papa to come home, frightened at his yelling at Tommy, being fiercely hugged, the night of his death, the funeral, the hoping for his return each evening.

150

Then there's a big hiatus, staying with aunts Minnie and Vera, I'm told. The stairway and roof at different times were familiar to me on revisiting, and once, recently, I visualized the doorway with transom at their house. I have no other memory of moving from Washington Heights to 124th Street in Harlem and going to school there, except for those two or three dark faces with frizzy hair which I remembered as gray, then transferring to a South Harlem School.

I do recall walking through Mt. Morris Park to school, imagining a family where I was the mother, and sledding in winter. Earlier, I would drag a big stuffed doll in red-checked bonnet and rompers, pretending it was my two-year-old child. I also recall pushing a baby carriage, a little too low for me, the best Ma could afford, I knew. But I can't really make a chronology of this and at this point I don't really want to. Why? These are not really unpleasant memories, but recalling and trying to recall bring considerable pain. At Pa's death? At my solitariness? Yet I did have occasional friends, walking home with a group of girls as far as 120th Street after school though I was never really part of their circle and envied their living near one another. So I do, in fact, have many memories.

June 4, 1993

Moved to write impressions of last night's Older Women's League enlarged executive committee meeting. Dorothy S. expressed very similar reactions to those of Debbie *re* GPs. Both seem to feel that dues-paying members who do not come to meetings or otherwise participate are just dead weight. Finally, I stressed that their paying dues was support and should be so regarded. There were nine people in that room, all willing to participate. Somehow, this seemed very different from the Gray Panther board, which, though desirous of continuing, is not a cohesive body. I think back to my feeling when distributing war toys fliers with Third Unitarian people, that knitted us together, if only for the moment. Of course GP conditions of working were much harder: a weak, seemingly indifferent national board and structure, paid staff at the national level not very helpful, and also a local leadership not caring or courteous in regard to the membership.

Personally, I was thinking bitterly the other day that for Henny Moore I initiated a grand acknowledgement and send off. Of course, I did not prop the organization up as she did for so long, but is the present collapse an acknowledgement of failure to develop other leadership?

I set out to sift last night's OWL discussion which had a good outcome. People arrived at a consensus to remain a chapter while suspending the bylaws, becoming more of a discussion group with fewer official responsibilities, and arranging for a special meeting in July to firm this up.

Is such a scenario possible for GPs? Can we develop Bob Wiebe's scenario for an occasional meeting? Can we dispense with our "world responsibilities" and think of a looser format, not carrying the world on our shoulders? Or are we too burned out even for that? It's becoming clearer to me that National has a big responsibility for this collapse, not to mention the political climate — Clinton's withdrawing his nomination of a Black woman lawyer who is pro Civil Rights.

That last is enough to make me bitter at all the people who voted for Clinton as representing a hope. So far, zilch, as even the watered-down program is being reduced to water. People will still staunchly insist, I bet, that there was no other choice, refusing to recognize that there was *no* choice. Isserman, in his *Nation* review of Dellinger's autobiography, *From Yale to Jail*, can't forego defending support of McGovern and instead attributes weaknesses to Dellinger. He can't believe his framework wasn't the correct one and calls Dave's stand on electoral politics, "moral rectitude" which of course Isserman doesn't believe in. So, though the review is largely positive, he can't help venting some near-spiteful digs, calling into question Dave's experience. I think that that is a disservice to history: his speculation/analysis of how sophisticated the Viet Namese were against Dave's account of what actually happened. I feel somehow I should clarify this but it requires work and thought and I keep hoping someone will answer Isserman to validate this point.

June 14, 1993

To what extent am I responsible for Chicago Gray Panthers? Alice Drell called and I realized with a sinking feeling that with Agnes gone for the summer and Deb involved in school, no one is going to the office except Ernestine. Although we posed the problem to a Board meeting and a committee wanting to continue emerged, there is really now no structure. . . . We have literally abandoned our posts. Except for several meetings with the committee, getting out the flyer and mailing it, I am on hold and though the room for the annual meeting is engaged, who is now even taking phone calls? Have we already buried it?

June 30, 1993

Waiting for clothes to dry, thinking of events of the weekend and this morning, feeling teary and torn up over GP dissolution Saturday and the Clinton attack on Iraq Saturday evening. Saturday night was the worst of all. My rage and anger and impotence at this unprovoked bloody "retaliation" is like the wrath of God being visited on me? us? for the GP dissolution. Saturday or Sunday night, dreamt I was lecturing some gathering on how every missile represented schools, homes, food being blown away as well as the war victims. Feel I have to hunker down for continued repression of all kinds.

Yet a couple of rewarding things happened. I called Faith Bissell yesterday and, talking about Iraq, she mentioned how sorry she was she'd voted for Clinton and thought of me and a neighbor of hers as having done the right thing by not voting. Then Renée Buecker called this morning and we had quite a talk about her and Gladys Knobel's anger and disappointment at our folding. She said she felt sorry for Ann Joyner who'd collected $80 to help and I replied it was not for nothing; it was an attempt to preserve and show support. I was very glad to get the call because I had been wondering what the fallout from the meeting would be.

Meanwhile, Jim Lynch came yesterday, we visited, I treated him to supper at Bakers Square in lieu of making supper, bought a pie for tonight's Social Action Committee potluck, and he'll call to see about driving me to Laurel Lambert's to see "Panama Deception." Also called Monica and Thursday we're meeting at the Holley Court Terrace dining room.

July 1, 1993

Evidently this whole period and the GP dissolution in particular keeps bothering me. Yesterday, at the Arboretum gift shop with Debbie, I bought a scratch pad as well as a letter kit as a gift for Violet and charged these, signing my name *Ruth Stamm* which of course disturbed me and continues to do so. It's as though events have charged something loose and it now seems perfectly natural to me to be Ruth Stamm rather than Ruth Dear, my post-Revolutionary Workers League, post-marriage, post-George name which I thought I liked. Am I reclaiming some identity? Am I no longer satisfied to be Ruth Dear? Does that contain too much of George?

Henny called from Maine this afternoon. This makes the fourth call to me *re* Chicago GPs folding. Glad to talk to her. Margaret Harder called Debbie and of course Renee and Bob Wiebe too. Henny feels we should give whatever money is left over to National Gray Panthers. I really don't feel strongly about this.

Glad I went to the Hiroshima Committee meeting tonight as Larry Armstrong, who's devoted himself to interviewing Hiroshima survivors and someone who was with a naval survey team two months after the bombing, described the devastation. Larry was asked to contribute to the 1995 War Resisters League calendar and intends to write up the Hiroshima "maidens" but first wants to get an okay from the women since they are leery of exploitation and invasion of privacy. It looks like a good program is shaping up.

Do I spend my time trying to forget, like Hiroshima residents? Bury my traumas? Is Ruth Stamm really emerging?

By the way, on the way out, Doris Bolef thanked me for coming and said she appreciated my help with identifying concisely the speakers for the leaflet and I realized I had taken the lead in that. How little I value what I do!

July 2, 1993

While writing *George*, thinking that was his authentic name, I felt again that Ruth Stamm was mine and that Ruth Dear wasn't quite authentic, both as to my beliefs and my real name. So am I indeed resurrecting or uncovering my true self, coming to terms with it? Feeling that it or I wasn't such a bad, to-be-buried person? What's in a name, indeed!

Yesterday at the Hiroshima meeting, I was content to go along with the framework though I'd prefer another. Since I wasn't organizing it and people were coming from different places, I went along and made suggestions within that framework. I recognized our decision not to feature the high school student was ignored, that all speakers but one are male except for Doris as MC. Glad to suggest songs to Mike Hayes. Very well pleased that Pope John Paul's quote: "To remember Hiroshima is to oppose war" on the flyer puts it firmly in an antiwar context. It was relaxing to be able to accept *faits accomplis* while influencing others nevertheless.

July 3, 1993

Odd — I awoke this morning feeling down, yet the first thing I did was to put the begonia planter on the balcony, potted two caladiums in the footed planter, measured the bench surface, washed out pots, etc. Then decided to pot the caladiums for the condo planter, called Lucy to tell her so and went down and did it. Suddenly I rejoice in the vivid colors of the coral, pink, salmon, white geraniums and gold marigolds. It's as though, in deciding to be less prissy about color combinations, I released something and took courage to experiment. Is this part of the Ruth Stamm identity bit?

July 4, 1993

Went to church ten a.m. to hear a nun talk about Cesar Chavez, the United Farm Workers, the grape boycott and pesticides. She asked whether anybody had recollections of previous boycotts and I remembered the mini-demonstration and guerrilla theater we did in Hyde Park. Then I further remembered the lettuce boycott, pressing the Hyde Park Co-op store, the direct action of moving S & W products from the shelves. The Co-op struck a chord with her as she lives in Hyde Park and said the Co-op has a sign about grapes being boycotted but still stocks them. It was good to hear union and solidarity talk and a vision of social justice as well as emphasis on nonviolence as a tool of resistance. To her and Chavez this was a basic philosophy though I can't quite say that. I recall union tactics of beating up scabs which, thinking of it now, seems a poor way to express solidarity.

I see the round moon behind a veil of clouds, now disappearing but still there. Now the moon is fully out and a faint breeze relieves me. If only I had the energy or will to enjoy more what is around me and what I have and to work on my writing! I do feel stymied, but then, like yesterday, I suddenly pick up and do things. Go figure!

July 5, 1993

I have lined the bench, put out and pruned the wandering jew, potted the two Rieger begonias, made eighteen zebrina (wandering jew) cuttings in case the pruning was too drastic, washed out pots, plastic sheets, etc. etc., swept and bagged debris and finally sat down to rest with a glass of iced tea.

Further reactions to *Possession* — how stimulating that Victorian period must have been — Darwin, Marx, Feuerbach, Mesmer. Gained new respect for this period and the intellectuals of it. And I thought of its relation to the rise of industrialism, capitalism, early imperialism in India, and the firm belief in Progress, which Marx and Engels of course shared, as well as the conviction that the West would show the way and the rest of the world would follow or develop in its model. This was true of the later Leninists too. And it was so obviously a product or concomitant of rising, developing capitalism. Has it really had its day? Is this why I cling to notions of solidarity while distrusting socialist blueprints?

Will this even more highly developed than ever imagined global imperialism present a new model for global organizing and solidarity? It seemed very clear to Marx and Lenin that there would be a global capitalist economy and it is even clearer today. But where are the global models in "ordinary" people's minds? There are some, as with solutions to environmental problems, but there seems, contradictorily, to be a narrowing of consciousness to national and ethnic concerns. Will an internationalism of sorts develop or will we see the same old alliances — global, regional, national for self-preservation, for national identity, for private enterprise? But won't people's consciousness at some time be driven to internationalism? How can one tell in the belly of the beast?

I suppose I'll go on striving for that vision — I can't really help it — but it's beginning to appear more as a religion or faith than a practical, scientific socialist vision. I have hooked on to one cause or another, tried to express resistance as well as vision. So how much now is personal depression? Which inhibits which: a bad social scene or a bad outlook/feeling?

I saw in the *Daily World*, left at Third Unitarian today, that there is a big DC rally and march scheduled for August 28, centering on unions, health, civil rights, etc. Sponsored by Coretta King, AFL-CIO, NAACP, etc. in commemoration of the 1963 rally. So someone out there is demonstrating. I hope the tone will be militant and internationalist but I'm not very sanguine about that. The gay/lesbian and women's rights rallies in DC were also very large. So many people out there want justice but they can't seem to get it all together under one social vision. The elements are there but the bureaucracies and concentrations on particular issues stand in the way. Well, let's hope they are seeding the ground.

Another thing that struck me in *Possession* was the Victorian writing style of the two correspondents and how careful they were to qualify every expression of opinion, to defer to each other, to hedge assertions and then to backtrack a little and sort of apologize. In a way, a fawning style. It reminded me of the way I tend to qualify expressions in these journals.

Acceptance seems to be a thing with me now as with the new flower combinations, the limitations on how much I can do with the plants on the balcony. In a way, I don't like it, but in another way, it's reality and can be freeing. One adjusts, but at what point does this become not possible?

July 7, 1993

Listening to part of a "Mostly Mozart" Lincoln Center concert, I thought of the one we attended in New York City one summer while visiting Ma who was in the Home, sick, remembering it nevertheless as a pleasant time, having Vi's studio to stay in, going off, not having to stay with someone else. Then thinking of loss and of this void and my emotional involvement in Gray Panthers for many years, I though back to the folding of Communist Workers Group, the void and loss of that in the 40s. I clenched and raised my fists and was moved to write it down. Of course, George is not here, nor Ma, so I do not have those support systems, but I have sought out my own. I do feel somehow more in control of my life, that there are options, though I do not seem them clearly. I guess pleasant moments like the time in New York can't be duplicated and should be (and are) treasured for what they were. Did we feel free to enjoy ourselves for a brief period? Was it because I no longer had the full responsibility of Ma? Sometimes I feel a bit guilty that that should have been the occasion for an enjoyable experience. And now I wish for more enjoyable occasions.

July 8, 1993

"The old order is dying, and the new cannot be born; in this interregnum there arises a great diversity of morbid symptoms." A quote from Gramsci by John Leonard in the *Nation*. How well that captures how I feel!

I thought that after the 40s and 50s experiences, I would not get so completely involved again, but evidently I did, although I realized it was not my whole life or the whole of life. Well, maybe I've acquired some wisdom in that respect. I am a political, social issues person, no matter how I slice it or what aspect I assume.

That quote from Gramsci which I find so apropos expresses my wondering, despair, fear, seeing a system working to destruction. Am I, as well as the society, suffering morbid symptoms? The Channel 11 program on the Nazis' "Degenerate art" expo and the destruction of works of art conveyed an atmosphere that exists in America today. Not officially maybe, but being voiced more loudly by politicians as well as religious fundamentalists. It was also an interesting analysis of Expressionism: what remains for me are the tortured images. Truly a nation in torment!

So my depression has a real base. I wonder at the figures and even at the notion and spread of clinical depression. It may be chemical, but what triggers what? The other day I could understand more clearly Paul and Laura Lafargue's suicide after the defeat of the Paris Commune.

July 9, 1993

Since I function with my plants in the morning, I start the day with chores which, in a way, press me but are also gratifying and enjoyable. I've managed to beat the heat in this way, to achieve some continuity and create a little beauty. I wish others could enjoy what I've created too.

July 10, 1993

So many things have come to a head during this separation from Gray Panthers. I thought I had adequate support systems and really wanted out from the burden of responsibility. So why am I not relieved? If the organization had continued while I withdrew from leadership, I would have been relieved, but when the relief is also the end of the entity, it is too much. I wanted *out*, not *down*, not the end.

July 12, 1993

A pleasant trip to Hyde Park with Debbie to a Palestinian Medical Rights picnic at a townhouse on Harper. Beautiful back gardens all around an inner area which we traipsed through, stopping to talk to a woman who was much absorbed in and quite talkative about hers. Such variety in so small a space! Then I noticed a woman looking vaguely familiar, evidently coming home. Then she and her husband were walking around with their grandson. I finally approached her: Barbara Greenberg who identified me from Circle Pines and asked about George. Bernard, her husband, was playing ball with the boy and I went up to him to chat mostly because Barbara and Debbie started to get into it about Israel and Arabs. Gratifying that both Greenbergs recognized me as an activist. For some reason, it gave me a lift to make these connections as I didn't know a soul at the picnic though I guess I'd met a few at that dinner, and no one seemed very communicative, including me.

Afterwards, Debbie drove us, torturously, circuitously, through one-way streets, and I got a glimpse of our back porch on Harper and the front of the building on 57th Street building where long-gone friends had lived.

Having done all this potting and planting, why don't the geraniums bloom? I saw a tiny wandering jew leaf this morning. The petunias have revived a bit and a few are blooming. Should I use plant food? The Hyde Park artist/gardener said she does. But I used to get bloom without enhancement and I thought some new soil would be enough. I do wish the balcony was comfortable to sit in during the day. I'd like a garden bower and I can't have that with the sun in full force there and a not very comfortable chair. Why don't I drink my juice out there, for example, when it's cool? No view? No vista? It's odd. The study windows are full of trees and even from the bedroom I see some trees, but the living room and dining room have no real view and the kitchen, none at all.

Am I saying I want to see more? Be out more? Partake of the outside more? Have I put the past — Hyde Park years — in some perspective? The decision to go to the picnic there was, of course, part of the process. I feel relieved and glad. I was going to write, "Is this a form of *schadenfreude*? but on looking up the meaning, I found it is joy at other's mistakes so that is not what I mean. I mean literally joy that has an under pricking or lining of sadness. Well, if that's the best I can do, so be it. Seize the day.

July 13, 1993

Reading about Cesar Chavez' one-man rule and its negative effect on the United Farm Workers and a review of a black minister in East Brooklyn who's done good things for the community, though hampered by his church's positions on abortion AIDS, gays, etc., struck me as sad, unfortunate. Good leaders do good things but they want it their way and so one doesn't find an altogether good working model. Maybe it's not possible. If only people wouldn't leave it to the leaders. An account of the Cooneys, an anarchist couple who tried various things like simple living, working in community was refreshing, but the man didn't get along well with people despite his searching and dedication. However, they tried to live out something and I guess that's the best that can be said.

I think I'm too Cassandra-ish about things, have lost my balance or footing and desperately want to feel I'm going somewhere again. Well, the writing is an option but it requires so much discipline. Where is satisfaction? Where?

July 14, 1993

Good day! Went to GP office with Debbie, discussed a letter and a final publication, called a GP in Wichita who will be here August 7 to 9 and arranged for her to call me when she gets in. Felt good about the blouse I'd ordered which fits well over tan pants. Lunched at Walnut Room at Field's, shopped for summer bag and sun hat at Carson's and got two sun hats very cheaply, with wider brims, one pink and one aqua.

In the office, discussed some personal things and when Deb asked me the date, I said, "Fourteenth at last," and realized that last evening I must have been reacting to the date — the thirteenth. This sparked her remark about similar feelings whose cause she didn't know until the next day when she realized it had been her first wedding anniversary date. Glad to share this and to find other people reacting similarly.

July 17, 1993

Yesterday I had a delightful day. Debbie called around noon: Did I want to got to 22nd Street with her to get a newsletter reproduced, have lunch, and then look at her weeds? Of course I said yes. We shopped at Office Max, I looking at notebooks, folders and she at desks. At her house, weeding surprisingly easy. I suggested she could have a garden similar to the delightful ones we saw in Hyde Park. She responded enthusiastically and outlined what she'd like, including a glider in a corner. I suggested a curved brick path, tearing out grass and evergreen shrubs. When I said I regarded my balcony as additional space, which was what she seemed to be looking for, she again agreed enthusiastically and repeated the phrase several times. Next week, she proposed, we should look for a glider and meanwhile she'd ask Mark to measure the plot. I promised to get out my graph paper and landscape books. This has given me a chance to plant a garden! At home I got out books and a garden encyclopedia but found little actually pictorial to stimulate ideas though I have them in the back of my mind: a small tree or a graceful shrub.

Didn't realize how big a surge for gardening was underneath! I'd still like the balcony to be more of a shady, green retreat but I guess that's utopian. However, I have achieved mostly what I planned this year. The next big thing would be to repot the sanseveria and decide where to put it in winter.

July 25, 1993

Returned from a very nice relaxing weekend at Sue L. and Tom Neumann's with Lucy. A small peaceful lake, half-choked with waterlilies, woods/trees on the opposite bank, comfortable house, pleasant canoe trip and restaurant. Now, a little sad — partly Sunday evening depression, partly bittersweet feelings about traveling a similar route to Circle Pines. Coming home, Route 131 signs struck a chord: we passed a red-painted Victorian house with looped white gingerbread trim which also looked very familiar, then the Chicago Skyway, Gary, Hammond, etc. etc. made me think of U.S. Steel mills where George worked.

August 8, 1993

Feeling low about Hiroshima commemoration today, sad thoughts of our initiating it and how George was an organizer and, to me, an enabler. I started thinking about history as against living and *relic* versus *survivor* and was stimulated by these insights and cheered by them. I wonder why — if emotions are so important — the insights/ideas galvanized me. Of course, they created a feeling, a stimulus. Survivors — George — Hiroshima — old age — survivors — relics — history — life — living.

Thinking about the difference between Hiroshima as history versus experience. What is history to younger people is living to older ones. This insight seemed to clarify for me also my faint negative reaction to *Sister Age*. In her description of the elderly characters M. K. Fisher tends to treat them sometimes as relics rather than survivors. Of course, the two are related, and though, originally, I did not like the term *survivor* because it meant to me to be one of a small band of people or even a lone person left alive, it is a stronger concept than *relic*, implying someone active rather than an artifact or the remains of something. Perhaps in her reverence for and devotion to old people, Fisher tends to treat them like the relic of the painting which she treasures.

Kathy Jeans called to offer me a lift to the Hiroshima meeting in Scoville Park yesterday. She really wanted to go to the Arboretum but felt she should go to the commemoration. I thought this over, especially how George and I learned to play hooky, so to speak, miss a meeting and go out there to enjoy ourselves. So I called Kathy back to suggest this and we did enjoy an early lunch there, a slow walk around the lake, and made it back to the meeting just in time.

August 12, 1993

Grief about George and Gray Panthers went/goes together. I wish I felt more positive about what to do. Lunches with friends are fine but they do not supply a need to be steadily involved in something though they do take me out of myself and I do have the opportunity to bounce ideas and reactions off people.

August 15, 1993

What do I want out of life? I really haven't dared to ask this question fully. The word comes to mind is *balance*. What do I mean by balance? I know that life isn't balanced, that shocks and changes keep occurring, so it's not an objective balance that I want. I want some worthwhile activity, some mutual working toward a goal or a concrete accomplishment. Even *concrete accomplishment* is abstract. I like the discipline of a regular commitment that will use my abilities and stimulate me. What comes to mind is the crew mailing the *Militant* in the early thirties. But that is long gone. That kind of activity is not required and it's really not the activity but the spirit of working together toward a goal and the optimism of achieving that goal. Many people give of themselves to various goals in various ways today and maybe they achieve that. That brief feeling of solidarity while distributing war toys flyers was like an echo from the past, but it was not sustained. I said I was grateful that I had made a difference on several occasions. That surely is a goal.

But what do I want for me? If I could come to grips with that, I might find that writing autobiographical background for my material would be easier. In addition to balance, rootedness is also something I want to feel. How does one achieve that? For a brief period, I felt that about Third Unitarian Church and maybe with fall activity, I will feel some of that again. I want to feel a steadiness (steadfastness?), a confidence in what I do. Reading is fine but not enough. Yet somehow I don't summon the energy to take a course, go on an Elderhostel. I'd like to travel some more with a congenial group or companion. My relations with people seem episodic. Do I wish to enter more into other people's lives and relationships since I have lost a life-long one?" It's eight years for godsakes!

I realize that depression colors my approaches and attitudes and I am struggling with it. The lack of zest hangs on. Well, it's been a brutal period what with GPs not performing and folding and some physical troubles. But the latter are here to stay and apparently so are periods of depression. So another goal is the ability to summon the will to function and reach out. It was sobering to see myself fall into a depressed state again though I've gotten support, etc. and am still getting it. It has enabled me to function and to see myself in a new light.

Another thing I'd like to do is have fun, to be able to enjoy myself. I did so with Debbie and I wonder what the quality is that enables it. Other people enjoy my company. Today I had a nice visit with Rosemary Dixon and Bobbi Perkins after eating at Peterson's, going to see the wildflower garden.

August 22, 1993

This week has been rather calm though I did see the ophthalmologist who said I should have an angiogram and after that, maybe removal of the cataract from the right eye or possibly laser treatment for macular degeneration if indicated. Another goddamn procedure.

How pretty the cherry pink impatiens look with the Fanny Munson caldiums behind them! I've made a nice corner there. Usually, I look more to the railing planters, which are scraggly except for the tub with pink and white geraniums. Yesterday, I finally transplanted the sanseveria and, using the very big pot as a *cache-pot*, put it in the outside hall. And today I hope to use the hexagonal ceramic planter to make a centerpiece for the coffee table with nephthytis and pothos.

Thursday, I spent the whole afternoon and evening with Debbie, going downtown to get labels reproduced, checking in at the old GP office, eating and discussing a letter to the members, going home with her and polishing the draft which she typed, then to Kinko's to reproduce it, picking up pizza, and, after the meal, sorting letters for third class mail. For me, a good day, though it looks like her garden planning is on hold. She's delighted with the display the impatiens are making, having taken over most of the plot.

September 6, 1993

Went to Third Unitarian for program of labor songs, mostly male-oriented of course, and a droning historical account between songs plus a livelier one by an IWW professional unionist. I asked for "Bread and Roses" which he did briefly and not very distinctly.

September 9, 1993

It occurred to me today, thinking of the GPs and of missing the peer-group aspect, that there seems to be a contradiction between that and saying I don't want to be housed only with old people. I then realized that it wasn't the age so much as the kind of old people, i.e. their alertness to social issues, and that (1) I should not stereotype all old people and (2) that the old people I relate to are those who don't fit the stereotype. A houseful of old lefties and liberals would be different, stimulating, I hope, from a houseful of seeming vegetables. I thought of this in the context of my projected talk to the Women's Alliance. Could I also introduce the brochure on Clinton's health care plan? There should be plenty of issues. Maybe I could look up early GP material on health care?

September 15, 1993

Interested in *Nation* article by R. Heilbroner, "Does Socialism Have a Future?" Not completely clear to me but somewhat hopeful though not in the usual Marxist terms. So I'm not the only one struggling with this concept! (I didn't really think I was, but it emphasizes that my concerns and lack of hope were not all depression-based. The interaction is much more complex!) Also received material for a health care reform party which I agreed to help organize, apparently OWL-inspired.

I also took in house plants from balcony since it's quite nippy out. Hope tomorrow to pot impatiens and remaining geraniums if they survive.

September 17, 1993

Yesterday, an unnerving experience. A woman claiming to be from some department of ageing in Chicago rang the bell and I let her in. Said she was checking on a call received from a neighbor about the apartment smelling and my always cadging money from neighbors. Psychologically, she put me in the position of showing I was in good shape, had an adequate income, etc., and feeling very down on such reported maliciousness. So that when she asked me to change a $50 bill I felt she was testing me to see if I had adequate cash. Writing this now, I see that was exactly what she was doing but not for any helpful reason! I was reluctant to exchange that bill but went to the bedroom to get the money and noted that she followed me halfway down the hall to look on. Previously she had asked, could she look at the apartment which, again, I interpreted as checking in my living conditions. She said the complainers were a couple.

What bothers me most is my naiveté. It was as though I was being seduced to open up. But as she left, I suggested we confront the couple together, but she ducked out of that one and said they'd call from downtown to warn them. Halfway through, I did ask her for identification and she showed me a driver's license and Illinois Department of Public Aid card but said she no longer worked for them. She asked me for identification and I showed her the driver's license and RTA card!

Immediately after she left, I called Village Hall and was referred to the police who sent out a cop right away. He examined the $50 bill, compared it to one of his and said it looked okay and that it was good I hadn't left her alone in a room, explaining also that he had such a large bill on him because he had received vacation pay. I feel such a fool.

September 19, 1993

Yesterday, returning from GP Board meeting and lunch, wrote a brief note and put it up on mailbox as a warning. I confirmed it certainly was a scam as the couple she mentioned had met her coming in. A smooth operator, very quick. Whew!

Quite a morning at Third Unitarian today! A reading of Dennis Brutus' poetry till he arrived, late, and spoke about currents and possibilities in South Africa. Erwin Knoll of the *Progressive* spoke well on his absolute devotion to the First Amendment as well as nonviolence and his socialist/anarchist beliefs. Then a bunch of us went to a barbecue at a member's house. There was some interesting political discussion. A Serbian man, basically a De Leonist, gave his syndicalist version of workers legislating power. A disillusioned Stalinist violinist held forth on the noninterest of the working class in change. Our hosts showed a video of the *Frontline* documentary on Hoover and the FBI.

Now I feel up, especially since yesterday's Board meeting went well and the eye angiogram is over with.

September 22, 1993

Heard the end of Clinton's health plan speech and certainly some of the goals were inspiring. Interesting that PBS has a Democrat and a Republican as commentators. No representatives of health organizations. And then the host tried to guide the discussion to the political/strategic/tactical angle.

Odd that Leningrad is being renamed St. Petersburg; they couldn't stop at Petrograd. It's as though they want to return to tsarist days! I guess it's symptomatic of my feelings about a revolution lost and the overwhelming success of capitalism to contain and dominate. Though I keep saying one can never tell at what point people will revolt in some way, do I really believe it? And if I cease to believe it, will I be failing those who do revolt and will I also be short-changing myself and my lifelong beliefs?

September 23, 1993

Why do I get a lift out of making a planter for Kathy Jeans, potting impatiens, cutting down geraniums and begonias, potting outside geraniums and then do nothing further about this? Why do I regard the rest of the day, when I return at four, as time preceding TV watching? Escapism, obviously, from loneliness and pain and grief. Why do I regard each day as a journey to be gotten through, preferably by lunching with someone or shopping or doing laundry? I do things but generally under pressure or the need to fulfill an obligation or a goal. That's why I like doing Spanish. It is a simple task of exercise, I learn from it, and it's easier because I've had some background. I do so like learning a language.

September 30, 1993

September ending already?

All of a sudden I've been busy with lunches and meetings. Tuesday night was book group; Wednesday, OWL health care preparation; tonight, Spanish; Monday night, Kurt and Marion Wahle and Kathy Jeans came: I ordered pizza, made a salad and had a nice visit. Ditto, Saturday night at Kathy Jean's Italian dinner. We started talking about the Pledge of Resistance, civil rights movement, specifically, Mississippi summer, psychiatry, juvenile offenders, house plants.

October 17, 1993

Yesterday, at the OWL meeting, undertook to organize a steering or planning committee on the spot after suggesting that the next meeting feature a Community Response speaker. Renée Buecker did make the meeting and might even join. It would be nice to have Gray Panthers sort of infiltrate and maybe move it a little more to the left. It was gratifying to see people's reaction to the *Families U.S.A.* film as simplistic, incomplete, directed to a very narrow audience of white middle class families. Also gratifying was the response to a single payer health system except for one woman who kept giving stock arguments against the Canadian system. Very

163

gratifying, too, was Rita's picking up on my point about the tendency to overlook societal and public health issues in talking about health care. There were a few women from the Women's Alliance and Third Church which helped considerably.

October 24, 1993

Maybe it's time to write in here again. A lot has happened emotionally and maybe, indirectly, physically. Tuesday, went to urologist at West Suburban who recommended surgery this coming Tuesday. I came away in semi-shock for this reason and because he said he would use a local anesthetic as the procedure was "only a half hour."

Well, at first I tried to adjust to the idea of a local and then had visions of another time when I had to have one instead of being put under because I had been given breakfast by mistake kept growing stronger. My first impulse was to call someone, feeling I was being rushed to surgery without really knowing what was involved, what the results would be, if any, both long and short term. Finally, after a bad night, I decided I would call and hold it off.

This weekend has given me a vacation from it, so to speak. Saturday, after attending a memorial for Bill Hammack at Third Church, went out to Indian Head Park for a Women for Peace reunion, and today went to the church forum and this evening, a movie and a bite at a Thai restaurant.

November 4, 1993

Have a date to see a woman urogynecologist for a second opinion. Renée called and, feeling overwhelmed, I told of the situation and she was quite supportive. We met for lunch and then came here and outlined the final Gray Panther newsletter. We have a date to take it down to the printer's on Monday.

November 6, 1993

Yesterday, Debbie drove us to the GP office and I started going through the files, oodles of them. I decided to use the creation of a montage for our reunion lunch to guide me and looked for appropriate reports of actions. In the process, was recalled to people I'd forgotten, many of them now dead. George appeared quite often, including the *Reader* interview covering representatives of three generations of peace workers.

November 11, 1993

Margaret Labadie will be here about 10 a.m. but I wanted to write feelings about my flap over the suggested surgery. The doctor recommended against any operation and will so inform the other doctors. I went through so much unnecessary hell during these two weeks, both the discomfort and the internal debate over the wisdom of getting another opinion, thinking this woman doctor would probably confirm the original suggestion. Felt an upsurge of gratitude and appreciation at the way I was treated by her and the staff. It confirmed my feeling that male urologists were mostly interested in penises and prostates and seemed to have little sensitivity to women's problems. Thinking of this, I could not avoid a spontaneous grin that I and others had at Mr. Bobbit's penectomy(?).

Tonight I'd written about Herb Lind's demise, suddenly, of a heart attack, driving in North Carolina. The Linds' son called to tell me this and said Ruth would be staying with him, in Oak Park. A great shock. I called around to Women Mobilized for Change people, much shaken by the news. Then, yesterday, Ruth called, saying she'd like to go to Third Unitarian with me as her Baptist church was in Palos Hills. I empathized strongly, thinking she had no real base now and must be in shock. I want to help but I'm a little wary.

November 14, 1993

Ruth Lind's visit to Third Unitarian went very nicely. I'd warned her that this was different from formal service and that we'd be mostly practicing from the new Unitarian song book. Though there was too much God in several of them, Valerie DePriest did an excellent job of leading and the choir was good. Ruth exchanged with several people before and afterwards. Then we went for a long lunch. Told her I wouldn't be able to go to the memorial for Herb. I feel bad about this but, though torn, enough is enough for me.

The coffee hour was particularly pleasant. Don Wheat made a point to speak to Ruth, Aldine Gunn celebrated her 80th birthday, I bought a ticket to a Medical Aid for Palestinians dinner. I was told the Religious Education director was delighted at the idea of kids turning in their war toys, and Tom Neumann invited me for Thanksgiving dinner.

November 25, 1993

Tuesday, I hosted a small gathering of Women Mobilized for Change for Ruth L: Henny Moore, Yorika Hohri, Bea Stuart and the two of us.

December 4, 1993

On awaking, thought of the panel on Clinton's first year I'm to be on at Third Unitarian forum. It occurred to me that I could perhaps handle it best by remarking on how journalists zero in on the strategies and physical performances and their prejudices rather than the content and would like to set all that aside in order to look at the facts. Also, regardless of what people believe, we should evaluate it objectively.

December 7, 1993

Got a call from Ruth Lind yesterday and agreed to go over after lunch with Renée. I want to help but I should not use it as a vehicle to go through all those emotions again. There are a great many points of similarity: subject to depression, losing a lifelong companion, not realizing the loss, as with Ruth saying she kept feeling she was only visiting her son and would return and things would be as before. Now she is writing acknowledgements and my first thought was how grim, but she said it kept her aware he wasn't there. My impulse was to bring her the sheets on grief that I was given but I think that's reaching and somewhat officious. I want to help her over this quickly but it can't be done, so it's best just to stand by.

December 9, 1993

I've got to go for a mammogram. I don't think much about it except that every once in a while, if I consider it, I get a feeling of apprehension as to outcome. Also, as it's not the pleasantest procedure in the world, I'm a bit reluctant, but at the same time, want to get it over with before seeing the doctor on the 30th. Quite like being a good girl and doing my homework for the teacher. I do wish I could shake that attitude!

December 23, 1993

Reading *Looking Back at the Sixties*, an anthology which Gert Rubin sent me — she has two poems in it — I was at first stimulated and then saddened by the memories of some of doping, dropping out completely, apparently now with some contempt for their condition. There are such different aspects of this era, the above-mentioned and the movements, the spirit of liberation and the spirit of despair of all society. I guess if the individuals reminiscing did nothing positive, then they're entitled to be ashamed or disdainful of the experience.

In fact, this anthology is very good for that reason, showing these two currents. Of course, there was a general loosening of bonds and a search for coherence, relatedness on the one hand, and a shedding of all taboos, on the other. I suppose every radical movement will be accompanied by this: people on the fringes taking advantage of the new, heady atmosphere to experiment personally.

Gert's inscription was her gladness at having shared this time with me. The biographical entry at the back refers to her as a septuagenarian! True, but irrelevant. People are still surprised that 70-year olds walk, breathe, and create! Really an ageist attitude.

Chapter Five
The Process of Writing It Out

January 9, 1994

Last Sunday, on the forum panel on Clinton's first year, I apparently did well and received quite a few compliments. Don Wheat sent me a rapturous note about my speaking just from notes and answering aptly off the cuff.

Vicky Combs did a smashing sermon on diversity and long-range planning involving the Austin community. She was taking Don's place as he's in hospital, recovering from surgery on a split palate. I sent him a card at the hospital and also signed a huge card with all kinds of inscriptions, writing, "I hope it's ok to tell you to keep a stiff upper lip." Don had his fingers in so many different things that I wonder if it would fall apart without him. It has become important to me as a community, as a place for expression, as a medium to carry out some of my ideas.

During the coffee hour, what depressed me was that I had to decide not to go to the anti-Klan rally in Springfield on January 16 as it will be outdoors. A lesser consideration was that that is my birthday and Deb seems to be planning something, but I'd call that off if I could go.

This Wednesday Monica wants to take me to the Art Institute dining room or, if that's not open, to a Greek restaurant nearby.

This business of reaching 80 is enfeebling me, I think, as I regard it as ancient, just as once I so regarded 70. However, this is entering old, old age and I keep thinking of it every time I have a physical difficulty. I'll get over it as I discover things are not radically different . . . .

Henny called earlier and encouraged me to get on with my writing as she had gone through, or was going through, papers she had with an intention of making her story known.

January 14, 1994

Today, Deb treated me to lunch and explained that she'd ordered a cake with an army eagle with a slash through it in white frosting and the word *Peace* below it. A really novel approach, honoring my commitment rather than my age.

Thursday, Vicky Combs, Third Unitarian intern, came for lunch and we hit it off. She said she had a block to pastoral visiting and people had advised her to see me — start with me? She seemed glad to exchange about administration, cliquism, etc. Though she calls herself a theologian and certain of her beliefs are not my bag at all, I like her sharpness and active role and interactive style.

Ambivalence at turning 80: I do feel it's an achievement in a way but also feel I should not feel that way about a chronological age. Maybe I'm looking somewhere for some political correctness and that's why I liked more and more the idea of the cake decoration. It tickled both of us, especially as she described to the bakery what she wanted originally, picketers, but that was beyond them.

January 21, 1994

Still struggling with a formula without defensiveness for explaining joining Third Unitarian to relatives and others. Psychologically, it goes way back to childhood, believing or wanting to believe, in God, to be part of the Gentile mainstream, to belong. However, this eventually suppressed desire was not what precipitated it. I think a major contributor was the dedication and courage of radical Catholics. Come to think of it, I defended Dorothy Day way back in the women's lit. history group, 20 years ago or so, for her participation and resistance during a strike on the West Coast while others were sneering at her for her non-Marxist beliefs. So, in a word, I admired dedication to radical class struggle causes and celebrated it wherever it occurred.

Working with religious people broke through the wall that Marxist philosophy had erected together with my Jewish atheist background. Sometimes I regret losing the surety that religion is the opium of the people, but how can I maintain that in the face of my experiences and observations of religious people I know, including ministers and priests? If they want to call it faith, that's okay with me as long as they don't impose that on me. I might call it humanitarianism, solidarity, commitment, dedication even. They have their jargon and I have mine though I've accommodated somewhat to theirs. And at Third Unitarian Don, in a sense, accommodates to mine and those of other atheists. I'm willing to meet on the grounds of humanism though that seems a bit wishy-washy. However, do I want a Marxist church? No, I'd have preferred the Sunday meetings of the Pledge people in Elgin.

Do I really need a formula or an explanation? Why should I have to go into a long song and dance? Why not announce it as meeting certain needs, the conclusion of many experiences?

As a result of the process of writing it out, I've established a consistency — for myself, anyway. Is not traveling a path that one recognizes, consistency? It may be inconsistent with preceding expressions of belief and disbelief, but what if the original formula no longer sustains me and appears inconsistent with what I've observed? Am I bothered as much by re-examining Marxist beliefs and finding some were not true or were inadequate? Didn't I go through a similar struggle during the 60s? Didn't I adjust rhetoric to the new circumstances and modify views? Yet a core has remained.

Odd, that having passed my 80th birthday happily, I feel good about being in the 80s!

January 24, 1994

Ruth Lind called last evening, finding it somewhat difficult to talk and not wanting to make commitments which I fully understood. I tried to reassure her that the worst would pass and was reassured by her saying she was going to a widows' support group. Altogether, a moving conversation and of course it tears me up, consciously or unconsciously. I think, in trying to respond to her, I was also seeking to answer my need to share my experience. I feel I should be helping her, not for my needs but for hers. I tried to enumerate the stages of grief and damned if I didn't forget the fourth. I remembered anger, realization, and making new relationships. I think I'll look it up right now: it's experiencing the pain of grief.

Well, I seem to have done all this, but when I put down the phone, I felt the need to contact someone and I called Henny which helped me a great deal because I not only told her about Ruth and suggested she call but also shared events of my 80th birthday. She told me her daughter who had first answered the phone had recognized my voice because she had put together a video of a Women Mobilized for Change exchange and was about to play it. So we had a nice conversation and a little help for Ruth, I hope.

Impelled to discuss feeling/impulse that I would or could put my writing together and that it might be fun to try. A re-awakening of interest, in short. It still seems overwhelming but maybe the interest in organizing the material will serve me. I think this impulse may be the result of having come to terms with joining Third Unitarian and a way of handling it. Also, Gerda Lerner's introduction in *The Creation of Patriarchy*, on women's history having to follow its own logic, find its own coherence, has also opened a way for me, writing my own history and what guided me. Thinking about Ruth Lind's grief, I also realized that commitment had helped carry me through my grief. Lerner, also, by describing how she realized what was blocking her and how this enabled her to overcome it, touched me and apparently I've applied it.

January 31, 1994

Enjoyed Vicky Combs' sermon yesterday, attacking the idea of monotheism and a patriarchal god as going together and asking, why not a plurality of deities? I liked it for the strong feminist message, a link I hadn't thought of, and for the crafting of it too. Told Vicky it was mind-opening. Thought how I would have closed this out at one time. I'm really sorry Vicky's leaving as she provides structure, adds dimension, and appeals to a different population.

February 4, 1994

Today I bought an electronic typewriter, a Smith Corona, which I'd been thinking about, disliking the second-hand IBM I got, yearning for my old Sears electric. This one at Office Max seemed accessible, easy to operate, clear, and with correctional features and easily visible typed material. It was only $90, so I got it! It types pica, elite and even smaller!

After buying the typewriter, bought 400-sheet package of typing paper, so I am moving in at least the symbolic direction of writing.

February 7, 1994

Thinking about various terms for religious or committed states, the metaphor occurred to me of the materialists' dressing these conditions, emotions, awarenesses in straight plain clothes. Whatever the emotional response, the depth of feeling, it was labeled a reaction to conditions, shying away from any taint of the supernatural. There was acknowledgement and some appreciation of the psychological impact, an awareness of how conditions and feelings interacted, but all was accounted for within the parameters of Marxism or dialectical materialism.

February 12, 1994

At last, a rally about health care at the Blue Cross building in the Loop, Thursday at 12:30. Can't make it as I have an appointment for individual health care, though if the weather is warmer, I might. Agnes called to ask me to call the three gubernatorial candidates about the Illinois single payer bill but did not know about the rally which is sponsored by Jobs with Justice, Democratic Socialists of America and others. Looks like groups are not getting their act together for a change!

February 18, 1994

Re-reading the entries, wonder if a journal wouldn't be more appropriate than an autobiographical account? That journal idea teases me but seems to be in contradiction with a chronology. Well, chronology is mostly for me, to get a clearer picture of involvements and from that will hopefully flow ideas and decisions. I realize that the typing-out of selected articles are samples of an ability to write interestingly, both topically and personally. Having established that, I can proceed to broaden out and place them within a personal/political history.

But what to do about my Trotskyist past, the years before the late 50s and the 60s? I realize I'm one of the few living members of the Left Opposition and have been asserting this political past more and more, feeling safer as time has obscured or dimmed the issues and their immediacy. So, painful though it may be, I cannot really sever those bonds and connections or subsume them under general phrases about a radical past. It is not so much a question of integrating them, as my radical beliefs and involvements cover a 63-year span, including the dismal 50s. Does that mean I have to go back to those activities too? Well, for me, they make a coherent past. I'm not very comfortable plumbing these depths and ultimately it will be up to me to decide how much or how little to include but at least I'll have a more seamless picture.

February 20, 1994

At Third Church I watched a short video on the second Cuba caravan last summer and the hunger strikers in the school bus at the Mexican border. The two young women presenters who'd been on the bus lost their jobs when they returned. Watching civil disobedience, direct action, I wanted to relate more closely to that. Said, "Congratulations!" to the young woman who was explaining the video. It made me live again the Pledge of Resistance Civil Disobedience actions and the feeling of sisterhood and brotherhood in doing them, working for peace and justice together.

February 26, 1994

After all that thrashing about, settled down to writing cards (notes on my writing) three days in a row, enjoying it, winnowing material, throwing away a lot. I do like cataloging and organizing but I have to tell myself to keep at it as if I were doing a job on someone else's material. Experience has shown me that from such a process, a picture emerges of how to handle it. In any case, reading through and listing stuff stresses a vast continuous involvement although I'm not sure of the specific relevance.

February 28, 1994

Going over 1978 "Partial Recalls" for the GP radio program, I realized how much pleasure, researching, writing and delivering them gave and gives me now, re-reading and reviewing these pieces.

* * *

What is an autobiography? As I certainly don't want just to write a life story, should I write a political biography? Now that I've seriously started on this, I need some guidance. How to use writings, reports, talks? As I do with short quotes in a talk or article? Turning over these approaches stimulates possibilities. I see the line between a personal and a writing journal is being crossed here. It would be really great to achieve an interesting tapestry or Persian rug to stand on (Henry James' advice to monologist Ruth Draper when she asked if she should widen her acting). Come to think of it, each of Draper's pieces was a literary composition too, but without her acting them out, they would probably have been lifeless. Maybe that's a good insight about Partial Recalls which were, after all, written for public presentation.

Goddammit, I feel I'm on a path, making a wished-for journey. I must not let doubts, even grieving, get me down!! Let me ride this wave and worry about drying up if and when it comes. I am encouraged by the desire to resume, by getting on it, by my enjoyment. After all, a few days ago I was shook by going through old *Peace Actions*, probably because of the loss of George and the WRL group, but these last few days, the opposite has happened. I've been encouraged, turned on, stimulated by "Partial Recalls," maybe because they were my own, my very own? If only I could convey well, clearly, stimulatingly my pleasure in this as I've tried to do here!

March 6, 1994

Friday, to Arboretum with Mark and Deb. A most enjoyable visit: the snow-covered terrain, the feathering-out trees, the still green pachysandra, the long yellow willow stems. The lake looked even more beautiful covered with ice, as it made an unbroken white landscape. Walking around it and then driving through, one could appreciate how beautifully landscaped the Arboretum is. The true shapes stand out more in winter against the white ground. The red and yellow twig dogwood bushes too were picturesque. So this was my renewal and my holy (?) experience.

Seeing that my notes under "Activities" were fewer than those under "Writings" or "Interviews," brought me back on track as to what my heaviest involvement was: writing about activism, mine or someone else's. So, moving or nostalgic or personally important though other things were, they have to be handled very lightly as they apply to my theme.

I wish I had the record of the 30s and 40s years, from the National Student League to the Washington Park Open Forum. I'm still tempted to sit down with those later snapshots stapled to the garden diary pages and note them on the back for a memorabilia file. What sticks with me is the one of George in brown coat and Russian fur hat at the Milwaukee Conservatory. It's a nice picture and a nice memory, and, I suppose, a necessary part of generally orienting my life, just as notes do for involvement. I had started to write *fulfillment!* Yes, in a way, I am fulfilling it, rounding it off, so to speak. Living from day to day or cause to cause, one loses sight of what went before and how this contributed to where one is.

March 9, 1994

Yesterday afternoon went to an International Women's Day commemoration at a WILPF meeting at Dole Library where Rima Schultz gave a neat, well-ordered paper on Jane Addams, "From Hull House to the Hague." Impressed by her social vision and objectivity. Afterwards, spoke to her about my project and she offered to call this morning to make an appointment to discuss it. Whether she will, I do not know, but it has nudged me to go over passages in this journal.

Continuing the note taking of files has had very different effects: (1) I'm beginning to get a grasp of types of involvements on a continuum with still-vague ideas about shaping a work. (2) It is emotionally very uneven, recalling events I'd half forgotten, a positive enrichment. (3) At the same time, this reliving stimulates pain, since so much was done with others and especially with George, as well as nostalgia for the depth and pace of involvement. (4) This, in turn, creates a hunger for such involvements and an empty feeling now. So some of this reviewing and winnowing and recording is scary.

Parts of this task are exciting, though: the Women For Peace material on the HUAC hearings supply a grounding of the dramatization so that I can flesh out a personal recollection, especially the organization of our trip to DC and Shelia Wexler's account of the hearing, maybe even quote from it. Sometimes the amount of material and the editorial tasks seem forbidding and at other times, stimulating.

March 10, 1994

Have been trying to list questions and ideas for meeting with Rima Sunday and am again moved by how much went into "Partial Recall;" yet have no way of conveying this except perhaps by one or two examples like the Alice Herz piece plus a description of what this meant to me as a creative

172

process: the love of writing small, finished, interesting research pieces of substance or of linking facts and alternate-news items into a connected chain. So two things seem in opposition: a spare style to convey emotions or atmosphere by exemplification and the emotional, poetic descriptions of feelings often exemplified by nature. How much writing is required to get down to the actual task of writing!

March 14, 1994

A big break? In fact, good news about my writing: Rima Schultz had volunteered to come over yesterday when I approached her at the Women's International league for Peace and Freedom International Women's Day meeting on Jane Addams, much to my surprise. She did, I showed her the xeroxed pieces which she took home with her, and we arranged to meet Thursday afternoon for her to tape/interview me. I was gratified because this is just what I've been longing for: someone to interview me as a means of sharing my reactions to events. She made a very important point that personal interviewing — oral history — gives a whole different quality to one's history, that, in fact, it supplies the personal accounts which fill out or make unique one's involvements.

So I felt very elated, hard to take in my good fortune, surprised at her readiness and buoyed by a very good, lively exchange. She's a red diaper baby, started in civil rights, went through an electoral phase, realized that movements were important rather than outstanding individuals. I got some of that, without so labeling it, from her Jane Addams presentation.

March 16, 1994

Looked through materials I'd already selected for possible reproduction, overwhelmed by mass of it. This seems now like a gold mine in contrast to the minutiae I'd been gathering.

I can see how a "real" autobiography would take years, yet people have written about parts of their lives, too: Margaret Mead in *Blackberry Winter*, Jill Conway in *Road from Coorain*, Lillian Hellman in *Scoundrel Time*. So I could take a certain period — from the late 50s to now — and deal with preceding years in a sketch, as indeed I have in interviews. If memories of earlier years are stimulated, so much the better.

I'm very lucky to have the time and leisure to do this though I do feel a certain pressure to get it done; at my age, the future is so unpredictable.

This week I got a certificate of lifetime achievement from the Illinois Department of Ageing. Anita Miller had nominated me.

March 18, 1994

National OWL has endorsed Clinton's health plan on purely self-interest grounds, the aspects affecting older women. Their press release says its "virtually" the only plan covering these things, but in the *Field Advocate* they admit Wellstone's and McDermott's plans do so too. What really gets me is that they paint themselves into a corner, looking at only what's possible legislatively and then not even supporting the good legislation. In addition,

Anita and I have egg on our faces, having participated for OWL in the single payer coalition. Will anyone else be outraged? [Yes, local chapters were. RD]

Also very discouraged by the limited issues National suggests dealing with. It occurs to me that it's a big mistake having a national organization impose priorities on its chapters because this means conceiving chapters as clones and this allows for no local differences or interests. This means for a dead — if effective on its terms — organization.

What I miss is the accepting, principled, broad outlook and atmosphere of Gray Panthers where we were ready to take on any issue. Well, look who was involved.

March 23, 1994

Reading sculptor Janet Scudder's account of her persistence till she found her true metier (in *Written by Herself*, edited by Jill Conway) also encourages me because, surprisingly, I feel a similar determination to carve something out of my life and doings. If I could only decided on a clear focus as she finally did! I have to overcome this tendency to include everything. How to develop strict criteria? and how to evaluate what is contributory, usable, useful? It's interesting that despite this big break from Rima, I do want to shape my own life and history, in much the same way I clung to and pursued it when George was sick and then when he died. I want to do my own thing as those independents did.

March 25, 1994

Sometimes it seems to me that history is very dishonest. One does or expresses things as removed from each other, but when one records or recalls, one hits the high spots so that the accumulation has a much greater impact on the reader and an impression of high-powered activity, for example, is achieved. Similarly, the longer one lives, the greater the number of events though they may have taken place at the same pace or time intervals or even become more widely spaced. So I'm still struggling with what is honestly impressive and what is sheer longevity. But I must admit I am impressed. This file reviewing recalls what I don't ordinarily talk about: the emotional involvement. I see how much certain periods of activity, certain actions, meant and still mean to me. I guess that's where the commitment comes in.

I must learn to convey these emotions to others as I realize more and more clearly that the total experience has to be conveyed. Well, personal interviewing should supply at least some of that.

It just occurs to me that our final Trotskyist involvement, a split-off from the Oehler group, was a brave and crazy thing to do. Thinking about those women who were for total, unconditional disarmament and kept at it for years, growing smaller and older, reminded me of our holding on. We even had less of a base, less money and less impact. But it is not something to be totally ashamed of. We just carried our commitment to an impossible dead end. How could we have existed in such isolated fashion? Where did we get the chutzpah, the sectarianism? Well, we were not the first to do something crazy and it was better than committing suicide a la the Lafargues, though they suffered a more crushing defeat, actually seeing a seizure of power and then the Paris Commune and their comrades bloodily crushed. Emotionally, of course, we suffered an end to our hopes but we were not then in a real struggle.

To whom does one listen? When we OWLers went to the residential hotel Oak Park Arms to look at possible meeting rooms, a little old woman with a cane said this was not a good place to be and I think we all dismissed her. Thinking about it later, I realized that my approach had been to think her attitude/remark irrelevant and to identify with the institution and the bureaucracy. I feel now we should have stopped and asked her why, treated her as a human being whose opinion was as important, if not more so, than the salaried representatives we were to see. One should not dismiss old people, but one does.

March 27, 1994

Realize that Rima's very firm proposal must be based on her reading of my material which she had put in chronological order. This included some of the material I'd submitted to Gert who'd also liked it. So I have her and Wayne and Rima to thank for this encouragement as well as Margaret's friend, Caroline.

We talked for over an hour, Rima finally plugged in the machine and began by asking how I met George and segued into early political past. I tried to avoid going into relations with Ma and Tommy. It seems like a rocky start but I suppose she'll keep probing till she gets what she wants. I said emphatically that I didn't want to get into a therapy-like interview.

April 5, 1994

At Rima's urging, read a good part of *I Came A Stranger* by Hilda Polacheck yesterday, and have been turning it over in my mind ever since. I approached it, at first, with the feeling that this was an account of someone who did something, knew and worked with someone famous (Jane Addams) and had first-hand accounts of life at Hull House. In fact, reading, the conviction grew that her recollections paralleled Jane Addams' autobiographies and I wondered how much they had influenced her. Such parallelism I suppose is inevitable and wondered how much my recollections reflected others' accounts.

Anyway, my original awe turned to reality when I tried to make parallels with my life and approach. I was raised in a very different milieu, forty years later, and though poor, never experienced the bone-chilling poverty and the need to sweat blood for a few dollars' sustenance. Also, my background was radical and intellectual while she had to make that journey by herself. Hull House to her was what the movement was to me: an opportunity for self-realization.

Most of the "names" who came to Hull House are known to me as names while, to her, they were people she met and heard. Similarly, to my experience, once she discovered them she went through the classics of literature while I discovered them through my mother's guidance. I was put off at times by Polacheck's clumsy style though occasionally her expressions were very apt. Actually, I remember her in WILPF as rather bluff and a bit intimidating. But I realize, from this book, she certainly deserved the standing she had in WILPF. Proud of being an American and a reformer, she does not appear here as a radical.

* * *

Should I include recollections of mailing the *Militant*, the arrest in New Jersey and earlier, as a child, reading while overlooking Mt. Morris Park? My reading, in general? More on living quarters? Should we map out what to look at, and when to include columns, etc.? There is a timeline of events in Hilda's life, a guide.

Just read the "Afterword" and realize the Polacheck autobiography is quite a construct from many versions and attempts. Too bad she never lived to see it published.

I hope I do.

April 7, 1994

I'm uncomfortable with details of meeting George in last Thursday's taping as I don't quite see the relevance except for the fact that he was lifelong companion and enabler in the struggle. So that part is OK, but how we personally linked is not really what I want to share. I do realize that in going over that, I covered early movement days and I suppose I should share the enjoyable emotions of solidarity, companionship, purpose, which for a while totally absorbed me and through this, I met boyfriend and husband. Unfortunately when this world fell apart, so did mine for a time.

April 10, 1994

Today, got out memorabilia box, looking for Circle Pines Center and Hyde Park Co-op and Credit Union stuff to fill in what I was doing in the 50s as last Thursday's tape with Rima was a very halting, inadequate, seemingly blank recollection. Quite an experience, sorting family pictures, pictures of George and me, movement pictures as well as yet-to-be sorted printed material all over the desk and chair. This last batch, "Opera of the Elite," a collection of verse, was written while fooling around in the instructors' office at the American School, finally threw out sad attempts at poems, reflections on relations with George, as not contributing to the kind of record I want to construct. I did keep some doggerel as representing my feelings at American School and some "poems" about plants as well as one piece on "Spin, World," with anti-war content.

Where I get stuck is not wanting to put only a positive sheen on the past. Up to now, except for going over the 70s diaries, I've been OK except for that momentary feeling, when being interviewed, of wanting to turn to George to verify a recollection.

And there are good things coming out. It was a busy period, I/we were involved and neither friendless nor uncommitted, and isn't that a good thing to establish instead of just saying the 50s were a black hole?

April 12, 1994

I really don't want to "write a woman's life" and I don't want to do a public analysis of mine. What I want is to weave a tapestry of my activity, the events that moved me and others and that were woven into my life and being. So I could perhaps have a brief sketch of parentage, background, ideas, marriage, — I was also a Red Diaper baby! — the radical political years, the war, McCarthy, the gradual seeking out and opening up of political life again, finding somewhat like-minded people around the Co-op, Credit Union, University community: liberal Democrats, some socialists, some CPers, always with a radical consciousness, wanting more than this. The discovery of Circle Pines: the stimulation of Milton Mayer's presentation and workshop, the finding of an integrated place and a more radical milieu. Then passionately following the civil rights struggle, then the 60s, 70s, 80s, providing a continuum of involvement, action and much writing.

Writing was involvement even when just observing and reporting. Even when not participating, emotionally I was deeply involved, following events.

This is a period of examination, re-examination, although not unique since that goes on continuously, but the visceral movements — civil rights, student upheavals, anti-Viet Nam war — caused the deepest reevaluation and the most liberating from dogmatic hangovers.

April 16, 1994

I've had a hard time reading over Women for Peace stuff and the night before last, unable to sleep after having done the struggle to get local support for going to the HUAC hearings, I had to tell myself that this was over, reliving it while going through need not mean I'm still living it. Even last night, going through the Terre des Hommes rejection by WILPF and my subsequent resignation as special projects chair was a bit painful.

But why do I dwell on the struggles rather than the excitement of going to Washington and being with over 400 others in supporting Dagmar? Of course, there were doubts about the tactic of testifying before the Committee which I'm glad to recall because this rounds out the introduction I want to write for the piece. I am proud of what I did. Why can't I distance myself more, though?

I did pick up on the question posed by Rima as to when peace became a strong motif/issue, sat down and typed an account of this thread in my history up to the Viet Nam War. It was a pleasure to use the machine — the first time, really — so easily and to use it for a first draft of experiences. The material flowed, but somehow I'm reluctant to complete it with later experiences. The thread did continue through the anti-draft years through civil disobedience actions on Central America, including the arrest at the

Arlington Heights army base, the Gulf War coalition, Hiroshima Day last year.

What to do with the material? How to overcome this tendency to respond to a rush of impressions with a slightly frenetic desire to get it all down somewhere in case I miss a precious point? Experience tells me that if I overlook something at one point, it surfaces at another time.

I'm trying to arrive at a balance amid a great deal of turmoil over the past and achieve a more positive approach to this. After all, I do want to write about a life well spent in the service of social justice.

April 17, 1994

Have done quite a bit this evening. Went over HUAC notes for an introduction, becoming quite absorbed. Then, about an hour ago, took up "Peace As An Overriding Issue" to proof and correct and was somewhat disappointed in it. Worked on it and wrote out a conclusion, though feeling my interest and involvement has been so over-riding and in so many aspects, that I could never cover it all. I should do more on the 50s. Have to keep reminding myself to bring in the personal more.

Ruth Dear in forefront, George Dear holding sign, at anti-Nazi Counter-Demonstrations, Spirng 1978, Chicago.

May 8, 1994

Reading Jane Addams' My *Twenty Years at Hull House*, at Rima's suggestion, further stirred me up as I see her point which the editor's introduction underlines: Very little about personal life, especially crises, and living through Hull House. So I tried once again to outline stages in my career but felt overwhelmed again by the many facets and an inability to reduce them to manageable size or framework.

Making progress going through files. As today, I occasionally rediscover something: the interview in *Gay Life* by Marie Kuda, and the announcement of the agenda of OWL's charter meeting which Henny and I attended.

How is it that I poured so much of myself into these things and I don't seem able to convey that pouring? Oh, I wish something would click as the way to handle it — or am I too impatient?

May 10, 1994

In a way, the *idea* of being active in the women's peace movement, supplying that bit of history as well as local history appeals to me, but this has somehow faded. The deep wellspring of *emotion* concerns the 70s and 80s more. I said the last decade was a period of looking back and evaluating but this is also tied to having lost George, looking back on a life with him and adjusting to a life without him — looking at *myself*, in short, rather than *us* — *my* involvement rather than *ours* — establishing for myself a single identity. It's as if with George cleared away, I could look at personal and political history following a single thread. At the same time, finding it painful in a way to untwist it from George's. Yet when he died, one of my first impulses was to tell myself that I'd been independently active too, that I'd been in the movement before I met him, that I had an independent history as well as a joint one.

Similarly with writing: I began to regard myself as a writer in the late 70s and became more confident of this appellation gradually. And then, really after George's death, began to explore the meaning of this, examine and enjoy the feeling of creating with words, recognizing the ebb and flow of the instinct or drive to express myself, my reflections, my observations and participations, to see the rhythms of these feelings and the particular pleasure of finding the right word, the right characterization, the utilization of others' words also to express the idea or meaning.

July 1994

Finding the radical impulse: a core question to me. Sometimes I made connections through a burning desire to protest in person and I attached myself to whatever visible sign of protest there was as with the Viet Nam war, with WMC at the Mt. Greenwood school integration witness. I supported the SNCC voter registration drive despite feelings about electoral politics because it was a movement against the system of oppression in the South; in defiance of both law and police. In short, their resistance seemed to demand support.

Somewhere along the line, learned to look for the radical kernel in a campaign and to nourish that, aside from, or despite, rhetoric and beliefs of the participants. A very early insight: My remark that the U.S. working class would probably make the revolution singing the "Star Spangled Banner."

August 24, 1994

I've mislaid my small writing diary that I took to the Unitarian-Universalist conference on racism in North Carolina, August 8-13. It's a bit crazy-making, especially since the fear that I've thrown it out is somewhere in the background and I have to resist yet another impulse to search where I have already done so several times.

Things are not easier since I learned the left eye — the "good" eye — has some macular degeneration now though vision is 20-25. I get afraid I won't be able to see well in a few years — or less, or more. It's taken about six-seven years for the "bad" eye, the right one, to lose central detail.

During the week at "the mountain," I kept feeling good about something: a view, an event, and then I'd get a bad feeling as though something were inhibiting it, and only later, on the way home and afterward, did I realize this was sadness at not being there with George. I had looked forward to going to the Smokies because we'd liked it so. It felt good driving there this time, once again taking a scenic route. So, once again, I distanced myself from pain and sadness.

Had I faced this, would I have felt better at the retreat?

August 25, 1994

Somehow, I just can't adjust to being 80. It does seem a burden of years cutting me off, somehow from 79, say. Reaching 60 or 70, big though these events were, did not do so in the same way, it now seems to me. The consciousness and self-consciousness make me feel more dependent, less capable, more aware of even slightly discommoding aches and pains. Do I feel that my time is more limited? Yes, certainly. Do I feel I may be on the last stretch? Yes. Do I dread becoming more dependent? Of course! Why can't I shake some of this off? After all, I'm writing a book. I'm reading and will be studying Spanish again. I compose and agonize and note-take daily.

September 2, 1994

Outlining the 70s, I thought would be easier. Why so hard to tackle what was really a good period? A big change, moving to Oak Park, joining the newly-founded War Resisters League chapter.

September 8, 1994

Twice reminded of the same incident en route from "the mountain," while listening to tape of freedom songs: Driving East with George, listening spellbound, utterly absorbed, to speeches at a NAACP conference — a shared time, a shared interest going through the Smokies with unfolding vistas of mountains.

Reading "Marriage Perceived: English literature, 1873-1944" in Carolyn Heilbrun's *Hamlet's Mother and Other Women*. It emphasizes the need for friendship in marriage and the sharing of goals. "But they must share an intellectual and moral base," she quotes Nigel Nicholson.

Outlining the 80s, remembered a local action with the Pledge where we were arrested and later debated accepting a guilty plea and a $25 fine versus pleading not guilty and taking the consequences. The majority leaned to the former but the feeling welled up in me that this would make the whole action meaningless, so I decided to take the not guilty plea in order to assert the reasons for our action: U.S. support to the Salvadoran government. The irony is that I received the same penalty, a $25 fine, but got to say my piece. My decision swayed a few others. Felt this as a source of strength which carried me through a biopsy for possible cancer which, fortunately, was negative.

Well, I've mined it all. Reading the diary excerpts on nature has brought out the personal, emotional experience of some of those years at critical times with George's physical condition. I feel now that the dryness and schematicism of just listing events from cards make no distinction among them and held me up in an impossible catalog. The realization that the house purchase and the move to Oak Park were a big part of our life, evoking as they did, feelings about age, property, finances, physical space, etc., convinces me I cannot dismiss them. They are part of my growth and change and living.

September 16, 1994

It occurred to me this morning, lying in bed, that my delight in organizing the garden is like my delight in shaping a talk or an article, a painful delight at times. These are challenges which I can meet and like the process of meeting. Right now, I'm engaged in shaping the space of my life which, though far from a delight, fascinates so that I keep working at it. Surely, something good and coherent will come.

* * *

Thinking over the anti-interference law directed against right-to-lifers and how it will surely be used against us. A result of one-issue politics and organization. A failure of perspective. A part of the ideology that you can manipulate the system. Actually, a "good" law — any such law — is the result of tremendous grassroots pressure or a desire by the authorities to stave this off. By itself, a law can be manipulated any way and will be, as with the Sherman anti-trust act which was later used against unions.

So struggle should be in the streets and from the outside and should be continuous. To rest after such passage is to give the game away. To try to manipulate the system, as with Bork and marijuana, is to betray one set of ideas — decriminalizing drugs, for example — for another, immediate one. However, I do see a difference between Neighbor to Neighbor targeting support for a single payer health system and putting energy, legislative and otherwise, to achieving this because it is a great social gain for all. The irony of the process is, that once enacted, it still has to be watch-dogged, implemented, made to work against powerful interests.

181

Last night, hearing of U.S. readiness to invade Haiti, had the chilling feeling that this was a dress rehearsal for Cuba. Once arguments for intervention against a cruel dictatorship are swallowed, what's to prevent U.S. from using them against Cuba? It will have established that since they did a "good" intervention, they can now consistently proceed against Cuba. Can't people see beyond the rhetoric to the arrogant imperialist content and assumptions? The government is here manipulating the race issue too. Again, single issue politics! Odd, at one time I was resigned to this single-issue approach, accepted it, but events, time and again, show its vulnerability. The defeat of the Cuban government would mean terrible repercussions here at home as there would then be no challenge to U.S. hegemony, unless, of course, Central and South American countries offer one.

How to convey the pain, unrest, impulse to do something, to act on this insight, to communicate this to someone as did Henny and Margaret during the Gulf War? Is there sentiment for resistance? Is this another case of using oppression of Jews to justify an imperialist war? Are these insights to be put down on paper, after the fact? The agony of impotence, as has occurred so many times.

Thinking over the Reagan years as the breaking of a consensus on government responsibility for public welfare. Contrast the War on Poverty with Reagan's denial that it even exists. This required an adjustment of expectations, a more hostile environment to even liberal ideas and a growing atmosphere of greed and selfishness. People blame Generation X or any other for what the new ruling philosophy fathered. Here too I feel a tightening noose, watching helplessly, as ideas, premises and lives are destroyed. Society builds prisons for law-breakers, decides who breaks the law, and criminalizes everything. That is the road to a reign of terror and suppression. Now it is being done economically and against crime, but the target is the mass of the people. Will they allow this, organize, break this trend? What new forms will arise if they do? I can't help carrying in my head some idea of restoration of strong union, unemployed and homeless organizations, but, as with the 60s, who knows?

Why do we now use only the word *homeless* and *homelessness* when we really are describing a general condition of being poor, of poverty? A more genteel word?

September 21, 1994

Coming across my "Bread and Roses" columns for *WIN* in 1982, struck by difference in contrast to 1970s "Dovetales" columns. These are sober, straight announcements and quotes while "Dovetales" contents are about far-out actions, direct actions popping up all over. A commentary on the change in atmosphere with the end of the Viet Nam War, people hunkering down for a long haul.

A note from plant journal, 8/17/84: Barbara Deming died on August 1, 1984. Wish I'd thought of dedicating a plant to her. Would like something delicate looking but sturdy, a perennial that would lend grace but not be flamboyant. Coreopsis perhaps? Lilac? An azalea?

September 27, 1994

Thinking over my time at the American School (over 25 years!) grading English papers: Despite its tedium and repetitiveness, the work shaped my editorial skills while correcting compositions and paragraphs. The parsing and diagramming appealed to my love of analysis and gave me a solid background in English grammar. I was raised in an atmosphere of work as a necessity, not a career, and not necessarily to one's liking. One took a job, worked hard, and brought home money to live on. So to me, even today, people's ability to work at chosen careers seems something of a luxury and relates to the question of choices and options. Sure, one pursued one's interests if one could, but that was not part of the daily job. Now, when people are bounced out of professional or executive jobs part of me feels that that's tough but not tragic. George's enjoyment of his job at Midwest Committee for Military Counseling after he "retired," was the first one he said he could give himself wholly to and get real satisfaction from social as against factory work. Though he had liked being a machinist, this filled only part of his need to be socially productive.

October 8, 1994

"If I suffer from my lacks, and I do daily, I also feel elated at what I have become." (p.75)

"Is life a pregnancy? That would make death a birth." (p. 76) From *The Measure of My Days* by Florida Scott-Maxwell.

Thinking over reactions to the Radical Therapy conference in 1980 and its effect on viewing resistance in Gray Panther steering committee to new ideas and arguments. I persisted in GP, despite rebuffs, until George and I attended this conference in May 1980, I believe, as workshop leaders, George on war taxes and I on ageism. Here we were treated with great respect and I asked myself, "Why am I taking this shit?" and decided to withdraw from the steering committee and I did not return to leadership until a new, larger, more inclusive board was formed, mostly through the efforts of Henny Moore.

I have this feeling that in typing out excerpts from my late 1980s journals, I was presenting me, and if this doesn't work, I don't know what else to do. I have been wondering about making the book more of a journal. These excerpts are my platform from which I say a number of things about books, politics, personal reactions, etc. Of interest? Or is there interest only when combined with actions?

October 11, 1994

Last evening went to Mozart benefit concert at Symphony Hall for Staley strikers, an enjoyable evening. Felt stirrings of solidarity though at first put off by an uninspiring presentation. These workers have been taking it on the chin for 15 months. Present were mostly older radicals and militants. Some of the 50 who had been arrested in a blockade were asked to stand. Then, as an encore, the Chicago Symphony orchestra did a beautiful performance of "Solidarity Forever" and the audience eventually joined in, standing up, holding hands high — a spark rekindled. I wish there was a less beleaguered movement, more people on the march. Do I carry an impossible picture of the 30s and 60s?

October 16, 1994

Just realized why these post-George journal entries are so meaningful, though this should have been obvious before. Formerly, I could express these ideas and vent these feelings to him, someone to validate them. At least two people held the same views most of the time. Now I confide them to a journal and they now seem to me a surprising record, coherent and well-expressed, more so, perhaps, than conversation would have been because they have to be formulated in order to be written. How I value these flashes of insight! The very process of going over these entries and then typing them leads to further illumination.

A while back, when I remarked to some people that I'd read somewhere that a diarist really writes to be read, they disagreed vehemently. However I was doing so half-consciously. I also see better how notes to myself to include this and that are really like journal entries, conversations with myself.

October 18, 1994

Much moved by Noam Chomsky's talk at University of Illinois last night. Went with Terry and Scott and saw other Third Churchers there. Every left group and her sister was there with publications, including Joffre Stewart and his anti-Semitic creed, which I turned away. The Illinois room was packed and we sneaked in a side door and sat in the aisle with others while still others stood all around, till, finally a man left and offered me his seat. Although increasingly uncomfortable, despite being carried away at times at some point Chomsky made, I was really glad to accept. Age has its advantages at times!

It was far from a cheerful message: world society becoming increasingly totalitarian and polarized, money going into speculations and only five to ten percent into production. He reviewed sections of the Universal Declaration of Human Rights and showed how they were being ignored or violated, his point being that soon, as with England at the start of the industrial revolution, there would be only the right to sell one's labor.

I especially liked his point that policy was made at the top in secret and had little to do with politics where people played out, in effect, illusions about changing things. I also liked his emphasis on the unions as being the last case of people working together instead of just for themselves and, of course, relates to the erosion of rights which union destruction accomplishes. I had realized this a while back and had entered it somewhere in my journal, I think, and felt good at his insight but a trifle miffed that he gets to express it to an audience of 1000 while I shared it with only a few people.

His conclusion was that he could make no predictions. Perhaps, as with the early 18th century English working class, there would be a revolt for rights, but he ended on a very quiet note: to do rather than to predict. Applause was tremendous. The attendance and enthusiasm demonstrated to me how hungry people were for clarity and radical insight.

It also throws into question, if not active distaste, the Coalition for New Priorities board game that the Third Unitarian Social Action Committee agreed to host on election night, tomorrow. Reading over the rules, I was put off by the strait-jacket rules about the representative having to decide for her/his electoral district how a given amount of money is to be spent. I don't like playing by capitalist electoral rules and now Chomsky's talk makes them seem downright silly. I wonder if there is some way of subverting them if I go tomorrow. He remarked several times that his analysis was unique, that this or that was his opinion alone. How often I have felt that!

November 2, 1994

Looking at "NYPD Blue" last night, struck once again by the acceptance of police brutality under the guise of realism. I don't doubt that real cops behave in this way and worse, but they are, in the story, essentially good guys. Why, once a cop makes a collar, does he have to push the arrestee forcefully into the car and even hit him? Logically, he has arrested someone, forcibly or not, and should not be inflicting further punishment or even discourtesy. Granted, the guy is his opponent, if violent or requiring a chase, but once the capture is accomplished, why beat on him? Is this the way cops vent their emotions on helpless people? Rodney King and many others certainly show that. Similarly, in this episode, two different cops interrogating prisoners graphically threatened each with a beating in order to force a confession — a bow, I guess, in the direction of acknowledging that real beatings do go on without going so far as to show them. So a form of torture is accepted. If the viewer is so naive as to think people are legally innocent till proven guilty, the police station becomes a nightmare of brutality, disregard for rights, punitive, ball-breaking — a perfect cosmos of order without law which is what characterizes a terrorist state.

November 17, 1994

Had a good meeting with Rima yesterday as she liked very much the '90s journal excerpts and we proceeded to Springer's on her initiative to xerox two copies of each page so that she could then start to edit with a view to showing them to interested parties for publication. This was a big boost as now I feel on solid ground and can proceed with the job.

Even for my review of the *Challenge of Shalom* our meeting was helpful as I was able to clarify how I felt about the religious emphasis in telling Rima about it; that I had always had the task of defining myself as a secular, cultural, ethnic Jew as against the general assumption that Judaism meant practicing the religion. In other words, the assumptions of these rabbis and others were disturbing, even threatening to my seemingly fragile stance. At one time I definitely did not want to be identified as Jewish and even remarked to someone that I had "passed," a term she could appreciate, being Black.

When I finally reclaimed my background, it was through a realization of Yiddish cultural heritage. Perhaps this is why I identified more with the fascists' oppression of the working class and radicals than the Jews. What brought about the change? I'm not sure. Certainly it occurred after the thirties, probably in the late 40s or early 50s when I had more time to think it through. And then I began to make it a practice to let people know I was Jewish in order to avoid having to deal with anti-Semitism or thoughtless assumptions.

I remember when Gert, Midge, and I went down to Cairo, Illinois, to show support for the boycott there at the same time that two Black women from Chicago arrived. When a local woman organizer said she was disappointed in the lack of Jewish support, I asked why she singled out Jews and she replied she'd expected more of them. My demurral unleashed an emotional anti-Semitic attack from the younger of the two Chicago visitors and we really got into it. Afterwards, Gert seemed glad I'd spoken up which made me feel better because I'd been wondering was I wrong to do so as though I was in some way responsible for the unpleasantness.

What touches me greatly from the *Challenge* is the observation of the woman who wrote about going to the Seneca women's peace camp with a delegation from Maine and taking comfort from the fact that there was another Jewish woman in the delegation. Like her, I've often looked around the room at a committee meeting or other gathering and realized I was the only Jew there. I was fascinated also by another woman's account of her visit to Nicaragua and the contacting of Jews there.

I wish I could make these two women's contributions the theme of my review and also Michael Young's overview of the Israeli peace movements as well as the account of the Jewish Peace Fellowship, the many references to international solidarity, humanity, peace with the Palestinians, the grasp of Germany's victimization by the Allies after World War I, and using the Holocaust because these are the things that resonate with me. I guess I'm trying to work out a way of handling the ten pages or so of material I've typed up, largely quotes from the book. It's amazing how I felt impelled to type out these people's words when I would ordinarily have summarized in writing, usually on cards. The subject and issues raised were so overwhelming that I had somehow to anchor them on paper. There were so many disparate points of view, so much searching, whereas in previous reviews, there was a more easily graspable theme and even when I disagreed, it was relatively easy to do. This, on the other hand, though it has a theme of course, made me uncertain: So much rabbinical scholarly discourse and who was I to question it, certainly not being a Biblical scholar myself. And what if I offended some people? So I guess ghosts from the past on what it means to be a Jew kept haunting me, though I believe I've laid some of them to rest with the help of the other sectors of the book which deal more with the realities I know.

Meeting with Rima, seeing her enthusiasm and her feeling that here she had something she could present and discussing with her this particular "Jewish question" have helped me to see my way clearer on the *Shalom* problem.

November 23, 1994

Why can't I mention what I like and what I dislike and not get caught up in a web of emotions and ideas plus my usual difficulty finishing a piece which involves bringing together all the elements? My dealing with this is also encumbered by positions on Zionism and pacifism. I did realize that the people who supported the "war against Hitler" or the military defense of Israel, despite their pacifist and peace stances, are not too different from my qualifying support of pacifism by support of people's revolts. So I guess that pushes a tender button, as does the realization that I can't condemn them from a position of absolute pacifism as I don't occupy that position. That should make me more tolerant! But it is an unpleasant realization since I do not agree with the issues these contributors have chosen to take exception to.

November 11, 1994

A little while ago, finished going through *Shalom* notes feeling, finally, I had a handle on an approach to the review. How many stages I've gone through! The first, reading, underlining and writing comments. Then the written notes and typing 14 pages of quotes which I cut up and stapled to cards. And, today, seeing more clearly how to arrange all this material, how themes overlapped and could be organized into fewer and clearer categories.

I've discarded almost all my personal objections, arguments, difficulties with religion, Israel, Zionism as well as attempts at self-definition, as not really dealing with the book. But at least and at last, I'm beginning to see the light at the end of this tunnel. What an experience! For an ultimate review of 500 words, I wrote and annotated and agonized and self-examined. A helluva lot of work, but I was obviously determined to probe, to assert a position, to deal with what moved me so.

Never has material proved so slippery, elusive, so fraught as this. Yes, I went through a crisis with "Perspectives," but that was at least around an issue that was clearly posed to me though that also unexpectedly involved coming to terms with my Trotskyist past. Before I could deal with this book, I also had to deal with my past. And though neither piece includes this struggle, "Perspectives" at least represented my voice, whereas the review has to be objective, reflecting my perspective only in passing.

Well, was it worth it? "Perspectives" certainly was but on *Shalom* the jury is out. I suppose to the extent that it yielded a better grasp of where I and the contributors were coming from and a better knowledge of Jewish peace activity here, in Nazi Germany and in Israel, the experience was certainly valuable. Anyway, for now, "Peace" or should I say, "Shalom"?

December 12, 1994

Received a Christmas letter from Larry Gara in which he mentions he is working or going to work on an autobiography. Are all aged radicals doing it? I guess it's logical, having gone through so much, active in the public sphere, meeting many people and facing many crises. Early this evening, finished typing out 1990 excerpts, including a next-to-last bit about therapy and the inability of clients to communicate to others what really goes on there. That's two references to therapy, something I thought I'd never mention, but since these observations are part of summing up, I feel they belong. Who would have thought it?

December 13, 1994

Read Isserman's review in *The Nation* of *The Sixties*, an anthology. Half of his review consists of his opinions and recollections and setting the record straight. It has made me waver a bit on my decision to keep *Shalom* a straight review.

December 21, 1994

One very valuable insight: What were so important to me originally, the finished pieces, I see now as secondary. The real part was the struggle, each time, previous to the writing, the process. So I have a clearer fix on the relation of one to the other as well as seeing the proper place for these pieces. To me this is fascinating, rich in the throes of creation and composition and, hopefully, of interest to others too.

This year I got started on the book, struggled with emotional blocks to autobiography, finally sweated out a first chapter and then, after much frustration, found an unexpected source and medium — the journals!

At first, when Rima proposed working on a book, I was walking on a cloud, unbelieving my good fortune. Then came not very satisfactory interviews and some frustration, a working out of proposed outlines of chapters on the decades from the 40s on which Rima correctly observed were not really reflecting me. They were, rather, outlines of the events with some personal touches. Quite a setback as the purpose was to show them to publishing contacts. But out of *my* depression and frustration came the seemingly desperate, last-stand decision to mine my journals, and lo and behold, this worked. Pay dirt!

In the process, what really made it viable was the instant connection between Rima and me, sharing our similar backgrounds, taking to each other, a real bond. I also offered a sympathetic ear which was apparently important to her and which I was glad to do. I have been enriched and encouraged by her steady help, though at times, as with the criticism of the outlines, somewhat angry. And, in the end, the writing will be mine and a lot of the structural underpinning, hers.

December 25, 1994

Last night, enjoyed being able to listen to real Christmas music, much moved by the candle-lit choirs surrounding St. Olaf church at the conclusion of the concert. Just this morning, thinking about what moved me so, I realized one emotion was celebratory of a great event; another, was of commitment and devotion. A bit uncomfortable with "O Come All Ye Faithful," which, despite all the "adore Hims," gave me such a feeling of uplift, marching towards something, a summon to the faithful to proclaim. That could be translated into devotion to going forward, joy at achievement. The shining path? The radiant way, as used by radicals in Central and South America?

I enjoyed last night particularly because I had this celebration to myself, could hear the music fully, not in tantalizing snatches in restaurants and shopping malls. I guess, at heart, I have a real religious impulse and from time to time regret not having been born in that tradition which is ridiculous since it is mine to enjoy when I wish and when I'm able. Maybe if I'd been born to it I'd regard it with less awe and appreciation. Remember asking a co-worker from Liverpool to sing "Good King Wenceslas" and struck by her bored rendering.

I suppose I'm still haunted by that *contretemps* with Beverly and our dutiful, miserable attendance at a carol singing afterward. So last night was a real return, on my terms, regaining my pleasure at the music and even turned on the radio this morning and got a Mozart flute concerto as a bonus. I had also thought about turning on "The Midnight Special" but decided it would still be too painful and maybe a bit stereotyped and dated. Besides, such humor is much enhanced by listening with someone else in the same mood. Maybe next year I'll go that step further.

If only I could rid myself of that childish feeling of being excluded and barred. Sorry I never took Faith up on her suggestion that we get out of the U.S. for Christmas. Foolishly, I'd held back because all tours seemed to highlight it in one way or another and I wanted to escape it completely — a pretty impossible task since it is wherever there is Western influence. Of course, the best alternative was a WRL potluck or other movement thing, a counter-Christmas, so to speak, with support from a nonreligious radical community.

Thought earlier it would be nice if I could "celebrate" today by finishing the *Shalom* review. It would be a real assertion, a raising of one's arm and hand above the encompassing seasonal waters, saying, "Here I am, not totally submerged, standing my ground. You haven't got all of me and I have another tradition to celebrate, more meaningful and more substantial than all the projections and appropriations of music and its emotional content." This seems to me very positive and somewhat empowering rather than one person standing alone in a sea of Christianity or otherness, triumphing over this and through this.

December 28, 1994

Yesterday was Tommy's birthday and I wondered how Karen was taking it, what with her mother now also beyond her, with Alzheimer's. I actually typed up and mailed the *Challenge of Shalom* review. The intense joy came on Monday, the 26th (day after Christmas!) when I actually finally assembled, shaped, and typed the first draft. It began with feelings that having weathered Christmas and still depressed, I'd never finish it. But I sat down with it, looked at the introduction I'd written, found it coherent and valid, and put together the rest, having carried around in my head the points I wanted to make and the notes to highlight. Reading the blurb about it in New Society Publishers book list and seeing how they summarized it, crystallized for me how to approach it. I was put off by their stressing the (weakest) environmental section in their reference to its coverage and by its citing of only one woman. So in a way it focussed what I wanted to say and whom to quote. I managed to work in my tradition, wanting to establish that I was Jewish, precluding fantasized objections to my authority as a Jew. I felt very good about quoting two women. I also feel proud that I was finally able to work in the religionist aspect without hostility, that I touched base on all the aspects I resonated to, and brought into prominence those two intelligent, thoughtful, ethnic-transcending women, Helen Fein and Helen Lipstadt — not Buber, not Einstein, not Heschel. Perhaps I'll be criticized for doing that or for other omissions and perhaps feminists will respond to these women as I did.

Started *Between Women*, an anthology of women writers/biographers writing about their subjects, their identifications with them, how they handled them, grew, etc. In a way, a book about how these women subjects became mentors or had been mentors for their biographers. The first one by Alix K. Schulman who wrote a biography of Emma Goldman was a powerful expression of this relationship and a good, powerful description of the demons of doubt that assail a writer.

I approached Goldman always with a kind of stand-off, judgmental attitude, influenced no doubt by my mother's attitude to her. A shy, reserved woman, she disliked Emma's brashness and, perhaps puritanically, objected to what she considered her promiscuity. A study in contrasts! Both anarchists, both midwives, one an organizer and agitator leading a very open life, the other, retiring, homebound with first one child and then, ten years later, another. Evidently my feisty father's enlightenment on domestic issues did not extend beyond insisting we eat out every Sunday. Am I somewhere between the two women? Agitating and propagandizing, but painfully shy and introspective. Certainly no sex pot! But living within and for a cause.

December 31, 1994

More on Emma: Have been thinking over Blanche Wiesen Cook's characterization of her as "mendacious, cruel, self-stuffed" and "occasionally delightful and flamboyant, she is ultimately narrow-minded and vicious to both enemies and allies." (p. 400, *Between Women*). This jolted me and at the same time made Ma's dislike of her more understandable and accurate.

Goldman was, in fact, a perhaps brilliant agitator and an independent woman and a radical but not necessarily a "nice" person. I had tended to discount Ma's evaluation, especially in the years when Emma became an icon of the women's movement. From Cook's description, I realize she was a person I too would have heartily disliked and I am grateful to Ma for this insight and can now identify with her dislike.

Yesterday, had 17 more pages of this journal xeroxed, after completing three pages on musings and questionings on nationalism, racism, police cruelty and violence, looking for answers, dotted with a myriad of questions, working my way through the question of bonding, both good and bad.

I can look back on 1994 with some satisfaction, even great satisfaction at the working on the book, the stages of realization and self-realization this has involved and continues so to do, at coming to terms with feelings about Judaism, church, at good personal relations with friends and, of course, with Rima as our conversations and interviews and exchanges developed. How much easier it is to see the positive as, right now, a few physical problems seem to have cleared up or are under better control!

Well, happy New Year to me, I hope! The doctor's observation that I've a good ten years yet, though encouraging in part, also tends to make me start a count down. Typical! I resolve to pursue the project as long and as best as I can and hope my faculties will permit this — things I never would have considered ten years ago!

Ruth Dear receives a National Organization of Women (N.O.W.) Award for political activism.

Chapter Six
To Free Myself From Ghosts

January 1, 1995

In one week I'll be eighty-one! Feel quite up today. Even got to do back exercises this a.m. Was planning to cook when Monica called to ask for a lift to West Suburban as her heart has been acting up. Went down to make sure the car would start and then took her to the hospital. Driving away from the hospital, down Austin Boulevard, realized the similarity to the many times I'd taken George there, the sometimes sudden need to get ready to go, and I saw more clearly why I did not want to wait there.

Reading last night Sarah Ruddick on Virginia Woolf, got a strong negative reaction to this constant probing of the subject and the biographer and this intertwining of their emotional lives.

What these probings reveal is that one can never write the definitive biography of someone else as there are always more avenues to be explored, different tools and approaches as times change, different writers with different sensibilities. It surprises me that anyone can use that phrase, "definitive biography." The most that can be said is that a biography is thoughtful, intelligent, and a reasonable sounding approximation.

January 2, 1995

Thinking about Ma's prejudice against Poles and general remarks about "Galitzianers" (Galician Jews) as well as the conviction that I inherited that Arabs were threatening and dangerous, I marveled at these contradictions to her internationalist position. But then I realized that I built upon that internationalist position and learned to reject those contradictory prejudices or to try to. I related it also to Marx's prejudice against Asians and Asian societies and how, similarly, one built on the basic internationalism and went beyond those restrictive preconceptions, a continuous process of learning from a solid base.

January 9, 1995

In January 1995 *Harper's* "Reading" on multiculturalism struck a chord. I've been feeling vaguely uneasy at all this loving diversity and multiculturalism emphasis which is drowning real issues in a sea of good will and acceptance. Though I disagree with Rorty's too simplistic answers, I do feel, as he does, that teaching people about oppression and disparity in power is a better answer to racism rather than cultural identity and sensitivity. Evidently, the right is attacking academia for multiculturalism and political correctness, reminiscent of the attacks on eggheads by Spiro Agnew. Such a strain of anti-intellectualism, know-nothingness surfaces in U.S. society from time to time!

How well put! Catie Doyle of Milwaukee Clinic Protection Coalition, quoted in *Violent Certainties* by Verlyn Klinkenborg, 1/95 *Harper's*:

"There is something in me, I realize lately, I really long in a way. It's to be involved in some kind of movement that just takes over your life, sweeps you up, gives you a focus from which to make judgments about everything else in the world. There's really a nice feeling about being caught up in something like that and knowing, for example, that you can just talk to people and they'll understand completely everything you're talking about."

January 11, 1995

I see the themes emerging from these journals as the process of writing/ creation, the mourning over George, the process of political and personal evaluation, an older feminist's take on age and feminism, and political involvements. I've been letting a little more of the personal creep in from time to time — a real evolution for me. As I've done this and dealt with thoughts and process of creation, the finished pieces pale in comparison and even begin to seem irrelevant at times. Yet they also constitute a record and this record should not be omitted. Occasionally, I begin to see how a piece like the one for *The Midwest Pacifist* on the Oak Park peace movement during the Gulf War could click right into place with my discussion of that. What of earlier stuff? Should a sampling be included at the end?

If I were younger, a well known writer, madly successful with a published journal, perhaps I could contemplate publishing these earlier pieces as a follow up. Fantasy? Yes, and it's the first, or one of the first times I've confided this even to my journal. Besides, I've learned, from the early entries that first thoughts, impulses, seeming impossibilities are taking shape. So why not dream further?

Last night, re-read *Violent Certainties* about the Milwaukee anti-abortion network and the fanaticism. What impelled, I'm not sure, though there are layers of feeling about my abortion underneath. I was most fascinated by a description of the procedure in the doctor's office, how he and the nurse handled it, or rather, handled the woman; one tends to overlook this in fascination with what is done. The entrance blocking and threatening and murderousness of the opposition with its emphasis on the fetus, tend to take away the focus of all this: the sufferer, the woman involved. The piece is a beautifully written, philosophical rumination as well as sensitive description and reportage.

My abortion I tend to tell about in clipped form: the office, the trip home in the cab with Ma, the hemorrhaging, the cab drive back to the office, the stocky, blunt doctor, a nurse somewhere in the background and, finally, the agony of the repeat procedure. I've tried to put the whole messy business behind me and never latched onto a single-issue stance on abortion, but I've given to NARAL, especially when abortion was under legislative attack. I wanted to rip that anti-abortion "pregnant counseling" service announcement from the door of the Medical Arts building and even tracked down their office, but I never quite had the courage to tear it off.

January 19, 1995

Re-reading Amanda Cross's *Sweet Death, Kind Death*, appalled by her woman author's ageism, fear of age, her feeling that one loses creativity and should live to only 70. That contradicted everything I knew and experienced, such as feelings of empowerment and looking back at the age of 60. Whereas she considers life at 50 as perhaps offering possibilities but overshadowed by the approach of death. What she really feared was the unknown, the loss of powers — as who does not — and anticipated this by flirting with ideas of death. Why so quick to cut out of life? Well, that was her *mishugas* or neurosis, fictional, at that, so I should not fight with it. But in a way, her approach is threatening.

In fact, when I read about this character, Patrice Umphelby, I feel proud that at 81 I'm working on something creatively. So why the doubts now? Monday, out with Deb for my birthday, went to the NOW feminist book group in the evening. Tuesday and Wednesday, also out to lunch, shopped, etc. and Thursday evening to Spanish class. Tomorrow will also be a day out. Each of these last few days, I thought I'd get back to typing but didn't.

We did lunch at the Medici in Hyde Park Friday, drove all around the area and Kenwood, including several places where George and I had lived. Enjoyed the tour, located the original co-op townhouses, noted the Co-op shopping mall, completely unrecognizable, as was University Bank in its new (to me) cladding, remembered going there weekly to weigh ourselves when George and I were each losing half a pound a week. A pleasant exercise in nostalgia.

January 23, 1995

From "Lowell Weicker — Third Party of One," Bruce Shapiro in *Nation*, 2/6/95: "As Weicker sees it, both Democrats and Republicans have drawn a circle around middle-class Americans — isolating them politically and preventing them from making common cause with any other constituencies."

Very apropos Claire's comment yesterday about the middle class being victimized. It underlines the emphasis on middle class people who are homeless, have lost jobs, pensions, health care, etc. Somehow this seems to make such concern over economic conditions more respectable while the poor and unemployed are somehow outside concern, "the great unwashed."

January 27, 1995

I feel I now have a sufficient sample for Rima to work on. Though I do have an urge to do more, I should call a halt till I consult with her. I need tuning up and affirmation/confirmation.

This is a period of growth and accomplishment in this field, no matter what the outcome. Some of the hardest work organizing early material got me started looking at my roots and of course has resonated in my later journals, after the fact.

I am seated in my armchair, watching the snow falling in the light of the street lamp, feeling tucked in here, considering what today's xeroxing constitutes — meant — means. Somehow, the flakes are comforting, something ongoing, outside this niche. They seem in tune with my decision to let further journal typing rest, while life/weather flows on. A needed corrective, perhaps, to the feeling today that absorption in this typing, making this my main work, is not unlike self-absorption in therapy. So the snow is comforting also as a sign that nature goes on, is there outside me, is a real world.

That's why I am glad to go to the installation of the new NARAL Chicago director, Brenetta Howell Barrett, at Malcolm X College. As she is also a member of Third Unitarian, I'd like to support her, but, more important, it gives me a chance to celebrate something outside of myself.

This writing is of course a different kind of self-absorption from therapy because there I was probing personality and personal influences and emotional reactions and experiences while now I am more engaged in personal-political history and thought. For me, they both have their place and, certainly, I couldn't have arrived at one without the first, at least with the same awareness and confidence. So who shall say? Introspection certainly has its uses! But it's good to let it rest too. Besides, this allows breathing room for thoughts to percolate and perspective to reassert itself.

So, by and large, I am content with the day, with the accomplishments, including at last a hooded scarf that stays on my head without electrifying my hair or slipping off, and, now, a good mystery to keep demons at bay.

February 3, 1995

Did attend the NARAL reception at Malcolm X, a disappointingly attended event in a large bare dining room. Introductory speeches were boring. Brenetta, however, delivered a moving talk about the plight of women on welfare, the stereotyping and the racism involved. Quite a few Third Church people were there and were also listed as sponsors. Somehow, let down at lack of spirit and people. When I expressed surprise at there being no sponsorship from NOW, someone indicated that NARAL was trying to play it safe. Why no coalition with Planned Parenthood or is that, too, keeping its skirts clean?

It's like a vicious circle! As times grow hard and the atmosphere more reactionary, organizations leave an even wider gap between themselves and the people's interests and the widening of this gap, in turn, underlines their isolation and impels them even further to the right.

February 4, 1995

Just came across two articles by Vivian Gornick; one, "The Next Great Moment in History is Theirs" in the *Village Voice*, 11/27/69, and the other, "The Light of Liberation Can Be Blinding," 12/20/70. A real find but I couldn't locate a precise quotation that liberated me from preening myself on being on a par with males, serving on national committees with them, etc. She did throw a blinding light on this attitude and made me ashamed of using that as my measure, shaking me to my roots. I have treasured that insight ever since as one of the significant moments of radical consciousness.

I resonated particularly to the second one, "The Light of Liberation Can Be Blinding," because of the depths of consciousness it probes, the hailing of feminism as a truly revolutionary movement and her tolerance and perspective on the various factions and splits. This tolerance manifests itself also in the first article, "The Next Great Movement in History Is Theirs," which opposes focussing on man as the enemy and looks to a true liberation for people of both genders.

I can see how much of her general approach influenced me and from time to time I'm surprised that others have either not heard of her or do not seem to think her particularly significant. Well, she certainly was to me and I suppose she caught me at the right moment — an individual experience which I should not expect others to share. Following generations have other gurus. It gives one a feeling of being on a broad, long path with different landmarks on the way, moving toward a common end. A not surprising observation since Gornick describes this process of the movement: creating, splitting, re-forming, refining positions and goals.

". . . Those terms of description sometimes harden into dogma, and dogma in time becomes a kind of shorthand — first for explanation and then for response. When that happens experience is on its way to becoming institutionalized and the life at the center of that experience is being sucked away." How true!

"To travel down that ideological road [rigidity] is not fatal — nothing can be fatal to the feminist movement, for it is alive in all its parts and its desire for more life is omnivorous, feeding itself on anything and everything. . . ." ("Light of Liberation").

February 6, 1995

Waiting for Scott Smith-Taylor, intern at Third, to go over use of *Challenge of Shalom* for Sunday service. Impressed by my fourteen pages of notes and how they enabled me to grasp the scope of the book, plus some good comments. A bit puzzled as to the type of material to use for readings — preferably longer quotes and mainly inspirational ones rather than historical.

Called Karen yesterday and had a long talk, ending up with an offer to accompany her to see her mother, May, maybe in March. I indicated I'm not too good at visiting a "home" for long and she said the surroundings there are very pleasant. Exchanged about journal, relations with Rima, NARAL, etc. She disliked mystery writer Piesman very much as giving an inaccurate, false impression of the courts and talked a bit about the dependency the system fosters — as with the single room occupancy clients she represents for the city of New York.

Sometimes I feel very oppressed by this dependency/victim characterization. Why is dependency the main evil? It's as though rugged individualism is in this society's bones and the middle class, which survives between upper and lower strata, often precariously, fiercely holds on to its ability to get by, to its superior knowledge etc. etc.

February 7, 1995

Had a good, interesting discussion with Scott yesterday and he suggested I emphasize the resistance and social justice angles of peace. I could link my support of resistance to the Viet Nam war with this as part of the resistance movement, not to mention the Pledge of Resistance activity, and how this involves the Holocaust, setting it in an international context as these contributors do.

February 10, 1995

Drafted a short version of a presentation, liked the outline, and then when Scott called, like an idiot I tried to give him a rundown. So of course he had suggestions which disoriented me. I could kick myself for yielding to that desire that disrupted my preparations. *I should not try to carry out someone else's idea* — it doesn't work for me. However, as a result of rethinking what I actually want to convey, I think I have something stronger though it involves the risk of sharing feelings about the Seneca women's peace camp, peace, etc. Now it has a strong feminist emphasis, partly intended, partly feelings just coming out. Right now, the draft looks jerky to me but I know that when one speaks, it is easier to move from one topic to another without the logical transition one needs in writing. Somehow the voice and the emotion and the directness to the audience allow leeway. But of course I like to produce something seamless.

This will be one of the very few times I reveal myself as a Jew and I am still not totally comfortable with that as with any self-revelation.

February 11, 1995

Right now, feeling good, having drafted the talk last night and now retyped half of the finished product. But about five a.m. woke from a distressing dream which, luckily, the light of day and the feeling of having accomplished a solid draft have dispelled.

It was a peculiar dream of being part of a number of people under some kind of Nazi terror which involved each one being individually watched and checked to see if each was doing things the right way. Any infraction or slip incurred death by shooting. Since no matter how hard people tried, they would inevitably break some rule, they were in great fear of death. Not I, apparently, observing and horrified, particularly at one of the guardians taking out a nickel-colored pistol and shooting a friend who was lying on the ground in the head. Somewhere, the Spanish subjunctive had something to do with it: Were people getting their tenses and endings right? A weird combination of anxieties: the fear of not getting my talk right and suffering arbitrary, severe, life-threatening consequences. Waking, I begin to jitter about the double whammy of sharing feelings about roots and from a church pulpit!

February 13, 1995

Sunday I did it! The talk on the *Challenge of Shalom* ("A Tapestry of Commitment") was well-received, and in fact, the whole service was very nice in its devotion to peace.

Around nine last night Sue Lodgen called to talk about the committee for the annual Robeson memorial at Third Unitarian and I agreed to serve. However, there is not one African-American on the committee. Sue suggested getting Austin High School students to talk about Paul Robeson as an example of achievement. Later, I thought, why not also try to involve the Oak Park High School African-American student group or get someone to talk about the Mississippi Freedom Summer of 1964? It's fine to honor the man and the artist, but the problem is that Martin Luther King is already history and Malcolm X is the hero of the moment. What possible living relation to young people does Robeson have? We can't expect them to share our experience and our consciousness.

At yesterday's forum Adolph Reed spoke for the Coalition for New Priorities on the "Contract on America" and underlined for me why I shouldn't join Democratic Socialists of America which he also represents. He referred several times to the 200 people the Left musters at a demonstration, is all for a national labor party but still has an agenda that includes influencing the Democratic party and politicians. I realized I would feel marginalized, as he was repeating James Weinstein's opinion of the "sectarian left." Then I wondered would someone ask why, if I could join a church, I couldn't accept DSA. I think the difference is that in DSA people I disagreed with would be speaking for me whereas the church generally does not do that, so I am freer to maintain my own stance.

A Tapestry of Commitment

A Talk At Third Unitarian Church, Chicago, February 11, 1995
by Ruth Dear

In the peace movement of the 60s, I was conscious, of course, of the involvement of large numbers of Jews, but I never thought specifically about Jewish pacifism as a phenomenon in itself until I had occasion to read and review a new anthology, *The Challenge of Shalom: The Jewish Tradition of Peace and Justice*, which is a comprehensive, in-depth view of Jewish pacifism and pacifists. Starting with "The Tradition," in which various religionists cite Biblical sources, it proceeds to the Holocaust and its implications, Jewish resistance during two world wars, an analysis of Jewish peace movements here and in Israel, up to and including the Middle East wars. Both secular and religious Jews will find ample background for their beliefs, as will all manner of peaceniks. Direct actionists will respond to the network of Jewish resistance efforts; feminists will resonate to women's anti-war organization; socialists and internationalists will identify with the deep-rooted concern for peace and social justice.

For me, this has been an intense emotional experience, a coming home to certain roots a struggle, as a secular Jew, with accepting people's reliance on the Old Testament and the Talmud to bolster their views, much as I accepted socialist internationalism to bolster mine. And I could only deal with the other rich contents of the collection when I had, so to speak, made my peace with them.

This work highlights three things for me. It punctures the myth of Jewish passivity under fascism. It describes people's grasp of the social forces behind war and oppression. And it outlines the extent and history of the Jewish peace movement here and in Israel.

In a chapter, "Impossible Pacifism: Jews, the Holocaust, and Nonviolence," Evelyn Wilcock remarks: "It is not surprising that many of those who actively opposed the Holocaust were themselves objectors of conscience or linked to peace movements." And she points to the fact that the network of resistance was made possible by the cooperation of others. Probably most of us are familiar with the story of Le Chambon, the Huguenot village that sheltered Jews throughout the war. These people were led by a pacifist minister and others.

The resistance network included a kind of Underground Railroad, mothers who sent their children out of the country when possible, individual acts of heroism by single men who offered to replace family men who were targeted for arrest and/or transportation. And of course, there was the Warsaw Ghetto uprising. But Helen Fein, in "Meanings and Misuses of the

Holocaust," emphasizes also that "Neither Jewish evaders nor Jewish rebels survived by their cunning and daring alone."

Some may feel that there should have been more uprisings, and possibly there were. Others may feel that this was only a last-ditch stand and not in the pacifist tradition. But whatever our hindsight, the fact is that under conditions of terrorism and murder, people *acted*. Fein draws the lessons from that, concluding, "It is not enough to say 'Never Again!' unless one refuses to create new victims and throws out a lifeline when boat people are sighted on the horizon."

Today, this willingness to act extends to the Middle East. In addition to Peace Now and Yesh G'Vul, there are movements by Israeli women who have formed Jewish Women to End the Occupation and Women in Black who mourn the war's destruction. Breira and New Jewish Agenda in the US forged links with those peace movements. And in the last section of the book, there are testimonies by people who have gone to Central America, joined Witness for Peace, and a host of peace and anti-imperialist movements here.

To me, one of the most inspiring statements comes from Helen Lipstadt who went to the Women's Peace Encampment at Seneca, New York, to join in the protest against deployment of Cruise and Pershing missiles in Europe: "in World War II, the Nazis aimed to eradicate some of us — Jews, homosexuals, radicals, gypsies. Today that same mentality pulls out all the stops. We're all earmarked in nuclear holocaust" and, a little later, " . . . we have made a choice this time, to come to this place. My family in the ghetto didn't have that option . . . . a Jew riding on the edge, saying never again, not to me, not to any of my people, not to my home. Over my live body."

I, too, visited the Seneca peace encampment with a group of women from War Resisters league, but it never occurred to me to relate it to the Holocaust or to myself as a Jew. This was just part of an ongoing involvement in the women's peace movement. But we were both there!

And Wednesday night, as I was preparing this talk, someone called to invite me to attend a Hiroshima Day committee meeting some time next month. Immersed as I was in this account, I readily agreed, thinking this is the 50th year that the threat of another nuclear holocaust is still with us.

In this period of horrible, imperialistic, ethnic and religious wars we need these affirmations, these visions of a common humanity. Rabbi Isidor B. Hoffman, a founder of the Jewish Peace Fellowship, organized to help Jewish war resisters in 1941, a time of much agony and soul searching among pacifists, feels that " . . . it is the people who kept their eye on the cause of war — how can we reorder society that there won't be another such occasion — who, as pacifists, were effective beyond their number in studying and understanding the longtime struggle for the elimination of war."

I have come from this work with a renewed feeling for my roots, with a deeper understanding of what these contributors have done and advocated, and an encouragement to continue in their tradition. I would especially like to thank the editors, Murray Polner and Naomi Goodman, for constructing such a rich tapestry of commitments to Shalom.

Gray Panther Maggie Kuhn with Ruth Dear, Oak Park, Illinois, c. 1990. Credit: Stanley Rosen Photo.

February 18, 1995

Finished Betty Friedan's *Fountain of Age* last night in preparation for Connie's report at the OWL meeting today. I found the last part much more interesting and she finally gives Maggie Kuhn and the Gray Panthers their due, accurately describing our stance and quoting Maggie, something that should have been at the beginning since so many of Friedan's ideas were prefigured by us. I was particularly interested in what she said about journaling, Jungian theory on this.

Quoting Suzanne Wagner, a Jungian analyst (p. 576):

"In fact your body may be slowing down, different energy goes into self-reflection now, a deeper understanding of what you have lived, there's a gathering of all the parts, to knit them together consciously."

Friedan also validated my reason for joining Third Unitarian which I've expressed as a desire for a community of support, filling part of the need of old people as other personal supports drop away. Also interesting was the idea that older people's cognitive intelligence is as good as, if not better, than younger people's in experience, perspective and skill, according to a study by the Max Planck Institute in Berlin. The older woman who celebrated her 75th birthday by a parachute jump "because that's something I haven't done before" reminded me of the decision to do my first civil disobedience at 71.

February 20, 1995

When I do a double-crostic, not only do I misread numbers and the small letters, but when I try to go over a letter I've sketched in, I do not do it neatly, following the outline, and finally, I realized this was another evidence of sight failure. Underneath, of course, is a panic which I keep a lid on but it does drive me to finish the project. I had the awful thought the other day that even if I do, and there is eventual publication, I might not be able to read it! The right eye took about eight years to get to this point. Though I can see a written part of the page by raising my head and looking down, I can't distinguish the words with it. So I can see where it would be helpful — if not vital — to be in a sheltered place with transportation and food available. A real downer! I am so involved in books, book groups, writing, reading, TV — I guess I'd have to rely on radio and tapes so it would not be all desert.

February 23, 1995

As I pick my way over the minefield of reactions, emotions, accounts personal, observational and philosophical, I sometimes get lost and the minefield becomes more of a thicket of pointed sword ends on which I sometimes prick myself and bleed a little at the memory. And sometimes I think an episode is significant and try to re-record it and find it too confusing, too full of friends' and acquaintances' names and so whatever point I originally had in mind is lost in this detail. Yet Rima said don't edit and I bear that in mind too. Then I grow weary of the process, the burden of these decisions. It is hard work, especially the going back, reading of turmoil and pain, being thrust into previous situations, exhuming them only to bury them again. An exhausting process!

February 24, 1995

Day before yesterday, copies of the *Non Violent Activist* came with my *Shalom* review which, on re-reading in print, seemed cold and somewhat abrupt at the start, in contrast to the emotional, more personally detailed talk at Third. When I sent it off, I thought I had presented a good, neat, solid job — an accomplishment, considering the emotional paths I'd traveled. But the talk at Third enabled me to say more of what it meant to me. I'm really beginning to prefer the personal/emotional over the concise understated article — quite a development, the result of all this journaling.

Interesting that Rima never thought of ageism till she gave a talk to OWL and realized how many older women were in movements, achievers. So this group opened up consciousness. Interesting, since at times I feel it is limited and not very imaginative. I was surprised and even shocked that the committee investigating hospital social services, particularly for outgoing patients, didn't go beyond vainly trying to interview West Suburban honchos when, to me, the next step would have been to go in a body and maybe eventually sit in till they get a satisfactory hearing or reply. Sometimes this unwillingness to go beyond conferences and calls and letters seems stifling.

February 27, 1995

Trying to obey Rima's injunction not to edit, remembering the struggle I had over including a personal note, in fact, beginning with it in the review of Brad Lyttle's book, *The Chicago Anti-Viet Nam War Movement.* How glad I was that I did, a break-through which convinced me of the value of these personal experiences for. enriching a piece. But where to draw the line? How guard against slipping into self-pity and suffering?

Scott Smith-Tayler's sermon yesterday reached me both because of his talk about authenticity and his description of Generation X youth and young adults up to thirty. He made an excellent point about young people's being in revolt against their parents' values and seeking, like them, escape and distraction but being bored with this. Not unlike sixties' youth rejecting their parents' life style, but they are not revolting against the system. Also excellent was his sensitive distinguishing between hippies who took drugs to enhance experience and young people today who take them out of boredom and unhappiness, to escape.

Today's disillusionment of youth makes them ripe for a fascist philosophy, perhaps, especially since many sixties people were red-diaper babies and these obviously are not.

March 2, 1995

Fell asleep last night, trying to visualize an extension of my fantasy about a young girl going forth from a place between hills (like a birth?) and going up a steep, bare hill with great effort and coming to the peak and then plunging down the smooth, steep, dark other side, down to darkness and depression. I was, in effect, making up a story, extending the original fantasy to later developments of childhood and young adulthood perhaps? What intrigues me is that I was telling myself a story and wondered if one would really develop. Much stirred by an essay in *Harper's* on the limitations of the "objective" scientific view and the search for explanation of the universe. We need to recognize that humans are the center of whatever construct they make or how they regard what they discover, as well as what, in fact, they do discover. Especially liked the reference to the fact that someone, on viewing the heavens, feels an expansion of spirit rather than only his/her smallness in the universe.

March 3, 1995

A very busy week: Tuesday, Wednesday, Thursday meetings for all of which I had to prepare, including two book groups and Spanish so that last night, at Spanish class, very, very tired.

In bed, tried to extend the story of the girl on a journey and imagined her landing from the slide down the hill into darkness, being underground where I had to negotiate spikes that seemed to come at me. Imagined gnomes being there, too, or some small people, but couldn't satisfactorily bring myself to see a way out though I did imagine a round opening to the light. At least I was dealing with the underground, the dark room/area/cave and giving it some detail as with the spikes and the people.

March 8, 1995

Today, or maybe next Wednesday, depending on Monica's wish, I'm to treat her to lunch in honor of her birthday. Next Tuesday morning, plan to go to demonstration against the incinerator in Austin which came up at last night's Social Action Committee meeting. This year's SAC has somewhat younger people, livelier, more open to activity. Caused much merriment by suggesting we combine the ELF announcement of their walk from Chicago to Clam Lake, Wisconsin, with the forum on Ireland because of elves.

Terry also invited me to a potluck for Scott's birthday, March 18, and I remarked it was the anniversary of the Paris Commune of 1870. This morning, thinking about it, realized how few people now know of it and how I must seem knowledgeable even though I can't supply detail except to relate it to the Franco-Prussian war. What I grew up with in the movement, celebrated or commemorated as part of our yearly rituals, has blown away, receded in time, uncelebrated and uncommemorated here as if it never was. My reality compared to younger people's reality.

March 9, 1995

The thought just popped into my head that the tendency today is to condemn the idle poor rather than the idle rich! Quite an inversion and a commentary on this punitive, acquisitive society. Some of the above has been stimulated by reading about the founding of Commonwealth College in the twenties and thirties in Mena, Arkansas (*Educational Commune* by Raymond and Charlotte Koch, published in the early seventies).

Particularly like the conclusion of the preface: "We were politically involved. So are many of today's young people. Most of our old ideas are reflected in the yearnings and darings of each new generation among the white, black, red, yellow or brown. To the extent that the young will permit us oldsters to participate in their strivings to reverse today's madness, we should be encouraging and assisting them in any way we can. The young generation of today is, after all, the inheritor of what we did not achieve sufficiently, or in time — in *our* time." (p. 11)

March 11, 1995

Beautiful sunny day. Yesterday at the Arboretum, saw some trees or shrubs with thin red stalks and tiny leaf buds and daffodil shoots. Spring is springing! The view from the lunchroom was unusually clear as to the various colors of trees and shrubbery: dark evergreens, red twig dogwoods, yellowish lawns, dark brown tree trunks and limbs.

Stirred yesterday, finishing Kochs' *Educational Experiment*, which describes well the misery, struggle, brutality of the time and the tremendous organizing impulse among farmers, miners, etc. These people had everything taken away — jobs, farms, rights, food, housing — and were forced to act, but there were also purposeful organizers who made it their business to work with them. Nostalgic, in a way, refreshing historically, as I'd forgotten terms like "Southern wage differential."

Commonwealth was all white, however, as a Black student or faculty member would surely have been threatened, punished, even lynched. But they did eventually work with the Southern Tenant Farmers Union.

The Kochs also bring out the rawness of radicals coming from the North with an attitude of derision toward the religious attitudes and beliefs of the native people and how they had to learn to disregard this and work to alleviate conditions, especially since ministers became involved or were organizing on their own. In contrast, they realized the social role of the church as a community for people who had little else.

Most moving is the epilogue about their return to view the site in the early 70s, thirty years or so after it had folded. They saw nothing of what they had helped to build. I was going to refer to it as a failed experiment but that is definitely not so! It was a center for learning, for expansion of mental and physical horizons, for organizing and contributing to the poor people of the South.

When I think of this time when everyone was organizing or had the impulse to do so, were driven and ready for action out of desperation, and then finding hope and dignity in struggle, I wish with all my heart I could recognize those impulses here and see more of them. Certainly there are desperation and mounting deprivation today. Will fixing up Dearborn Homes be enough? Will anti-incinerator demonstrations progress? People in the Thirties had to deal with the same kind of demagogy and bullshit on the part of politicians and entrenched leaders, such as union bosses, but they broke through this with the aid of radicals.

Hope I can make the demonstration against the Austin incinerator Tuesday and the Flower and Garden Show, not to mention Rima's Thursday. Yesterday xeroxed 32 more pages of journal.

March 14, 1995

Yesterday, I did go out later and was rewarded by seeing new lavender crocus in front, Dutchman's breeches in Austin Gardens and a forsythia in the old lady's front yard on Marion. An elderly man in a baseball cap overtook me in the park and asked was I out for the exercise and told me not to overdo it. Shortly thereafter, he sat down on a bench and I passed him. Got a *TV Guide* at Kroch's and then ate conveniently at the Golden Door. It was practically empty at 5 p.m. but then three, four old men drifted in, regulars perhaps. At lunch hour I'd seen mostly old women and wondered about the gender division. Should think, like me, women would not be up to cooking and would want to eat out, but perhaps they are afraid to go out at night, perceptions being what they are. Since I'd eaten little all day, the food seemed surprisingly good.

March 15, 1995

"Pick any strand and snap, and history comes unraveled." — *The Robber Bride*, Margaret Atwood, p.4.

Reading this in the library today, it struck a sharp note, making me think of the accounts in this journal, constituting threads of history, how one makes constructs of events, weaves or braids them into strands. Putting one event with another, trying to discern an outline or a thread running through them, one wonders finally at the validity. All it takes is another person's version to invalidate or weaken one's description/perception of the whole. Someone may take the same components, have gone through the experience with you, or paralleled it, and, like a kaleidoscope, a different pattern emerges. Of course with a kaleidoscope there are just so many patterns possible and this may be so of history, personal or "objective." How slippery then is the process, how subjective, but, somehow, within limits. So a history can be constructed but never the definitive one, though reviewers and PR people often so label it.

This speaks to my doubts and hesitancies as to accuracy of facts, validity of interpretations. It depends, too, on what one reads for: a writer's unique view, a description of the times, or the significance of events.

It's fine to use the metaphor of weaving — up to a point. The threads, the combinations, do not yield a set piece because they are elusive, changeable, and not necessarily a finished product, though often we try to present it as such.

March 16, 1995

Semi-dozing in chair, feeling need of comfort, had this vision of a Roman aqueduct or multi-arched bridge crumbling, as though some structure were falling beneath me though not precipitously. And had the thought which impelled this entry: I wish I could create rather than record. I'm not sure of the significance of the fantasy unless I want to abandon the structure or support or feel it is going. To enable something new? Creation? Am I not telling a story through this journal excerpting? Isn't that the framework I've chosen? The removal of a cast? Certainly the George cast has long crumbled. Is this then a further step? What will removal of this cast uncover? Is something waiting to push through?

Do I really want the aqueduct/bridge to crumble? Am I at a crossroads, left in the air? Was the urge to further creativity a wish to push past structures, shake loose of them, pursue my own path, an untrammeled one? That could be scary.

March 18, 1995

Quotes from *Between Women*:

From Gerald Brennan's review of artist Dora Carrington's letters: "Who could ever have supposed that these rapidly scrawled, badly spelled sheets that she was continuously sending off to her friends could look so well in print?" (p. 333)

From J. J. Wilson's essay on Carrington (in which the above is quoted): "I am wiser now to the ways in which women artists, especially, describe themselves and their work with such self-deprecation, such diffidence, such despair...." (p. 335)

"Indeed, it has been an important lesson for me in my own friendships with artists and other women workers: I do not take them at their word so easily when they tell me how little they have accomplished." (p. 337)

March 24, 1995

Sitting here, very sad after visit today with a friend who seems very vague at times. It seems so unfair, as well as threatening, that someone I worked with so closely who was so full of life and enterprise should be affected in this way. On top of that, we were joined by another friend who told me her good eye, after nine years, went just like that, a month or two after the doctor had found nothing serious yet. On the other hand, she has helped organize a macular degeneration support group and told me about a connection I could make. She gets about, judging what's on either side of her by peripheral vision and reads large print. That at least opened some possibilities.

I've been going over the many things we shared, her affection for George, her tribute at his memorial, Women Mobilized for Change days, Gray Panthers, even clashes, and it all seems too damned bad that she may not recall those shared moments. How tenuous relations, well-being, existence are! I suppose I should take comfort in the ability — so far — to see, though I get very fussed indeed, doing a double-crostic in the morning, looking at a list of definitions, nothing clicks. But then, gradually, it does and other mornings I click right away. Some slowness may be attributable to the various medicines I take. Studying Spanish, I refuse to try to memorize verb endings

— too much of a burden. Repetition in class and in writing should help to etch some of this in my memory. I do better at vocabulary. This is by no means unproductive.

I hope to share some of this Monday with Rima in order to underline the feeling that I don't have all that much time. One of the sadnesses of seeing someone's memory going is that if I ever do get published, she might not be able to share in the accomplishment. It's all very well to have younger friends but they can't take away the sting of seeing old ones deteriorate. It's also easy to be glib about the tribulations of old age when it is a generalization, but the specifics of losing touch with a friend make it very hard.

March 27, 1995

When I conveyed this to Rima today, she called it "a sense of urgency." She did give me her type-up of some 90 pages of the journal with suggestions and questions for clarification. So I am once again encouraged to proceed. We also talked about how to introduce it and she'll think about what to show to a publisher. She characterized these journals as starting with desolation and grief and proceeding to a searching, probing, assessing.

What's eating me now? I think the fact that I expressed my demons about Alzheimer's and sight. Nakedness? Nonsense! Isn't that what I wanted to convey? Sometimes I feel I've lost something, part of myself, my dignity, my facade when I do this, though why honestly expressing fear should cause this is puzzling. Perhaps because it brings it to the surface each time and is very real?

March 30, 1995

Read in *Rivington Street* by Meredith Tax last night, description of a pogrom, very graphic, very brutal. This a.m., thinking of the horrors, it occurred to me that there is really no way to grade holocausts with adjectives like worst, biggest etc. Each has its own horror, each includes torture, destruction, orgies of brutality directed against everyone. Like Toni Morrison who made slavery real in *Beloved*, Tax makes a pogrom real. And though we often compare it to a lynching party, a pogrom was directed against a whole settlement including looting, utter destruction of dwellings, stores etc. plus widespread rape. So here I go, quantifying!

What saddens is that these events are forgotten, glossed over, even obliterated, so that each new one appears as a fresh horror and to younger people, the first they experience and therefore the worst. It would be well to put alongside Holocaust mementos, those of pogroms, lynchings, mass bombings, nuclear holocausts.

Since, in the book, this pogrom occurred at Easter time when the superstition and propaganda was that Jews sacrificed Christian babies and drank their blood as a Passover rite, I wondered how Jews could ever celebrate Easter even with eggs and children's games. Or how people could celebrate a springtime resurrection and then go out and slaughter. Who were, in fact, the bloodthirsty ones?

Although I found the beginning of the book a little pat, I got drawn into it. It struck at first the same false note that the historical part of Marge Piercy's futuristic novel did: a reconstruction of something neither author experienced. Tax does it better, I feel, though this may be because the Russian background and history are more familiar and familial to me.

Writing now, seeing ideas flow, I feel a bit restored from the funk about old age, loss of faculties. The sun being out for the first time this week also helps. I guess I looked on those changes as a sentence — and still do — but I feel today there's life in me yet.

April 1, 1995

Had a good afternoon with Deb, driving through the Arboretum, seeing some viburnums blooming, tiny red blossoms, leaf buds, green leaflets on shrubs, graceful long yellow wands on willows, delicate golden yellow blooms on a shrub which she compared to the color of baby poop, much to my dislike and her regret, but at the same time delighting in these signs of spring. That sort of dry, humorous comment characterizes us both, sort of a sarcastic take on real enjoyment. Just tried to locate shrubs in the Time-Life *Flowering Shrubs* book. Had this swelling desire for a flowering almond followed by a defeatist feeling about lack of success with flowers in the house this year. Of course, I've been absorbed elsewhere and am very slow about feeding plants. Tomorrow, if something blooms again, I'll feel very differently!

April 16, 1995

Unexpectedly strong reaction to beginning of Easter service today, so I left. The first song was "Jesu etc." by Bach, followed by a hymn also about Jesus. Some of this feeling was fueled by the Friday seder service which I felt was something to celebrate (Freedom) and by the Easter pogrom described in *Rivington Street*. All this on top of the forum on "Welfare Reform" where a landlord almost had the last word, complaining of drugs, vandalism, a young woman renter who had four kids in four years with four different fathers. He'd quizzed her about further pregnancies and asked — shouldn't such people be sterilized, imprisoned, given heavier sentences, etc. etc.? I couldn't stand it and burst out about regulating the lives of women.

Sitting beside me at the forum, Sue said that in Massachusetts where she grew up, she was taunted at Easter made to feel an outsider. So that went into the mix too.

As she and Tom didn't attend the service either, on the way out, I suggested going for something to eat and we picnicked in their new house on Thatcher. Looking out from the second floor turret room was a heady experience. One could see Thatcher Woods. It created a yearning again to be in an environment with a view of trees and a garden, to see the possibilities and the variety of plants as yet unknown!

Now, looking at the forsythia cuttings in the dark green glass vase, one of a pair George gave me for a birthday, I remember our one forsythia bush and that first spring in the house, looking at the flowering cherry in bloom from my study window — an unexpected delight. And the astilbe I'd put in the spring before George died and which I never got to see in full flower.

Well, something has been resurrected on this beautiful spring day, both the good and the bad.

I must remember to preface the journals with an explanation that they served mainly as a vehicle for expressing upset and depressions and helped me to come through grief and self-doubt.

April 23, 1995

Feeling uncomfortable and at loose ends.

Heard yesterday that Maggie Kuhn died and though I didn't react af first, a little later, watching TV, felt a great sadness and an impulse to do something about it. Called around.

April 26, 1995

I have to hold fast to the news of student revolts in New York, San Francisco, *et al* as well as the occasional strikes, to keep from feeling washed down the drain by this punitive society.

They're still hyping the Oklahoma City tragedy, and by doing so, lose all sense of perspective and proportion as to tragedies elsewhere as well as poverty, disease, homelessness here, not to mention mass starvation and slaughter around the world, and U.S. government preparations for war on Third World "rogue" states. And of course now comes the threat of legislative approval of infiltrating "terrorist" groups, extending conspiracy laws, etc.

Am I just another elder thinking the world has gone mad? Evidently students at New York colleges don't think so as they protest against further hardship and withdrawal of learning opportunities. Equal opportunity? Ha!

I said to Margaret on Monday, I wonder at what psychological point will people crack and organizers spring up. In saying this, realized that I was, so to speak, laying down the burden or pressure to do something, say something. That role will have to be filled by others who are more directly affected, younger, able to mobilize and organize. Rationally, of course, I knew I could not fill that role and have realized it for a long time, but now I was saying it emotionally and psychologically. I was also saying it's up to the younger generations. Relief from a burden, perhaps, but regret that that's the way it has to be.

Of course, if a movement arose, I'd support it in some way, if only with money and petition signing and speaking out in my circles.

April 27, 1995

Though a few pages back I resolved to keep this for more personal entries, not for publication, I can't help also reacting to events and this is so much a part of me that I can't separate it, influencing and influenced by moods and feelings. So I guess it will remain such a record to the end.

May 1, 1995

Slight uneasiness at yesterday evening's discussion of Unitarian beliefs at one of the orientation sessions plus further uneasiness at what was projected for next time: discussion of God and Jesus.

Finally got an answer from Claire, who was there, as to what she had meant a good while back that I was one of the most religious persons she knew. She explained that she was characterizing a life of acting on my beliefs — what I would call commitment. I was pleased of course but still jib a little at being called religious.

We discussed loaded words (to nonbelievers, non-Christians) like salvation, faith, sin, Jesus, God, religion, church. For a while I thought I was the only Jew present but there were two others and I relaxed a bit realizing this. Repelled somewhat by a chalice symbol on the cover of the readings: very like a cross. A shamefaced cross? A compromise? Interesting that though Buddhism was mentioned, Islam was not. Considering the Austin area where the church is located, this seems insensitive. There was great discussion but no resolution on defining a creed which some say Unitarianism doesn't have. As to vocabulary, words like *beliefs* or even *principles* which were suggested were more acceptable to some of us.

Well, I had to learn a different political vocabulary in the 60s and maybe I'll get over my queasiness at what I consider Christian terms though, somehow, this seems harder, perhaps because mine are very early basic attitudes and I do not have the desire to learn this rhetoric as I did when I *became* involved in the radical movement. And this rhetoric was not nearly so foreign to me as religious rhetoric.

* * *

Feel somewhat better after spending a good part of the day with Rima who said she intends to set aside a block of time to devote to my stuff in midsummer. She mentioned several people to whom she'd like to show it and also discussed the introduction she'd write about why this is a valuable work.

As this was May Day, I was thinking on the way over and before that our whole movement calendar was meaningless now to people and that new movements would construct new ones — both a sad and a hopeful note to end this copybook on.

May 3, 1995

Reading "A Downwinder In Hiroshima" by Terry Tempest Weems in *The Nation*, moved to write down last night's dream which has been haunting me but which I've been avoiding describing here: I heard someone moving in the house at night while in bed and I thought, "George has returned," and sure enough, he had, younger looking, with a full head of hair. Felt good and comforted that he was back and then someone suggested he had Alzheimer's which I refused to believe. But when I tried to exchange with him, I noticed there was nothing there, as though behind his good, attractive facade there was a vacancy and I sadly acknowledged that the diagnosis must be true. So I moved in the dream from being greatly comforted to a feeling of near-desolation and awoke, wishing the first part of the dream were true.

Maybe the dream was in a sense coming to terms with George's absence despite the desire for things to be as they once were.

May 15, 1995

Good! Haven't written here for nearly two weeks, hoping to enter little so that I'll have little to select for typing. But today is George's birthday and I've finished a tribute to Maggie Kuhn at NVA editor's request and was glad of the opportunity to do it. *The Nation* had a nice comment and even Don Wheat mentioned her yesterday in his sermon.

I was reluctant to attend Third on Mother's Day, fearing there'd be a lot of sentimental glop but Don made it into a tribute to unusual women. A woman who spoke afterward remarked that her mother hated Mother's Day as a commercial device, just as Ma had.

Last week was the last session of Unitarianism 101 which I finally decided not to attend since it was to be on people's beliefs, how they came to Unitarianism. I was really on the fence, on the one hand, not wanting to go into my journey for the nth time and, on the other, curious as to other people's journeys. What partly put me off was someone saying the time before that she was very interested in where I was coming from. I asked did she want all 80 years of it and then reassured her I wouldn't cover them. Someone else had also indicated that other people were interested too. Later, I was sorry I hadn't replied, they should wait for my book.

May 24, 1995

Going through a 1993 journal, marking it for typing, I became overwhelmed with the turmoil and thrashing about that this represented. Covered about 90 pages and then had a reaction/repulsion to all this emotional engagement and repetition. Later, I reflected that this was the main purpose of the journal: to record and analyze these reactions, a diving into the book for venting when the need arose.

I am juggling so many considerations: to record honest emotions, to give some picture of daily life as a counterbalance or grounding, to record opinions of books, talks, articles, speakers, political/social/economic situations. I try to keep a more or less straight line, showing interaction of personal/political as well as the day to day contact with people, the role of nature and gardening and, especially necessary, the up periods to counterbalance so much down-ness.

Troubling at times is not knowing how to handle praise I receive. I record it faithfully because it means so much to me but at times it seems gauche and boastful to record it for publication.

Despite all the above, I do plug away and regardless of the exclusion or inclusion of this or that, there has emerged a body of work which probably gives as honest a picture as anyone else's.

May 26, 1995

Late yesterday afternoon at Deb's house where she put in a great number of varied plants which posed problems of size, color, arrangement etc. with my help as consultant. Enjoyed it thoroughly as she did the physical work and I had the problem only of advising placement of nine different flowering plant types of differing sizes, shapes, colors. It was like putting together a "Dovetales" column for *WIN*. All the odd bits and pieces of material I would weave into a whole, with introductory comments, juxtaposition, which could segue into which item. It was challenging and exciting as there was so much going on in the 70s, so announcements, mini-reports, quotations all had to be fitted in.

Right now, I have a much simpler task of positioning petunias and geraniums in window boxes for the balcony: how to fit the dark rose red petunias with lightish blue ones and whites as accents, guessing about colors of nonblooming geraniums from last year as well as the eventual placement of some houseplants outside. This year I decided to cut down a little.

Odd that I am so wedded to this basic color scheme for petunias, though shades and intensities vary from year to year. Last year, I had some marigolds too but though I liked the contrast provided by the yellow, and still do, elsewhere in other people's boxes and gardens, it seemed too much! I do love intensely the splash of color I achieved.

In a way, we are so different in approach. She'll see a lovely plant, get it forthwith, with little plan for the overall look, whereas I like to have a more detailed plan and though I'm seduced by color, I stick to it. At Luur's nursery in Hillside, resting, I felt I could bury myself and roll around in all that color and lushness spread out before me, wishing I could take and use it all. The drawback of balcony gardening is that there's no room to experiment, no new plants to try out in some corner, no perennials except for geraniums which are taken into the house over winter. Here's hoping the hibiscus, when transplanted outside, will provide some shade this summer!

May 28, 1995

Yesterday, did as I'd resolved, deciding the plants would give me pleasure all summer so worth devoting the day to. Arranged five planters on the rail with approximately equal spaces between and very much liked the look as it gave unity to the display although at first I'd objected to the neat, contained units evenly lined up. Because I was able to avoid bending, I cleaned up after a rest.

Slept soundly and woke up early, still feeling set up at having accomplished something, and this morning, before going to Third Unitarian forum, edited the last six pages I had typed which further enhanced that feeling.

At the fiesta dinner for Nicaragua, had a nice exchange with Doree Kent, starting with asking if her son was in Generation Y at Oak Park River Forest high school with a view to contacting the group for Hiroshima Day. He had graduated, she said, and joined the army, much to her dismay. She suggested calling someone from Students for Peace and Justice.

Now I intend to resume typing after a quick look around to see how the plants are doing.

June 2, 1995

Have been trying to deal with the tenth anniversary of George's death on the 13th and last night, tried to list/evaluate changes. Though I noted a number of things, felt that such enumerating didn't quite cover the change which is profounder than I can describe.

In grappling with changes, I listed greater self-confidence and assertiveness; finding a community of support through which to function; new friendships; this big project; living alone and making a new place for myself.

I guess we both would have changed. Though I have the burden of loneliness, I do not have the burden of his various handicaps and crises. Though I do miss the exchange and companionship very keenly at times, it is less as time passes and sometimes it is subliminal. There are exchange and stimuli elsewhere. "There are other people to be loved," to quote Freud. If not loved, then enjoyed.

I have a sense of accomplishment in having survived, functioned, created, withstood, and recognized better my own worth. Isn't that enough?

Watching the Blackside piece on the War on Poverty vicissitudes as reflected in the Newark civil rights movement added a dimension to the 60s which I tend to forget: the tremendous effort, rage, organizing, and downright resistance it takes to accomplish simple demands. Which of course were not so simple since they involved lobbying and massing against the city government and the feds, a rebellion causing great damage and empowering people as the local authorities ran scared and national sentiment shifted.

It made me think of driving through the West Side, seeing the decay and abandonment and miserable physical environment. This Newark history pointed up the mass will and anger and leadership it takes to improve conditions, far transcending a simple solution like cleaning up one's backyard or front stoop or sidewalk. Such a "solution" brings the problem down to the level of blaming individuals, the victims, in fact.

In the same way, I was offended by a remark that higher school achievement, a valuing of education, was a middle class prerogative. Bullshit! I know from past experience of the real hunger for knowledge of Blacks, how eagerly they picked up any literature we put out, as opposed to whites who often threw leaflets away, unread. Because people are not given the opportunity to develop and express this, being neglected, underfunded, crowded and looked down on, there is an erroneous tendency to assume they don't want education. Who fights for schools, protests closings, struggles to support kids and yet has to stand by and see them discriminated against and oppressed?

The emotions aroused are so deep and so often kept to myself that I cannot immediately channel them into a reasoned reply. Instead, I brood over the injustice of this.

June 5, 1995

Thinking over the fact that I never really dealt with the connection of my first civil disobedience action and George's death: on the one hand, an affirmation, a new step, and on the other, an ending and an emotional backstep. Too numb? Yet I was glad I had done this before he died, wondering after if I'd have had the courage to break ground on this alone. There is no entry at the time of the action because of the catastrophe almost immediately following. But I did go on from there to the Arlington Heights arrest, two years later. I did have a feeling of guilt at delaying taking George to the hospital on my triumphant return and finally went, at his urging, after a lie-down.

That feeling of triumph was nipped in the bud, overwhelmed, and though the fact that I'd done it remained with me, it was under a damper. Before I went downtown he expressed regret that he couldn't go to support me. I regretted it too but I had the support of an affinity group and the meetings and considerations that had helped me to a decision, so I was not setting out alone. Yet I remember how much sweeter it would have been had he been there.

What still comforts me in a way is the last memory of him sitting up in bed, reading the *Progressive*, and my leaving to go to the book group. Again, a feeling of triumph at my determination all through his illness to go on with my life and interests. Of course, I had no idea of the seriousness of his condition and the finality of that goodbye; rather, a resignation to more hospitalization and daily visits.

I wanted so much to help and remember my pleasure at getting large-print books from the library at his request and how he enjoyed getting them. That aspect of being needed and able to help, of taking him to Brookfield and Lilacea Park are good memories. Can I make my peace with bad memories?

As regards Mama, one of the hardest things was to serve her, to reverse our relationship which I never really did. She did have a home with us, I gave her company and we took her to meetings and entertainments. But I did this as a duty to a notion of indebtedness. That whole painful relationship contributes to shame and overshadows whatever I did for her. Yet as a child I loved her dearly, missed her terribly when she went on a long trip to Mexico. But can I ever forgive her nightmarish stories of her persecution at the hands of Grandma? Of course this gives rise to a pain at how needy she must have been to confide in a little girl.

On the other hand, she gave me a rich legacy of intellect, interests, social outlook and affection. A loving mother who probably overcompensated for having me at 43 by babying me. So I would like my feelings to uncurdle, to get back some of that loving atmosphere, to experience again the affection I once felt without the dependency and the feelings of entrapment.

Why does George who became dependent on me for many things seem not a burden as did she? Because I had the opportunity to choose to serve, to make a difference?

Originally, when George and I decided to live together, I thought, "Now I can go places!" I meant that movement-wise and personality-wise. So what stopped me? The war? The isolation? The 50s? Ma's constant presence? All of the above? At times I have that feeling of empowerment now. Interesting that this started as an evaluation of CD/death, relations with George, and segued into Ma. Guess I'm turning over important relationships and a desire to free myself from ghosts as well as demons.

June 14, 1995

Well, the 13th, tenth anniversary of George's death, has come and gone — a day I both dreaded and foolishly thought would put some period to my grief, I was distracted by involvements all day: car to garage at 10 a.m. where Renée picked me up and we went for her glasses at Sears and then for lunch followed by picking up my car. After a few hours' rest and a scratch meal, typed a page of the journal and then to the Hiroshima committee, a not bad meeting though the oral history project is probably dead for now.

All day, awareness of George came and went in little pricks and stabs. Then, in bed, I allowed grief to surface and had some bad times but eventually fell asleep. Thought I'd elaborate more on changes since his death but I didn't or couldn't. Yesterday I said nothing about it to Renee despite a long exchange, feeling she wouldn't know what to say and not wanting to embarrass her. In any case, I'm not sorry that I bore it alone.

The "bad times" mentioned above consisted of a feeling of agony about our being torn apart, thinking of us as Siamese twins who were separated. Certainly we were not literally attached bodily but we were attached emotionally, politically, physically at times. I thought again of the agony of the first, earlier grief and this was like a short replay. Now I feel this was a sort of catharsis, over the hump? of what? A ten-year milestone of survival minus my twin, a stability regarding the loss, a going on to live a full life in other aspects.

I guess I'll never really say goodbye in the sense of forgetting and I wouldn't want to, not because I want to hang on to grief but because I don't want to deny our 48-year companionship and collaboration and love. So the pain dulls, disappears, comes back, a necessary accompaniment, it seems, of that remembering.

What bothers me also is that only I know this is the tenth anniversary though probably his brother Douglas knows this too. Then I remember that two springs ago, in Florida, Kurt Wahle remembering us from Hyde Park days, so other people do remember. And I should remember that remarkable memorial, June 23, where so many people came and expressed their appreciation of him, an outpouring of tributes from diverse people and a remarkable picture of all that he'd been involved in. That should be comfort enough! I hope this journal, if it ever gets published, will also be a tribute to a co-worker.

July 27, 1995

Right now, almost half-through re-reading and noting *Always A Sister*. It's a short book, I have a short review to do, yet I crawl through it, conscientiously noting and reacting. I do do it the hard way! But particularly for something that puts me off, it's the only way. Trouble is that I don't resonate to Lillian Wald because she represents a different world and a reformist approach. I resent in a way the settlement house as a training ground and education for upper and middle class women. They receive center stage and the people they deal with, don't. It's interesting that despite all the help and training, there seems to be little written about it by the people who were served.

Always A Sister: The Feminism of Lillian D. Wald

by Doris Groshen Daniels
Reviewed by Ruth Dear
in "Activist Reviews," *TheNonViolent Activist*
November/December 1995

In the late 1800s and early 1900s, a group of gifted, independent, upper-class women defied the limited role assigned to them and realized themselves in working for social reform. Among them was Lillian Wald (1867-1940), founder of the famed Henry Street Settlement on New York City's Lower East Side.

Wald was an unceasing worker in many fields related to women's health, women's rights and peace. Her most significant innovations occurred in the field of nursing, where she pioneered in public health, founded the Visiting Nurses Association and achieved recognition and status for the profession.

In fact, the Henry Street Settlement originated as a nurses' center and then became a center and school for women immigrants, mostly from Eastern Europe. There the independent, unmarried Wald taught child-rearing and home care to the immigrant women who came to the settlement. (Interestingly, of German-Jewish extraction, she knew nothing of the history of the Eastern European Jewish women she tried to teach.)

Wald's concern for public health and the miserable working conditions of the time fueled her interest in labor legislation and led to the co-founding of the National Women's Trade Union League. As a (moderate) feminist, she supported the woman's suffrage movement; somewhat later she opposed U.S. entry into World War I and helped found Women's International League for Peace and Freedom.

A charming and persuasive woman, Wald was able to provide through her contacts money and support for her many causes. "A list of Henry Street supporters sounds like a Who's Who of American business and banking," notes Doris Groshen Daniels. Wald readily gave her name to many organizations, including the NAACP, but was neither a grass-roots activist nor a radical; at times she skirted issues in order not to antagonize donors. Yet she championed the 1912 Wobbly-led textile strike in Lawrence, Massachusetts, when the National Women's Trade Union League bowed out; sometimes she even supported Socialist candidates, though she herself was committed to working within the system. In the backlash against feminism, pacifism and radicalism that followed World War I, she found herself for the first time without the influence and access to the powerful she had once enjoyed. Nevertheless, she continued to work for labor legislation and the Women's Peace Party.

Daniels' book on Wald is decidedly a contribution to that branch of women's history that has fleshed out the lives and contributions of women leaders of the past. It is well-balanced, giving an honest picture of Wald. However, as the book deals with each aspect of Wald's involvement separately, rather than chronologically, at times context is lacking.

The book does raise some provocative questions about the settlement house movement and the role played by the women whom trade-unionist Rose Schneiderman called the "Mink Brigade" in teaching assimilation and acculturation. As Daniels puts it, "Being women and mothers, it seemed, was the natural state for all women except themselves." (Emma Goldman, though respectful of Wald's efforts, considered the work palliative rather than conducive to social struggle.)

Perhaps Wald herself summed up best: "My political attitude is making some of our generous friends uneasy . . . . It is foolish since, after all, . . . I am one insurance against unreasonable revolution in New York."

Photo on facing page: Ruth Dear speaking at the Oak Park Hiroshima Day, Scoville Park, August 1984.

August 1, 1995

Just occurred to me that to keep on an even keel as MC on Sunday, I should stick to what I want to say as introduction or between speakers and ignore the speakers' content as much as possible. Thus I'll avoid getting aggravated. Hope it doesn't reach 90 degrees and that I can rest in the shade between speakers since I'll have to pop up to introduce them and then open the mike.

Long dream last night about being in a big attic or store-room and finding many unusable things. One or two men and I went over old things, things that had not been bought and not used but were junky and useless. There was so much stuff that I felt it would occupy us for some time — a big task of examining and discarding.

Yesterday I finished the early 1994 journal and will start on a new one. So the dream of finding, examining, discarding, slight disappointment even at non-usability of things relates to this and seems now upbeat.

August 5, 1995

About an hour ago wrote out introduction for Sunday's Hiroshima commemoration. The words came smoothly as I'd been mulling over the contents all week and every publication I received had big articles on Hiroshima, including the *New Yorker*. I included concepts of total war, fire storm bombings of cities leading up to Hiroshima and Nagasaki plus the additional plague of radiation. Was able to relate that to victims at home. Thought of saying something about a niece and her husband dying of cancer after working at Oak Ridge.

Going over the WRL mailing with a listing of all the places in the U.S. where actions are and will be going on, impressed. I've had to condense a lot of stuff into about two minutes or three but maybe it will be the stronger for all that. Now that I've gotten into it, I don't mind doing it; the fear has mostly gone. I was doubtful of being able to get a sufficient message in but obviously I've constructed one.

August 6, 1995 Hiroshima Day!

Writing now to ward off nervousness. Maybe exercise to music will help. The other day, listened to the whole Emperor Concerto on WMFT, knew it was Beethoven, very familiar, but still couldn't place it. Miffed and puzzled: If I can place the composer, follow even from one movement to another, get so much pleasure from it, why can't I place it? No ear. Envy those who can recognize a melody or tune instantly while I, outside of a very few familiar favorites can't. Saddening.

Good vibes from the Hiroshima Day commemoration. The sun did come out from time to time but the platform around the vets' monument in Scoville Park was in the shade except for an occasional gleam poking through the trees. It was well attended — 125-150 people. Most gratifying were the eight or so who came from the People's Resource Center in Wheaton, old friends. Afterward two people called to state their appreciation of the event, saying it was moving. I got congratulations for running the meeting, also.

After the two main speakers, Fran Sullivan and John Philbin, Larry Armstrong said a few words about the Hiroshima Maidens and then a woman took the open mike with a petition against nukes. A vet justified the bombings with the usual rationalizations. Luckily I'd prepared the quotation from Gen. Curtis LeMay on the Tokyo bombings and after he spoke, merely said that it depends on the point of view and read it. Another vet also asked why we were not commemorating Iwo Jima. The vets were beautifully answered by historian Al Young who had returned from a conference where new material on Japan's previous willingness to surrender and the bomb's use as a warning to the Soviet Union were discussed.

The mood was peaceful, no disruption, a few vets clapped for the first one but that was all. (Afterward I was told that a man passed by, saying something about that "liberal bitch" while I was speaking but luckily no one else heard.) Valerie De Priest ended with a rousing "Study War No More," according to plan. As we were breaking up, someone suggested "We Shall Overcome" and we sang, holding hot, sweaty hands, sort of an anti-climax.

Afterwards, went to Erik's with Mark and Deb where he said that on the platform I looked 40 years younger. Have been pondering that remark and decided he meant I was animated and he had never seen me in that role as speaker/MC. Then today, in concluding *Always A Sister*, came upon this:

"When she felt well, [Lillian] Wald plunged back into action, claiming that she felt as 'young and ardent' as she 'did more than thirty years ago.'"

Altogether, felt elated and continued to do so after seeing Rima, Monday. She has retyped much more of my work and went over some of it, discussing what to do with writings like "Perspectives" which are needed to flesh out or illustrate entries.

Since the real emotional part of this journal begins with August 8, ten years ago, here is a good place to stop and on a much more positive note. I have come a long way.

Ruth Stamm Dear 10/29/95